MAURICE
Man and Moralist

MAURICE
Man and Moralist

Frank Mauldin McClain

LONDON

S · P · C · K

1972

First published in 1972
by S.P.C.K.
Holy Trinity Church
Marylebone Road
London NW1 4DU

Printed in Great Britain
at the St Ann's Press, Park Road, Altrincham, Cheshire WA14 5QQ

SBN 281 02651 3

For my Family

Contents

———— •◆•• ————

Preface

————◆————

Maurice, Man and Moralist attempts to relate the ethical teaching of Frederick Denison Maurice to the personal relationships of this eminent Victorian. Rather than the oft told tale of 1848–54, the book concentrates on Maurice's thought and the way in which inward tensions heightened his moral sensitivity and caused him to move towards an ethical statement important for the secular social ethics of today.

The book developed out of work leading to the degree of Doctor of Philosophy at Cambridge University. I am grateful to the Danforth Foundation of St Louis, Missouri, and the Episcopal Church Foundation of New York City whose generosity enabled me to pursue my research. The perceptive criticism, gentle humour, and kindliness of the Reverend Alec Vidler, and the Reverend David Edwards, as well as the stimulus of their learning, were invaluable. I am also indebted to former colleagues and students at Sweet Briar College, Virginia, for sustaining my original interest in F. D. Maurice.

The staffs of the libraries and archives represented in the list of manuscript sources have given me generous assistance. Miss H. Peek of the Cambridge University Archives and Miss C. Oliver of Queen's College, Harley Street, deserve specific acknowledgement. My particular thanks are due the staff of the Cambridge University Library, the Anderson Room, and especially to Miss Janice Houghton.

The Most Reverend A. M. Ramsey, and the Reverend Professor Owen Chadwick gave me helpful advice and showed me certain letters in their possession. I should also like to mention the graciousness of the Reverend Arthur Dowle, late chaplain of St Edward's

Church, Cambridge. His enthusiastic interest in my research was always a source of joy and strength.

I am grateful to Mr Robert Bayne-Powell for allowing me to use the memoirs of Lucilla Maurice Powell, and an incalculable debt is owed to Mr Frederick Michael Percival Maurice for making available a large collection of unpublished Maurice family correspondence. The number of unpublished manuscripts discovered indicates that other collections of letters and sermons might well be found.

Finally, the unflagging patience and understanding of my wife and my family made the work possible at all. They deserve thanks beyond any words of gratitude.

NOTE

Maurice's handwriting was notoriously bad, and in quotations from his letters and other manuscript material the use of empty square brackets indicates words which have remained illegible.

Introduction

———•◆•———

"How many men about to start on the adventure of death would have remembered to apologize to the barber?"[1] Consistent in the tension between genuine humility and hypersensitive self-efface-ment, Frederick Denison Maurice began the final hours of his life at five o'clock on Easter Monday, 1 April 1872. His physician, Dr Radcliffe, had been called; his friend Llewellyn Davies was asked to bring him the Communion. "You will explain to the barber", he inisisted, "why I cannot see him."[2]

Maurice, his wife carefully recorded, began talking very rapidly but very indistinctly. The Communion seemed to absorb all his thoughts. It was, he said, "for all nations and peoples, for men who were working like Dr Radcliffe."[3] "Something too we understood about its being *women's* work to teach men its meaning."[4] For a time they could not make out anything he said. The spirit of the man so often agitated, moments before nervous and afraid, had drawn into his inner being. For one trembling instant he opened his eyes. He suddenly raised himself upon the pillows and spread out his hands. Words poured forth from an internal depth of silence. "The knowledge of the love of God—the blessing of God Almighty, the Father, the Son, and the Holy Ghost be amongst *you*—amongst *us* —and remain with us for ever."[5] The blessing of the Trinitarian God caught up the whole of the life of Frederick Denison Maurice. He never spoke again.

A quiet radiance filled the room and no one, man or woman, who knelt about the bed failed to be struck by the beauty and dig-nity of his head and countenance. A look of calmness and of triumph settled down upon his face and remained.

It was an appropriate victory for a gentle warrior. Days before, sustained by the tenderness of women, like an ancient soldier, Maurice had been brought back to London, scene of the ceaseless struggles of his life, scene too of many victories of his spirit. An air of hushed finality surrounded the line of carriages which moved away from the tall, gray, terrace house in Cambridge. The hush surrounded the train and the small procession across the city. Maurice was taken to the house of Julia Sterling, 6, Bolton Row in Mayfair. There his niece could more easily supervise his care.

"Thank you much for the Recipe which you have taken such trouble to get for us. The Beef-juice has been our great stand by these two days—and much as he dislikes it, it certainly suits him at this stage better than anything else. His *pleasure* is in cold water and ice—he says he never knew the blessing of cold water before."[6] All food was painful and distressing to him. "I have learnt", he said, "that man does not live by bread alone . . . I feel now that I must take food solemnly."[7] "It is sacramental?" he was asked. "I did not wish to use that word, but that is what I mean."[8] Accustomed earnestness filled the last days of one who said, "Young men, *earnestness alone makes life eternity!*"[9] The juxtaposition of time and eternity, the sacramental quality of the world and human relationships, the nature of the Eucharist for all nations and people, formed the context of the theology and ethics of Frederick Denison Maurice.

In describing ethics, Maurice described a society, many societies perhaps, but ultimately the kingdom of Christ. The character of the society described is that of responsible freedom which can only exist or *become* because of the underlying activity of sacrificial love, found in the being of God as Trinity, and experienced by means of the work of the Holy Spirit, in all the innumerable sacrificial acts of history. How, then, did Maurice reach the position that the Eucharist, celebrated in Trinitarian faith, showed the whole of mankind its nature and destiny? Surely this is the heart of Maurice's ethics, his "secular" social morality.

The principal formative influences on Maurice's ethical teaching came from his own personal relationships. More subtle perhaps than the intellectual sources of his thought, they were far more important in a man for whom theology and ethics were primarily a matter of relations, essentially personal. Intimate domestic documents and correspondence, as far as possible unpublished material, have been used to indicate the ways in which Maurice's family, his friends, and his associates, influenced him, not only by making him the man that he was, but in providing that portion of the divine social order in which he expressed his identity.

Maurice's indebtedness to his teachers has often been acknowledged.[10] He himself was scrupulous, over-scrupulous perhaps, about acknowledging what he owed to other men.[11] Unquestionably the Unitarian influence of his father was a matter of lifelong importance, emphasizing the Unity of God whose nature is absolute unqualified love.[12] Calvinism—meditated, and tempered by that meditation, through his mother—was also important, emphasizing the divine majesty and all its implications.[13] Maurice's debt to Julius Hare for the vital influence of Plato cannot be overestimated.[14] Maurice felt himself to be particularly indebted to the Platonic method and self-consciously, if not always successfully, modelled his academic style on the dialectical system. According to C. R. Sanders, and indeed to Maurice himself, the greatest single influence on him was Samuel Taylor Coleridge.[15] The contributions to Maurice's thought made by Erskine of Linlathen and Edward Irving have been analysed in several studies.[16] Maurice was a man of his age; his reading was extensive and catholic. The extent to which he drew incidental hints from the general literature of the nineteenth century is far reaching.

An attempt has been made in this work to pay tribute to another less well known source of some of Maurice's distinctive ideas. He frequently mentioned how much he was indebted to the Millenarians for his belief in the fact that the kingdom of God had *already* been established and was a matter of present experience in time.[17] In a real sense, the quiet country clergyman Joseph Adam Stephenson, Millenarian rector of Lympsham, was important, not only for bringing Maurice to ordination in the Church of England, but in directing him along the line of thought which led to his greatest book, *The Kingdom of Christ*.

Maurice's own life was the best illustration of his ethics. For him it was basically part of the life of one who was the Head and King of the race, part of Christ's perfectly free, because perfectly sacrificial life. Maurice was acutely aware of the many faults in his life. Yet even imperfection may serve to draw attention to that which is without flaw, and the extent to which Maurice in his own human relations was able to apprehend, acknowledge, or express the freedom of sacrifice was eloquent to him, and to others, of his life's source. Hannes Leinonen observed that "Maurice's Christianity is essentially that of the First Commandment: a Christian does good deeds because he is inwardly bound to God. Here is one of the points in Maurice's theology and social ethics that unite him closely with Luther."[18] Maurice himself affirmed "We do not become God's children because we are good; but being the children of a good God, we can be like our Father in heaven."[19]

I

The Moralist
in the Making

————•◆•————

MICHAEL MAURICE
A GENTLE STRENGTH

"All human society," Maurice wrote, "is so constructed as to be an instrument by which the Divine Teacher acts upon man. Human relationships, laws, political events, are . . . the agencies whereby man is led to seek after a knowledge of his Maker and of himself."[1] Indeed, Maurice declared, "human relationships are not artificial types of something divine, but are actually the means, and the only means, through which man ascends to any knowledge of the divine;"[2] and he specially rejoiced that "most persons are constrained to admit that family relationships are in some sense or other an ordinance of God."[3] He himself regularly emphasized the significance of domestic relations. He affirmed that they were the dominant influences in bringing a person to self-awareness, and ultimately to the knowledge of God. It may well be imagined that his own relationships, particularly those of his early childhood, left a permanent impression on him.

C. R. Sanders says that it was from his father, Michael Maurice, that this theologian learnt the unity of God whose nature was of absolute unqualified love.[4] Most studies of Maurice acknowledge his debt to the Unitarian tradition and to Michael Maurice by whom that heritage was transmitted. He himself admitted that he owed a great deal to his father, far more than the simple statement of outward Unitarian belief. All that Maurice was to affirm about the nature of God as Father disclosed what he had learned about father-

5

hood from Michael Maurice. The basic principles which guided his distinctive response to the ethical demands of life were those which he had absorbed in the ordinary every day experience of life with his father. Michael Maurice provided an underlying certainty about God and life. The strength of this conviction made possible Maurice's gentleness and positive moral concern.

Maurice discussed his relationship with his father in a number of autobiographical letters. None of these sketches was ever finished though two were partially published in the *Life* of Maurice edited by his son.[5]

Maurice spoke of his father whose "Unitarianism was not of a fiercely dogmatic kind", and who was only

> intolerant of what he considered intolerance in Churchmen or Dissenters . . . I have inherited from him some haste of temper, and impatience of opposition to what he thought reasonable. I wish I had anything like his benevolence, generosity, and freedom from self-indulgence. As I grew up I became far too sensible of what seemed to me his narrowness, and of a certain incoherency in his mind; far too little sensible of his very noble qualities of heart. I have since come to the deep practical conviction that this insensibility was a sin against God, a refusal to recognize the operations of His Spirit. I held that thought while I was with my father, but it was not a firm belief in my mind which could withstand a certain pharisaical conceit that I knew more than he did, and that I was therefore in some sense better. Now I am very sure that if I had this knowledge it made my moral inferiority to him an additional reason for shame and repentance.[6]

There are several records of Michael Maurice's personal and religious integrity. If he could be spoken of as narrow and impatient of opposition, mention was made in the same breath of his tolerance, benevolence, and generosity. Lucilla Maurice Powell spoke of her father as heir to large estates and destined for Cambridge and Holy Orders. Instead, she said, he became a Unitarian and was disinherited.[7] John Frederick Maurice was more accurate. Michael Maurice was the son of an orthodox dissenting minister and intended to become an orthodox dissenting minister himself.[8] He was educated at Hoxton Academy and then at Hackney College. Instead of continuing in the orthodox faith, he became "sufficiently zealous in his Unitarian opinions to abandon a considerable property which would have been left to him had he been content to adhere to the faith of his forefathers."[9] This behaviour demonstrated his religious integrity and his willingness to run counter to his own interests in support of a conviction.

In spite of this indication of the firmness of his religious beliefs, Michael Maurice was accused of religious inconsistency by his fellow Unitarians. Edmund Kell wrote: "Notwithstanding this full conviction of the truth of his own religious faith, there was, however, a want of fidelity in the open profession of it. . ."[10] Two marks stood against him. Feeling that by mingling with others he spread truth, he worshipped with Trinitarians; and that the members of his family, attracted by "numbers" and "worldly advantages", left the Unitarian fold, said Kell, occurred because Michael Maurice was inconsistent and indulgent.[11] Kell mentioned the troubles of Michael's distinguished son at King's College, London. He wrote in explanation:

> O, it could not be that he could be brought up under the roof of his loving father, whose life was spent in labours for the good of others, and believe that *that* father would be everlastingly punished by the benevolent Being whose conduct he was so far striving to copy.[12]

Maurice's novel, *Eustace Conway,* provides the most unselfconscious guide into his early life and family relationships. C. F. G. Masterman suggests that the model for Eustace Conway was Maurice's friend, John Sterling, but there are many indications that the literary material is primarily autobiographical. Not the least important reason is the resolution of the hero's religious quest in the final passages of the book.[13] Sterling's religious restlessness was never resolved. In 1837, six years after the completion of *Eustace Conway,* Sterling's sister-in-law, Annie Barton, wrote to Maurice shortly after they were engaged:

> He (Sterling) spoke more of himself and of the struggle between good and evil that was still going on in him than I had ever heard him before; and he and his concern me too nearly for the subject not to have been a painfully interesting one to me.[14]

Sterling may have inspired certain aspects of the hero's character, but Eustace's religious quest helps us to understand Maurice's own religious development and enforces the novel's autobiographical nature. The publication of *Eustace Conway* in a special sense marked the culmination of its author's spiritual pilgrimage. *Eustace Conway,* in any case, provides insight into Maurice's own family life, particularly into his attitude toward his father and fatherhood.

The novel contrasts two specific types of fathers. A family portrait in his house might have been of Mr Vyvyan, Eustace Conway's uncle. It showed that mild expression in the upper lip which says so clearly that he loved his children well.[15] Mr. Vyvyan's generosity to the point of indulgence marked him out from other men. "He was literally born to be a father."[16] His character was similar to that of Lady Edward's father.

> His virtues in every relation—as a husband, a friend, a land-lord, and a legislator—were the theme of everyone's praise. In one point alone, he was thought to have erred: he was universally accused of injuring, by over-indulgence, the youngest of the girls, whom Providence had committed to his care.[17]

That his kindness was the cause of Lady Edward's troubles was doubtful.

> I fancy . . . that it was rather the capricious treatment she endured from the other branches of the family, than the unvary-ing kindness she experienced from him, which first awakened the evil passions of her character. From her infancy the child was lively, indiscreet, and volatile; acting sometimes upon good impulses, sometimes upon bad ones, but certainly never from any forethought about the consequences of her actions. Her father, I believe, was as anxious as the rest of her family that these impulses should be well directed, but it was never his wish to see them crushed . . . He seemed to think that, as self-denial is the greatest, the hardest of all duties, grown-up people should practice more of it than children; and so he made a great many more sacrifices to them than he expected from them.[18]

Such a father showed active sacrificial reticence about imposing his opinions. His direction was always positive, not negative. His personal integrity which was never capricious allowed his child to discover and acknowledge freedom rather than to be crushed.

Contrasted with this image of fatherhood was Captain Marryatt's father. "My father, as I told you," he said, "was a presbyterian,"[19] authoritarian, contentious, hypocritical, and lacking in charity toward other men. In a conversation about parental influences, Honoria, the heroine said "The impressions of our childhood are very strong . . . it is a great responsibility when they have all been in our favour."[20]

> I knew a wretch once, [replied Marryatt, her suitor] . . . whose cradle, I really believe, was cursed. He had a parent, Miss Conway, who made animating speeches at religious meetings about sending the words of truth and love through the whole family of man, and never spoke one loving and true word in his own family—who burnt Shakespeare in his study, and feasted on turtle-soup with horrible voracity—who forced his children to repeat a catechism twenty times as long as the one we use, and encouraged them to be spies upon each other—who revelled in the threatenings of the Bible, and outraged every one of its precepts—who would argue for hours to prove that some man, whom less pious persons thought a good Christian, belonged to the Prince of Darkness;—and, by a series of brutalities, murdered his wife.[21]

Later, Marryatt continued, "the indentures were sealed when I was in my cradle! I am that wretch whose father taught him before he could lisp to hate the only service of which the wages are not death."[22]

Michael Maurice appears in accounts of him to have resembled Mr Vyvyan rather than old Mr Marryatt, for he seems to have been eminently kind and generous, benevolent, lenient to a fault perhaps with his family. Maurice once recorded that his father was somewhat narrow in his views, but Michael Maurice was certainly not authoritarian with his children. The accusation of narrowness, which seems contradictory in the context of indulgence, may indicate no more than loyalty to principle, intolerance only of intolerance itself.

It is reported that Michael Maurice, because of his unbounded confidence in his son, always met any complaint against him with the invariable answer, " 'His intentions are excellent', and an explanation exculpatory of him."[23] Lest Michael Maurice's behaviour appear to indicate that the man was weak, it is important to take into account that he did make considerable sacrifices for causes to which he was loyal, Unitarianism and the Constitutional Party in Spain.[24] The personal expression of his integrity may have been subtle; its force was all the more telling for that. We may remember the story of Maurice's father walking into the room in which the pupils of his school slept and discovering that they were engaged in a pillow fight. He said nothing, he only stood, but one of the boys later remembered,

> I could not describe his look and I do not know what effect it had upon others, but I know that I myself . . . have never forgotten it to this day, and that during all the time I was with him I could not possibly have engaged in such a business again.[25]

It is more and more apparent that a child's conception of God, and to a large extent adult religious attitudes, are directly connected with the child's relation to its own parents, particularly its father. The broad outlines of Maurice's relationship with Michael Maurice, benevolent, open, yet firm in his convictions, help to explain some of the positive aspects of Maurice's theology and ethical teaching. Maurice himself is a living testimony to his father's parental wisdom. His own relation of obedience to his father's authority, notwithstanding his apparent contradiction of his father's Unitarianism, illustrates beautifully what Maurice called the ethos of the father-son relationship. Michael Maurice's method of education found its tribute in his son's freedom from the constrictions of public opinion and his son's "conscience of freedom", as Maurice liked to define freedom of conscience.

Maurice felt that the parental relationship produced either cowards or slaves. He was wary of "punishment."

> "The sentiment of the forbidden" may always be accompanied with the sentiment of trust in the person who has forbidden. If the child is taught . . . dread . . . not . . . reverence . . . then all has been done . . . to make it grow up a contemptible coward, crouching to every majority which threatens it with the punishments that it has learnt to regard as the greatest and only evils; . . . one who may . . . become the spontaneous agent of a majority in trampling out in others the freedom which has been so assiduously trampled out in him.[26]

A recently published letter from Daniel Macmillan to Thomas
Hughes refers to "Mr Maurice who has not had the least notion of
what cowardice means!"[27] Openness and freedom are the out-
standing qualities of Maurice's relations with his father. Candour is
the word which best describes his letters to Michael Maurice published in Maurice's biography. Candour learned in relationship
with his father enabled Maurice himself to welcome confidences on
the part of his own sons. "A parent who does not identify authority
with punishment wins the confidence of his child in his wisdom and
in his affection. The less he tries to worm any secrets from him the
more frankly they are told."[28] As an illustration, Maurice wrote to
his younger son

> You could not have given me a greater proof of your confidence
> than to tell me of the thoughts which are tormenting you. And
> you may be sure that there are very few of such temptations of
> which I have not known something; enough at least to take
> from me all right to condemn you, and to give me great con-
> fidence that you will be delivered out of them tremendous
> as they are and as you feel them to be.[29]

These words illustrate the whole tenor of the correspondence. It is
borne out by many other of Maurice's letters to Edmund.

> You need not fear, as you know, to tell me any difficulties or
> doubts of yours upon any subject. There is no closer bond
> between parent and child than confidence on such questions
> as those you raise in your letter. As I was brought up in the
> denial of Christ's divinity, these questions cannot be strange
> to me. And since I believe very firmly that it is the Spirit of
> God who awakens us out of mere acquiescence into enquiry
> that He may lead us to a true and solid faith I cannot wish
> that you should escape the struggles which are the usual—
> probably for young men in this day the inevitable—road to
> rest. And rest can *never* be mere repose; rest in God can never
> be rest in sleep.[30]

If the relationship between his father and himself helps account
for some of Maurice's strengths, it may help as well to pinpoint
some of his difficulties. A statement of the elder Maurice's belief
about the Divine relation between the Father and the Son appeared

in *The Christian Reformer*. Writing about Jesus of Nazareth, Michael Maurice said,

> I believe him to be what the Scriptures declare him to be,—the Son of God; sent by the Father of mercies to seek and to save. I regard him as the author and finisher of my faith; the publication of glad tidings; the teacher and perfect example of righteousness. I receive him, not only as proclaiming life and immortality, but as the faithful witness of our own resurrection in his own resurrection and ascension to glory . . . Life and immortality are not only taught, but confirmed, by the resurrection of Jesus.[31]

This declaration of faith illustrates with clarity both what Maurice called the good as well as the evil of Unitarianism, and his father's strengths and weaknesses. Many years later Maurice wrote about the Unitarians:

> The deeper my conviction of the truth of the name into which we are baptized as the ground and reconciliation of all truth has become, the more have I felt a desire to recognize that which I believe they hold or are trying to hold; the more strongly and passionately I believe in a universal atonement and sacrifice, the more do I desire to extricate them from some of the confusions into which the narrow and dark representations of that master-principle and key-note of social harmony have driven them.[32]

The question of personal assurance testified by a strong statement of the atonement and sacrifice could not be resolved among the members of the Maurice household. One by one, perhaps for different reasons, each of the Maurice women "was aroused to feel the need of a personal deliverer, such as her old system did not tell her of."[33] A "teacher and perfect example of righteousness" proclaiming life and immortality was not enough.

PRISCILLA MAURICE
SELF-CONSCIOUS SENSITIVITY

Their father's "benevolent indulgence" indirectly made his children's restlessness possible, but the source of the "morbid sensitivity"[34] which marred Maurice's life must be discovered elsewhere. There are many indications that its origin lies principally with his mother, although his elder sisters, Elizabeth, Anne, and Mary, contributed to his deep insecurity.

His biographer acknowledged a special relationship between F. D. Maurice and his mother.

> Mrs Michael Maurice's letters are the dictionary of her son's writings [he said]. In those which I have given, her use of "principles," "everlasting," "Gospel," "eternal life," are quite as unlike the conventional use of her day as her son's use of them was unlike the conventional use of his time. I believe I am right in saying that many other expressions such as "honest," "persons and things," etc., which he sometimes uses in a rather peculiar sense, might be similarly traced back to the habit of his boyhood.[35]

Maurice himself wrote "My mother had a far clearer intellect than my father, a much more lively imagination, a capacity for interests in a number of subjects, and an intense individual sympathy."[36] Maurice was never able to be objective enough about his relationship with his mother that he could speak, as he had done about his father, of "the conceit," if pharisaical, "that he knew more than [she] did."[37] It is not without significance that when he began his only attempt at what he called "a course of ethics," he wrote immediately after mentioning the first objects presented to the senses of the new born that "he has also human relations—a mother at all events, a father; perhaps brothers and sisters."[38]

Listing mother before father was unusual for Maurice, but that there was an unusually close connection between Maurice and his mother is certain. In one autobiographical letter, he wrote,

> I had three sisters older than myself. Two years before I was born my parents lost a little boy in croup. My mother could never utter his name; in all our intercourse I do not think she ever alluded to him; though I always perceived a shudder when

any of us or any child for whom she cared was said to have the complaint which carried him off. In her papers there are many references to the boy. I think I must owe part of the peculiar tenderness which she always showed me to my having come in a certain degree to supply his place, though she was such a mother to us all that the word peculiar is somewhat out of place.[39]

Mrs Maurice herself wrote about her children: "I think I love them all alike though sometimes interesting and amiable qualities may for a time have particularly attracted me—but I think it has been the same in all. I wish I could enlarge."[40] In his own teachings Maurice stressed the role of the mother as well as the role of the father. If "the authority which stamps itself on the life of a man" most obviously dwells with the father, "the union of the mother's influence with the father's helps to distinguish authority from dominion."[41] She must "counteract any disposition which there might be in the male parent to demand of his son mere agreement with his conclusions."[42] Maurice apparently joined motherhood with fatherhood in the parental relationship appointed by God to co-operate in the divine work. Certainly the child was immediately aware of the mother when he began to distinguish between persons and objects. For all that he had said about fatherhood, it was at the mother's knee, Maurice felt, that the child first was led to know God.

It would be interesting to know more about the role of Maurice's own mother in a household where none of the children eventually remained in agreement with the father's conclusions. The mother, Maurice said, "never can regard a child as a possession; she never can appeal exclusively or mainly to his intellect."[43] Her co-operation in authority (education) tempers it, divests it of its inhumanity, insures that it is effectual not just in one section but in the whole of the child's existence. Even where there is not co-operation, Maurice wrote in one pregnant phrase, "by the disorder which the collision produces" we discern "what the true order of the household is,"[44] for "all *disorder* implies an *order*",[45]—an unmistakably Maurician phrase.

Priscilla Hurry Maurice was, however, an apprehensive woman all her life, chronically worried about the welfare, physical and spiritual, not only of herself but others. Troubled by what she felt to be the weakness of the Unitarian creed, feeling the need of "a

personal deliverer" which she did not find in Unitarianism, Mrs
Maurice turned to what she called "the God revealed in the Scriptures."[46] While she adopted Calvinism in her sense of assuming "the
existence in the world of a select body who are known as the
'elect' ",[47] she was never able to be satisfied that she herself could
give the accredited proofs of belonging to that select body. Her
religious difficulties manifested the deep underlying personal insecurity which showed itself in her anxiety about her own health
and the health of her family. "My mother suffered from asthma,"[48]
Maurice recorded, mentioning as well "her fancy, which made her
very miserable by filling her with the most unnecessary fears about
all who were dear to her . . .".[49]

From time to time she became convinced that she was dying.
Then she would write long, careful letters of commendation and
counsel to her husband as well as to her children and her friends.[50]
An illustration of her concern appears in a story told by the old
family nurse. The woman had offered a plum to Frederick as she
had to the other children. "He drew himself up to his full height
and—giving her surname and Christian name in full instead of
the usual 'Betsy'—'Elizabeth'—, I did think *you* would have known
better than to do that, and would have remembered mamma wishes
us never to have fruit except she gives it herself." An undeserved
reproof, declared the servant, who was trusted by Mrs Maurice in
such matters, but she added, "I never forgot his look, nor have
I ever felt a reproof deeper."[51]

Once Mrs Maurice, "moved by the prospect of death",[52] wrote:

> Exhort my dear Frederick to attend to the One thing needful.
> I trust that already, it has pleased the gracious Saviour to select
> him as one who shall hereafter be a faithful minister of the
> Everlasting Gospel. May it be the end and object of his life to
> devote himself to Him who is able to do abundantly more for
> him that I can ask or wish. May the world have no allurements
> for my beloved Boy but may he stand up boldly, in the name
> of his Master, indifferent to every earthly pursuit. Tell him
> to remember that I cheerfully resigned him during a dangerous
> illness, to my God, wishing only, that dying or living he should
> be wholly His.[53]

This letter was not an isolated example; it indicated a consistent
attitude and illustrated a lasting quality of the relationship between

mother and son. Again, thinking she was dying, Mrs Maurice instructed her daughters:

> My dear Frederick will demand great affection and forbearance and watchfulness. Incline him, by affectionate attentions and study for his comfort, to be much with you, and watch over him that he may be kept from all dangerous companions, and from the peculiar temptations to which his circumstances expose him. I wish it were possible, that you might speak to him on the most important subjects with unreserve because I know that nothing but the principle produced by the real doctrines of the Gospel can have any effect in preserving from sin. That happy time may come, when his dear Father may wish this to be; but as it is, do all you can for my most darling Boy, who I trust will be a devoted Minister of the Everlasting Gospel, and I do most earnestly hope, that by the blessing of GOD on his study of the Scriptures, all truth will be revealed to him, without any human assistance.[54]

One more sample of her anxiety appeared in this letter when in reference to the youngest children, she adjured, "Watch over them incessantly . . . never leave them alone with any other young persons."[55]

In the apprehensions of his mother, religious and otherwise, Maurice experienced and understood at first hand what he called subjective (rather than personal) religion, the self-conscious study of "feelings, emotions, and states of mind . . . for the purpose of finding out what we are, of settling the question about our personal relation to God."[56] Such "subjective religion", Maurice said, was always haunted by the "fear of proving that the blessings and promises of the Gospel are not meant for us."[57] It is not surprising that a child as sensitive as Maurice should become morally self-conscious to a degree which sometimes bordered on being pathological.

ELIZABETH, MARY, ANNE
SEEDS OF CONTROVERSY

His parents were not the only influences in the Maurice household. Frederick Denison was the one surviving son in a family of eight sisters, three of them older and five of them younger than himself. Augustus Hare mentioned the Maurice sisters and "their tireless search after the motes in their brother's eyes."[58] Mrs Maurice wrote to them: "May levity and light inconsiderate conversation, contention and evil surmises of others give place . . ."[59] "Though I know you have numerous faults; many which have often deeply affected me, and more, which have grieved your own hearts; yet I feel assured you have given yourselves to God . . ."[60] The Maurices were no ordinary women. One ofter another the older girls and then their mother embraced different and conflicting religious beliefs. It was not unusual for members of the family to arise from the breakfast table, retire to their rooms, and write long explanatory letters to one another explaining why they were unable to share common religious worship.[61]

Maurice carried scars from his family's religious controversies all his life. It is true that he asserted that family relationship itself provided a unity which lay beneath what he called purely surface disagreements, different religious opinions. But the deep longing for an underlying unity and order which is such a characteristic of his thought may be the expression of an unconsious lack of ease in the presence of conflicting points of view dating back to his earliest years.

Something of the temper of the family even before open religious breaks appeared was captured in the earliest piece of Maurice's writing which has been preserved, a versified letter written when he was ten years old. He described in detail a typical evening at home in which the Maurice sisters were conducting a Bible class for the women of the neighbourhood.

> Oh Jones! how I wish that with equal discerning
> The *men* like the women were lovers of learning!
> "That the ladies are given to change" poets *say*
> But, as you my dear friend the remark won't betray
> In justice to them I must own in this letter
> That when they do change 'tis a change for the better. . . .

That when to their husbands at home they return
They sharply may say while he looks like a fool
"I am better than you, Sir! for I've been to school",
Well! Whilst in our study the wives made a riot
One hour in the week the poor men are in quiet.
Lamenting the troubles on wedlock that fall,
And advising their sons not to marry at all.[62]

The letter began interestingly:

As my sisters declare I must write
To relate the successes of yesterday night,
I have rather unwillingly taken to pen;
Which I hope very soon to relinquish again.[63]

A touch of self-consciousness about the influence of his sisters was
betrayed in a conversation between ladies in *Eustace Conway*.

"Your brother is a proof that intercourse with females does not
retard the growth of manliness in a character. Was he much
with Mr Vyvyan in his childhood?"

"Yes; his society must have been useful counteracting the weakness of ours."

"I should hardly have thought that," said Mrs Hartenfield.
"Does it strike you that Mr Vyvyan's character is remarkable
for strength?"[64]

In the conversation with the novel's heroine, Mrs Hartenfield had
just said, "It seems as if vigour and ferocity, weakness and benevolence, were betrothed to each other in our infancies."

"Neither marriage will ever take place in my brother's heart,"
said Honoria; "yet his reverence for strength amounts almost to
idolatry. 'I care not,' he sometimes says to me, 'for witty men,
for imaginative men, for reasoning men; I meet such at every
turn; and what comes of the meeting?—Nothing but vanity,
in both its senses. We try to seem clever to each other; and we
go away, seeming exceedingly clever to ourselves. What I want
is a strong man, one whom I may meet and grapple with in a
death embrace' "[65]

These words express Maurice's own need for the resolution of insecurity.

Maurice made several attempts to write an autobiographical account of his early years in answer to his son's request. All of them began bravely but broke off abruptly. One unpublished letter to "Freddy" ended with the sentences "I had more of the non-conformist feeling than probably most children of dissenters have. It was communicated to me both by my father and my mother and it entered into me strongly and appeared to penerate deeply." The word "appeared" in the last sentence was inserted later in Maurice's own hand. He altered the phrase from "it entered into me more strongly and penetrated deeply."[66]

More telling is the final sentence in one of the published letters:

> These events in my family influenced me powerfully; but not in the way which either of my parents or my sisters would have desired, nor in a way to which I can look back, so far as my then temper of mind was concerned, with the least complacency.
>
> These years were to me years of moral confusion and contradiction. I had none of the freedom . . .

So the manuscript ends.[67]

John Frederick Maurice appreciated the tension created when his father attempted to analyse the religious turmoil of his family in his early childhood.

> My father made repeated attempts during the last six years of his life to record the history of this change, but he always broke off abruptly. The effort was too great. The sense of the painful wrenches to which his father had been exposed, as the family gradually left him alone in his communion, was perhaps the chief, but was not quite the only cause that made those parts of the story which most influenced my father's career impossible for an affectionate son and brother to write. A sense that there had for a long time been a mere change in the objects of the intolerant expressions which passed his two eldest sisters' mouths, the intolerance of feeling remaining till a distinct and singular experience had softened it in each of them; the great love and even admiration which he entertained for his sisters; the difficulty for a brother to give in any kind of measure which should not appear exaggerated an account of the many high

qualities in them to which strangers have done such ample justice that almost each one of a large family has been spoken of by some whose judgements carry weight in terms of exceptional eulogy—these account at all events to some extent for my father's finding the task impossible. That, under the strain of trouble and perplexity, his father became captious and irritable, no doubt did not make it more easy.[68]

SCAR OF INWARD TURMOIL
OUTWARD SHYNESS

The inner lack of freedom which Maurice confessed appeared on the surface as shyness and self-effacing humility. Julius Hare, his tutor at Cambridge, later his brother-in-law, remembered him in 1822. There was, he said, in his classroom, "a pupil whose metaphysical powers were among the greatest he had ever come in contact with, but that the man was so shy that it was almost impossible to know him."[69] Various anecdotes are related in the biography of Maurice which give a picture of the little boy in the formative years. As a child, his later shyness appeared as an extraordinary "goodness". Apart from being bookish, Maurice was remembered as a "good" child. Shortly after his death, a cousin wrote from Australia;

> I remember my dear cousin Frederick when he was nearly six years old . . . such a bright clever little fellow, full of fun, with the sweetest temper; quite a boy, but never mischievous like most boys. I do not think it was even in his nature to play a mischievous trick; he was kind and gentle, as I ever remember him.[70]

His mother was fond of telling how Frederick Maurice, then five years old, entered the room with a biscuit in one hand and a flower in the other. A stranger who was present whispered to her, "Children always give up what they least care for: now we shall see which he likes best!" Then aloud, "Frederick! which will you give me, the flower or the biscuit?" Whereupon the child held out both hands, saying, "Choose which you like."[71]

Maurice's shyness seen in childhood docility or in adult reticence never left him. His biographer repeatedly made reference to it. Many years later when he returned to Cambridge as Knightbridge

Professor, he would generally invite some young lady to be present "to break the ice" when he entertained undergraduates.[72] His diffidence in pastoral visits was mentioned by his son who said that the habit of the famous "prophetic breakfasts" was "itself forced on him as much by his shyness as by his hospitality and by his kindliness of feeling towards all men. He wanted something to break the ice."[73]

Maurice's shyness was accompanied by an exaggerated if genuine humility.[74] "What books have since called 'the noble and pathetic monotone' of his life, which was 'like the burden of a Gregorian chaunt', describes him exactly, but was extremely depressing," wrote Augustus Hare. "He maundered over his own humility in a way which—even to a child—did not seem humble . . ."[75] Maurice's intense humility was a conspicuous element in his character. It explained his persistent refusal to visit Coleridge.[76] His "self-abasement" caused Joseph Adam Stephenson to offer him a title in Lympsham in 1832.[77]

Lack of confidence early along began to cripple his professional life; he declined the offer of a Downing College tutorship in 1836,[78] and in 1843 refused to stand for the preachership of Lincoln's Inn, or the Principalship of King's College, London.[79] By 1844, he was becoming sensitive to the fact that his classes were not popular with students.[80] Later he wrote that small classes had been a helpful stimulus to humiliation.[81]

In answer to a letter from Robert Scott about his efforts to organize classes for medical students at Guy's Hospital, he wrote

> I am sorry to say that my answer must be very unsatisfactory. My friends must have greatly exaggerated my attempts . . . Last year I was applied to by a few of the students to give them a course on Ecclesiastical History. I had about 12 or 14 hearers for two or three months, but this year I have not succeeded in getting a class.[82]

Even when he had accepted positions of authority, resignation was never far from his mind. His correspondence at Queen's College was filled with offers of resignation; when he actually resigned in 1853, he wrote that his class in moral philosophy was the smallest in the college, and his class in English literature had only been a substitute for Strettel.[83] In 1850 he suggested cancelling the moral philosophy lecture because the number of students was small and "likely to grow smaller."[84]

In a letter to the students at the Working Men's College, Maurice said that the dwindling away of his classes was an "admonition that I was not saying what I should have said."[85] He attributed his "failure" as a lecturer to his efforts "being too full of a thought", and from his not devoting enough time to considering how it may be best communicated to others.[86] Maurice as a teacher and preacher was selfconscious and critical of himself; he was always likely to misconstrue the reactions of others to his disadvantage. In 1869, about to withdraw from his chaplaincy at St Peter's, Vere Street, he wrote:

> I received minutes from the Trustees of the Chapel signifying that the rents of it have fallen from the year after I went to it. That I took as a notice to quit; my wife looking at it in the same light. I therefore placed my resignation in [Lloyds] hands and felt relieved.[87]

Maurice's lack of self-confidence made him peculiarly diffident about trying to impose his opinions upon others.

> ...He in the opinion of most of his friends carried to an almost criminal extent his determination not to do so—[wrote his biographer to Leslie Stephen]. In one very curious case he actually refused to see a young Jewess who had been much affected by what she had heard of him: and of whom a medical man warned him that the consequences might be very serious if he did not see her. It ended by her actually committing suicide. I am not of course here saying that he was right, but it shows the point to which he carried a view which he very definitely expressed in the Theological Essays themselves. "I am a very bad Proselytizer."[88]

Beneath outward shyness and extreme self-abasement all too frequently lies a tortured state of mind. Inner tensions, which Maurice confessed in letters of counsel to his sons, show that the influence of his mother's anxiety and his opinionated, suspicious sisters had taken its toll. He wrote a revealing letter at the time of the Colenso controversy when he finally withdrew his proposed resignation from St Peter's, Vere Street. His son had not been sympathetic with his father's decision to resign and took exception to what he supposed to be his father's, even more Mrs Maurice's, "insistence" on his sympathy. Maurice disclaimed any desire for sympathy. He continued:

But the mistake itself has worried me much less than the thought that you have inherited from me a habit of misconstruing words and attributing unkind motives which has been the curse and grievous sin of my life. Oh my dearest Freddy, if I have no right because I am free from the sin to cast stones at you for it, yet let me conjure you, by the anguish it has caused me, by the good from which it has cut me off, to fight against it as a very devil! I must speak if they were to be my last words; oh beware of it lest it should lead you to madness. For madness does lie in it. And every one of us has need to watch over the sanity of his own mind by every means which God gives him. I could tell you fearful things of the absolute necessity of watching and praying to our Father in Heaven against this temper of mind. . . . The need of not suspecting unkindness in them who care for us and would die for us. I say again; I blame myself much more than I blame you. But I am anxious to save you from this demon as I am to save myself. I am sure we may help each other in striving against it. The cruel perversions of our intentions in some of your late letters would have led me to speak harshly if I had yielded to my own impulses. Your mother would not let me yield to them, though your misrepresentations had been particularly directed against her and she had felt the smart of them keenly. She was right. I have to confess and implore not to find fault. I do confess that you have seen a bad example of those suspicions and perversions in me. I do implore you to let that nobler, truer, tender mind which your Father above has given you triumph over the tendencies you have derived from me. I speak very very earnestly. Do not put a wrong construction upon these words also. They are words of love if I ever wrote any.[89]

Several years later, Maurice also wrote to his younger son who thought he had been slighted by his older brother. Maurice assured him

The habit of brooding over unkind words that have been said to me, over unkind thoughts which I suppose others have

B

cherished towards me, has been one of those to which I have
yielded most, and which has interfered most with my attention
to what one time or another has demanded my attention. I
could accuse myself bitterly of having transmitted that habit to
you; still more of having done so little to warn you of it and to
cultivate the opposite habit in you. But no good would come of
that. I can help you far better by assuring you that the habit,
though it may never cease to be a plague, can be completely
overcome if we will dwell on that which is good and gracious
and lovely and use it to [   ] against those ugly and hideous
impressions which start up to separate us from those whom we
most desire to love . . ."[90]

"BED-RIDDEN WOMEN"
SELF-IMPOSED SERVITUDE

Apart from his shyness, exaggerated humility, his restlessness and
lack of self-confidence, Maurice apparently had a compulsive need
to care for unquestionably neurotic sick women. This compulsion
coupled with intense personal self-discipline amounted almost to
the point of caricature.[91] Leslie Stephen was not the only one to
notice and criticize Maurice's frequent appeal "against the opinions
of learned men" to the authority of "bed-ridden old women".[92]
His biographer noted how often he referred "back in thought to
the sick-beds of Guy's, of his sister Emma, or of others whom he
had known, and to speak of 'the bed-ridden woman' to whom
truth revealed itself because of her need and not because of her
intellect".[93] Save for the early, and all too few, years of his first
marriage, he was involved in essentially self-imposed attendance
upon chronic invalids.

Maurice returned home from London in 1829 to replace his
sister Mary at the bedside of his sister Emma.[94] Maurice's sister
Priscilla was another of the women he attended. Priscilla went with
him to his first parish, Bubbenhall in Warwickshire. She kept house
for him there from 1833 and continued as his housekeeper at
Guy's Hospital until his marriage in 1837.[95] After Annie Barton
died, Priscilla returned to stay with Maurice until his second marriage.[96] Priscilla was a sick woman for most of this period. She
wrote six books on sickness and death; one, *Sickness: its Trials and*

Blessings, ran to seven editions.[97] Among the subjects she discussed
was "Sickness, a vocation."[98] Augustus Hare, never predisposed to
the Maurices, mentioned "Priscilla, who . . . never left her bed,
and who was violently sick after everything she ate (yet with the
most enormous appetite), often for many months together."[99]
Though Augustus Hare was occasionally unreliable, his opinion of
Priscilla was accurate. Maurice's letters referred to his sister's health;
her meals were regularly taken upstairs to her rooms.

Worse however was to follow. Lucilla Powell recorded that

> in July 1849, Frederick Denison Maurice married Georgina
> Frances Hare . . . an intimate friend of his first wife. She was
> a great invalid, when he married her (having had bad health
> from her childhood) and has been so ever since, but that only
> served to enhance his tenderness, and until his last illness in
> 1872, he watched over her with the most chivalrous devotion,
> and self-denying love. He had chosen her, knowing his Annie's
> love for her, and justly believing that his two dear boys, would
> receive from their Mother's friend, the love of which they had
> been so early deprived.[100]

From the time of his marriage until his death, scarcely one of
Maurice's letters failed to make some reference to the bad or
deteriorating state of Georgina's health. Augustus Hare was
scarcely charitable about the second Mrs Maurice, his father's half-
sister. "Georgina Hare-Naylor", as he called her, had ruined her
health because of her fondness for dancing. After one ball when
she danced round the clock,

> she had to lie on her back for a year. From this time she defied
> the Italian proverb, "Let well alone", and dosed herself inces-
> santly. She had acquired "l'habitude d'être malade"; she liked
> the sympathy she excited, and henceforth *preferred* being ill.
> Once or twice every year she was dying, the family were
> summoned, everyone was in tears, they knelt around her bed;
> it was the most delicious excitement.[101]
>
> She was married during what was supposed to be her last ill-
> ness, but was so pleased with her nuptials that she recovered
> after the ceremony and lived for nearly half a century after-
> wards.[102]

Augustus Hare's evidence about the second Mrs Maurice was borne out in Maurice's correspondence and in the opinions of his friends. When Maurice was dismissed from King's College, London, Daniel Macmillan wrote his brother Alexander:

> I asked him about the future and half repent having done so. His answer was, "sufficient unto the day is the evil thereof". Mrs Maurice is rather a "cheeping body". I wish he had a more lively and braver wife. But pray don't whisper this to anyone. I may be mistaken.[103]

"I only remember her a sickly, discontented, petulant woman,"[104] wrote Augustus Hare.

There is evidence that Georgina was not only less than supportive. John Malcolm Ludlow felt that she was a decidedly negative influence on her husband. "Maurice had succumbed to the influence of his wife and her brother, Julius Hare, who wanted him to withdraw from the Christian Socialist movement, the radical views of which they did not share and which they thought damaging to his reputation".[105] Ludlow continued in his autobiography: "Observing her total want of interest in Co-operation as such, I have suspected that her influence had largely worked on Mr Maurice to dissever him from active connection with the movement".[106] Later Ludlow wrote:

> 'I may now say, what I should not have liked to say in Mrs Maurice's life-time, that I consider one powerful influence towards withdrawing Mr Maurice from any active part in the co-operative movement was the Hare influence, including her own. Archdeacon Hare, as I have said before, always disliked Christian Socialism; his sister,—tho' she was on the Committee of the Working Needlewomen's Association—certainly took not the slightest interest in it for its own sake. Often and often as I have seen her since her husband's death, I never but once remember her speaking to me about co-operation,—asking how it was getting on—and then she did not care to dwell on the subject'.[107]

Maurice denied Ludlow's accusation.

You think that I have become subject to some strange and perverse "influence". So far as *persons* are concerned I am sure that you are mistaken; no one has suggested to me the course which I have taken on any questions upon which I have been at issue with you; it is only rarely and by accident that anyone has known what they are.[108]

Maurice also wrote "You are wrong and I think hard in imputing my indolence to my wife's sickness. Whatever I have done in the way of Christian Socialism has been done since I married."[109]

Deny Ludlow's suspicion if he would, it is questionable if his second marriage to Georgina Hare-Naylor did anything to resolve the external and internal strains in his emotional life. His tensions appeared to increase and may explain what many feel to be a decline in the quality of his work after 1850. The second Mrs Maurice seemed only to leave her bedroom for her couch, and only to leave her house to travel to some place where the air, or the altitude, or the sea was hoped might improve her breathing, or her rheumatism, her dizziness, her palpitations, or her sciatica.

It was always uncertain if Mrs Maurice's health would allow her husband to be away from home overnight.[110] Their journeys together were interrupted for weeks at a time while she recovered strength to continue.[111] A carriage ride, a few hundred paces, from St Peter's Terrace, Cambridge to St Edward's Church for the baptism of Maurice's first grandson in 1871 was sufficient to confine Mrs Maurice to her bed for a week.[112]

The pattern in this marriage of never ending and never accomplished convalescence was only to be expected from the start; it reproduced the earlier pattern of Maurice's nine years of life with his sister Priscilla, and the months which he spent nursing Emma. There was something inescapably compulsive about the marriage, an extension of the atmosphere of his childhood relationships with his mother and sisters.

Maurice himself was not free from physical symptoms commonly associated with emotional stress. His mother's letters often noted her son's depression; in 1835, due to a "succession of carbuncles", Maurice had to leave Bubbenhall for a time and go to Milford for sea air and bathing.[113] It was agreed in order for him to escape from Warwickshire that he would return to London to take a church in Knightsbridge with Sterling.[114] Unfortunately,

Sterling's own deteriorating health compelled him to go abroad,
and Maurice accepted the chaplaincy of Guy's Hospital.

Maurice had been brought up in an atmosphere of intense, intro-
spective moral self-consciousness, which he called "subjective
religion", "finding out what we are, . . . settling the question about
our personal relation to God, . . . through fear" lest "the blessings
and promises of the Gospel are not meant for us".[115] He sensed
the bondage which inevitably resulted from such a form of extreme
moral scrupulousness, sensitive to be sure, yet patently self-centred.
In the context of such introspection there could be only bondage.
And Maurice did feel bound. He had "none of the freedom . . .".
His son remarked how curious it was that a man of his strongly
dramatic tastes only occasionally visited a theatre or opera even
when, as a critic, he was provided open entrance. The reasons
suggested were

> that he never could be content with the amount of work he
> had done, and was therefore unwilling to take a holiday; . . .
> that . . . he always thought someone else would do the criticism
> better than himself . . . [and] . . . a certain unwillingness to
> traverse the feelings of his mother and sisters, even in matters in
> which he did not think reasonable.[116]

Maurice's life was scattered with similar examples of scrupulousness. His son wrote:

> He was always an early riser. Hardly ever later than 6 a.m.,
> often much earlier than that, the sound of the splash of the
> cold tub, which summer and winter, down to the end of his
> life, he invariably took both the first thing in the morning and
> the last at night, was to be heard, and a curiously pathetic
> almost agonised 'shou-shou' followed, which seemed to tell
> that, for a frame that was kept so low as his by constant brain-
> work and a somewhat self-stinted diet, the shock was almost a
> penance endured rather than enjoyed.[117]

Maurice's life was marked by constant abstinence, fasting, and self-
denial. Many of his habits would be praised by all, such as his
regular fetching of cabs or delivering messages rather than letting a
maid-servant be exposed to bad weather.[118] As a duty to his servants,

he nearly always went round himself and paid the bills, both in London and Cambridge.[119] Yet it seems fair to say that the pattern of his habits indicated that the internal battle to which Maurice continually referred was never resolved.[120] He himself appeared never to be able to accept and manifest that peace of God about which he spoke to others.[121]

2

The Moralist
in Action

———— • ✦ • ————

OBSCURITY
OR AN HONEST QUEST FOR TRUTH?

The human face fascinated Maurice. Word portraits and descriptions of paintings often illustrated his works.[1] A typical example appeared in his correspondence with Edmund.

> I am glad that you have seen Gladstone and have been able to judge a little of what his face indicates. It is a very expressive one; hard worked as you say, and not perhaps specially happy; more indicative of struggle than of victory but not without promise of that.[2]

Maurice felt that an unlined face showed lack of inner earnestness, of not having wrestled adequately with life's problems. The description of Gladstone might well have described Maurice himself. He was actually a popular subject for painters, sculptors, and photographers. He and Carlyle inspired the two "brain-workers" in Ford Madox Brown's "Work".[3] Brown wrote a description of his subject,

> in friendly communion with the philosopher, smiling perhaps at some of his wild sallies and cynical thrusts . . . [He] is intended for a kindred and yet very dissimilar spirit. A clergyman, such as the Church of England offers examples of—a priest without guile—a gentleman without pride, much in communion with the working classes, "honouring all men",

"never weary in well doing". Scholar, author, philosopher, and teacher, too, in his way, but not above practical efforts, if even for a small resulting good. Deeply penetrated as he is with the axiom that each unit of humanity feels as much as all the rest combined, and impulsive and hopeful in nature, so that the remedy suggests itself to him concurrently with the evil.[4]

His face shows ordered outward calm, a half inward gentle smile, a look in his eye, some said, as if fixed upon a point just beyond ordinary vision.

"Work" may not be the only painting in which Brown used Maurice as a model. There is an opinion that Brown used him for the "reprobate" in "Last of England", who

> shakes his fist with curses at the land of his birth, as though that were answerable for *his* want of success; his old mother reproves him for his foul-mouthed profanity, while a boon companion, with flushed countenance, and got up in nautical togs for the voyage, signifies drunken approbation.[5]

"Last of England" is more a caricature of opposites than straightforward portraiture, but it indicates that the artist had an insight into the inward tension from which Maurice was never freed. That tension helps to explain some of Maurice's reputed obscurity. It has always been commonplace to think of Maurice as obscure; his tortuous style and apparent contradiction baffled and exasperated his contemporaries. Indeed he is spoken of as a seminal rather than a systematic theologian whose value lies in brilliant flashes of insight, rather than in a carefully ordered and integrated structure. Some admirers claim that valuable material was set like nuggets or jewels among much which might well be consigned to the flames. Maurice was doubtless difficult to understand. His obscurity arose in part out of inward tension which lasted throughout his life. In his work as a moralist Maurice required an external counter-irritant to draw him out of himself, compelling him to follow the conclusions of his inward conviction and to make those conclusions outwardly clear by being forced to live in accordance with them. When he was questioned in a setting of love and gentle support, his inner pressures could be directed into creative channels. Too often either he was not questioned at all, or there was an impersonal quality about his opposition which simply allowed or forced his internal pressures to be destructive.

Correspondence with Edmund disclosed that Maurice was aware of this difficulty.

> I have no doubt that it is very good for him and for all men to be associated in work with those who differ from them. It need not make them the least truckling; it may even bring out their own convictions more strongly, and yet may give them a respect for their opponents and a belief that they have convictions too which must be salutary. I have suffered from the want of this collision and have often become morbid and suspicious and opinionated because I have hugged my own thoughts too closely and not exposed them to the air.[6]

The sheer quantity of his writing gives another insight into the man and provides another possible reason for his obscurity. It is estimated that Maurice's published writings extend to more than 16,300 octavo pages and contain nearly 5,000,000 words.[7] Even Maurice's friends felt that he wrote too much. "Pray don't think of writing an Easter-day sermon for the subscription. We had too many sermons in last years series",[8] Ludlow once begged him. "Had we only such books as his we could not have lasted three years", Alexander Macmillan lamented. "Could I have guided Maurice's pen I would have published about three books for him instead of thirty."[9] Daniel Macmillan wrote,

> I would strongly advise Maurice not to publish any more books than those already projected. I know from something he said that he would like to say something about the war, but I took no notice of it. He has quite enough on his hands already. When he is writing on the Apocalypse, he can come out about the war.[10]

There is an opinion that Maurice was difficult to understand because he dictated his thoughts pacing up and down the room, but it is doubtful if dictation caused his obscurity.[11] Besides his unresolved tension and the quantity of his writing, the feverish rapidity of his composition may have contributed to his tortuous style. Maurice's biographer observed that "the rush of his start for a walk had gone" by the time of his Cambridge years as Knightbridge professor.[12] Quite an opposite situation appeared in his writing. The surviving manuscripts of Maurice's sermons, lectures, and correspondence show great care at the start. Letters were clearly formed and lines were regularly spaced and drawn out—in the beginning. But Maurice picked up momentum as he wrote. By the end of the second or third paragraph he was writing furiously, often illegibly; he used his own distinctive shorthand system of abbreviation, slashing out whole sections of the text, and filling the margins with alterations. Maurice was carried away by his thoughts which came too fast for him to write down; he was caught up in the sheer volume and flow of words. It seemed important for him to write and write and write, as if a compulsion drove him on to attempt to express, even to discover what he was trying to say. Only rarely was anyone able to curb him and force him to say less, but to say it more carefully. He was never able to hone his thoughts to a precision which made them instruments needed to express his ideas.

Maurice's reputation for being hard to understand did not go unchallenged. In comparison with the vivid visual literalness of his beloved pre-Raphaelite painters, Maurice might be said to be an "impressionist" theologian. Octavia Hill defended Maurice against Ruskin when he accused him of obscurity, but there is no indication that she was ever given the three quarters of an hour which she claimed was all she needed to make his style crystal clear to anyone.[13]

Defending himself, Maurice claimed that he refused to lay violent hands on truth, to dismember truth into its parts, supposedly to make it easier to understand, actually to destroy it altogether, killing that which is by its very nature alive. A. M. Ramsey touched this point when he wrote, "Things which we commonly grasp in one-sided antitheses, Maurice saw in their undivided oneness."[14] What Maurice said about his refusal to dissect the "wholeness" of "faith" is applicable in all his writing. "Our systematizers and logicians it seems to me must always have every notion by itself, fixed to the dissecting table ready to be anatomatized. Faith must stand all by itself when the glory of Faith as St. Paul and Luther understand it is that it cannot stand alone but in itself it [means] nothing."[15] This characteristic of Maurice's thought is equally illustrated by his discussion of two meanings of the word flesh, "the flesh, so far as it is identical with the body . . ." and

> . . . the flesh so far as it is identical with the corruption into which man has fallen . . . Neither of these senses of the word flesh can be exclusively adopted or rejected; something of the idea would perish if the ambiguity were removed from the expression; a consideration perpetually lost sight of by commentators and theologians in their eagerness to nail a word to one dead, invariable use, but most important for the clearness, the honesty and the vitality of our thoughts, really helping not hindering us to arrive at as simple a view of the case as the case itself permits.[16]

Maurice not only objected to the destructive compartmental analysis of truth in a moment in time, horizontally as it were; he equally affirmed the unity of truth in a dimension temporally vertical. Locke and others like him had interpreted stages of growth as "the senses awakening before the Understanding", but he had disastrously failed to acknowledge

> another stage of growth, the awakening of an inward eye, wherein we discern spiritual objects, corresponding to the outward eye of sense . . . because he only looks at the man in his *time* growth; precisely because the child *is* to him nothing save that which it has *become*. The existence of that which perceives an absolute truth and reality, the pure intuitive beholding is denied by them as a fact of experience because they cannot look beyond experience, because they have no notion of a tree being in the seed in any other sense than the material one of its actually carrying branches, leaves, bark within it (if I do not mistake this is Mr Coleridge's own illustration).[17]

Writing to Sara Coleridge, Maurice acclaimed those "passages in your father's writings which speak of the truths of the Reason as necessarily embodied, if expressed in our minds at all, in two contradictory propositions."[18] One of Maurice's grievances with parties and sectarian points of view was that the "husks and shells" of their opinions hid the opposite truth rather than led us to a "reconciliation of warring opinions". There is a real difficulty in any attempt to express with simple clarity, a truth which though simple must be acknowledged in depth and breadth, a fabric or tissue of many dimensions. That it was simple, Maurice never denied. Indeed he affirmed the ultimate simplicity of what he was trying to say.

For all its simplicity, Maurice admitted the difficulty which he, in any case, had in trying to express what he meant. He knew that many people found him difficult to understand. He apologized to Mrs Coleridge, explaining that

> The dread of saying something which I do not mean or of conveying an impression of what I mean entirely different from the actual thing or of giving that which may be in my mind at the moment but yet only half of the truth which lies at the root of my mind and perhaps the half that may damage the half which just then I ought most to sympathize with in the mind of a correspondent or friend; this dread, not unconfirmed by painful experience, often keeps me silent when I ought to speak and when any person of freer spirit and stronger faith would at once be able to speak. It is a very ignominious nightmare but one which it requires no slight effort of the will to shake off. If I could convey the full sense of it to you—which I should be sorry to do—you would perhaps enter more into the meaning of some of my phrases and modes of thinking which have puzzled you.[19]

ANNA BARTON
A MOMENT OF TRUST, ETERNITY

The years of Maurice's first marriage saw the publication of much of his best work: the first and second editions of the *Kingdom of Christ, Lectures on National Education,* and the essay which grew into *Moral and Metaphysical Philosophy.*[20] The reputation which Maurice gained during this time led to his appointment in 1845 both to the Boyle Lectureship and the Warburton Lectureship.[21] He became Professor of English Literature and Modern History at King's College, London, in 1840.[22] He was urged to become a candidate for the principalship in 1843, and on the establishment of a special theological department, he was invited by Dr Jelf to become a professor in that department.[23] He accepted the chair which was later entitled the Professorship of Ecclesiastical History.[24] If these years were rewarding, they were also the happiest years of Maurice's life, lending support to the view that he was stimulated to do his best work when he was able to carry on a dialogue in the context of loving understanding and personal support. Janet Elizabeth Courtney valued Annie Barton's contribution to Maurice's work, mentioning her "tranquillising and strengthening effect".[25] Lucilla Powell recorded Maurice's marriage to Anna Eleanor Stuart Barton, "the very joy and delight of our hearts."[26] That might be an expected evaluation of personality in the context of the *Annals,* but even Augustus Hare spoke highly of "Annie Barton, whom I remember as a very sweet and winning person."[27] Mrs Thomas Carlyle's tribute to Annie Barton is preserved.

> The *very best wife* that I have ever seen in this world, and you the very most affectionate husband that I have ever known—I have said it to my husband over and over again that you were the *only* pair in my whole acquaintance who seemed to me to make of married life what it was originally intended to be—a *"holy* estate of Matrimony" . . .

Carlyle himself said, "poor *good* Annie Maurice!—what *will* her husband do without her!"[28]

Maurice was indebted to his wife, if for no other reason, for her sense of humour. Her remark, "Mr Carlyle has been here talking for four hours in praise of silence", provided one of the all too few light touches in his whole biography.[29] Annie Barton knew German and helped introduce her husband to the unknown world of continental theology. In 1843, when Maurice wrote the first of a series of letters to Sara Coleridge, he said: "Mrs Maurice was pointing out to me yesterday a very striking discourse of Schleiermacher at a Confirmation."[30] During these years Maurice gained his reputation for composing books by dictation to avoid the labour of mechanical writing. Annie Barton herself was the source of the story that Maurice dictated his books; it was she who referred to the horsehair pillow which Maurice clutched whenever he was engaged in excited talk as his "black wife".[31] It is doubtful whether the luxury of dictation continued after their marriage. Extant manuscripts after 1845 are in Maurice's own difficult hand. His correspondence was filled with explanations that his second wife was unable even to write her own letters because of weakness or illness. It is hardly likely that she would have been strong enough to carry on Annie Barton's practice of writing down his spoken words.

Maurice's relationship with Annie Barton was fortuitous. The ease of their correspondence, the regular interchange of thoughts when they read together or talked over a growing manuscript provided Maurice with a ready, loyal, supportive, yet critical audience. Unfortunately the marriage was not to be a long one, only seven and a half years. In 1845, at what may well be the turning-point in his career, Annie Barton died of the disease she had contracted in nursing her sister, John Sterling's wife, then Sterling himself.[32] Maurice was thrown back on to his own resources. Inward pressures were heightened by the added responsibility of his two sons, no more than babies. Once again he had to call upon his sisters, particularly Priscilla, to supervise his household.

JOHN STERLING
THE ANVIL OF FRIENDSHIP

It is important to examine Maurice's adult associations for examples of the way in which a man's mature relationships provide the means and influence the manner in which he expresses his identity. An enquiry will be made into Maurice's friendship with John Sterling, and his relations with Charles Kingsley and John Malcolm Ludlow. The analysis must be cursory, but it will indicate the pattern of a moralist in action.

In later years Maurice sensed the dynamic attraction which bound him to Ludlow, the confrontation of "collision and sympathy" which directly and indirectly provided the moving force of much that he did in his life. Unquestionably in Maurice's youth it was Sterling who compelled him to write and attempt to express himself.[33] Sterling's relationship began at Cambridge and the story of their friendship appears both in the biographies of Maurice and Sterling.[34] Sterling was responsible for engineering Maurice's marriage to Annie Barton, his wife's sister.[35] Sterling had joined Maurice in his move from Trinity to Trinity Hall in Cambridge, had introduced Maurice in London, had tried to persuade him to go with him to Highgate to visit Coleridge.[36] Sterling's role was important in the initiation of *Eustace Conway*.[37] Maurice discussed the composition of the *Kingdom of Christ* with Sterling, as well as his contribution to the *Encyclopaedia Metropolitana*. Sterling tried to implement Maurice's move from Bubbenhall to London, proposing that they work together in Knightsbridge, a plan which unfortunately never materialized.[38]

After Maurice had moved to Guy's Hospital and had married, something began to go wrong in the friendship. Maurice sensed an inability to understand or to be understood. John Frederick Maurice said that his father bitterly reproached himself throughout his life on the subject of the relations between Sterling and himself. As Sterling passed more and more under Carlyle's influence, and as more and more his opinions diverged from his own, Maurice's

> anxiety and distress at the change in his friend's views of life, drove him again and again into indignant protest and, as he thought afterwards, into fierceness of expression for which he could find no excuse . . . . Always his conscience seems to have smitten him for not having been sufficiently gentle, sufficiently sympathetic, with not having helped instead of having disputed with his friend. One visit, in particular, to Clifton, which was, in fact, almost the termination of their intellectual intercourse, clung to his memory and seems to have left an ineradicable scar.[39]

This helps to explain Maurice's eagerness to be honest to Sterling's memory in the preface to the *Fable of the Bees*. Sterling had urged Maurice to undertake the business of republishing Law's works. "For myself," wrote Sterling, "I have never seen, in our language, the elementary grounds of a rational ideal philosophy, as opposed to empiricism, stated with nearly the same clearness, simplicity, and force."[40] But Maurice was cautious lest he put himself forward as expressing Sterling's views.

> I have expressed my own convictions in my own way; if he [Sterling] were considered responsible for them it would greatly disturb my gratification in being permitted for the last time to be connected in any earthly work with one from whom I have received more benefits and to whom I owe more love than any words can express.[41]

At Sterling's death, Maurice wrote to R. C. Trench:

> Had we all testified our love to him as you did, and been as true and faithful to him, I believe much would have come forth

from his heart—deeper and truer things than he himself almost knew were there. We did not deserve that he should utter them to us; and the lesson of submission and simple dependence on God's love in Christ is, I believe, deeper and more salutary, because it is accompanied with self-reproach and humiliation, than it could be if he had spoken many things which we should have delighted to hear.[42]

The Maurices became guardians of Sterling's daughters, Kate, Julia, and Hester. It was a personal blow that he left his son in the care of Francis Newman. "I need not say", wrote Maurice, "that the determination was painful to us; but the motives which led him to it were, I believe, most pure and right . . . . One point I feel very strongly, and my wife, who saw more of him, still more strongly than I: that his arrangement of sending Edward to Newman had nothing whatever to do with any sympathy which he might feel with him in some of his opinions . . ." but was due to his perplexities about the boy, "his sense of the friendship and kindness of Newman's offer to take charge of him . . . His [Newman's] honesty and earnestness . . . and . . . his being likely to cultivate in him self-denying and severe habits."[43]

STERLING'S SUCCESSOR
LUDLOW OR KINGSLEY?

It has been suggested that Maurice's friendship with Charles Kingsley, which began in the summer of 1844 just at the time of Sterling's death, took the place of his friendship with Sterling. Maurice's relation with Kingsley was profound and certainly lifelong. It can hardly be doubted that Kingsley, because of his devotion to his "Master", was instrumental in Maurice's election to the Knightbridge professorship at Cambridge.[44] But there was a quality of the relationship which would never permit Kingsley to serve as a counter-irritant for Maurice's thoughts. There could be no real "collision" between Maurice's ideas and those of a man who always began his letters to Maurice, "My dear Master". Kingsley's kindness knew no bounds and Maurice responded graciously and willingly to his attentions. Maurice's biographer paid tribute to the "delicate care with which Mr Kingsley attended him, and the smile of grateful appreciation which rewarded the little services, such as carrying some of his books back from the library, which Mr Kingsley often contrived to be at hand to render."[45]

> The last time I saw your father, [wrote a friend] he was leaving the Divinity Schools and met Kingsley, who had just come out of one of the other rooms. Kingsley ran to him and insisted on carrying his burden of books, and supporting him by the arm. The gracious smile with which the little act of kindness was acknowledged seems stamped on my memory.

"Anyone who knew my father will know well that smile," wrote Maurice's son.[46] Maurice and Kingsley did not always agree, but no basic disagreement ever troubled the waters of their relationship. The disciple never really questioned the master. The fact that Maurice obliquely sent Kingsley the memorandum about the suppression of *Duty of the Age* is half an indication that at least in that quarter he would find uncontested acceptance of what he had done.[47]

It was in fact Ludlow, whom Maurice met in 1848, who best filled Sterling's place, the role of stimulus, of counter-attraction. Ludlow found in Maurice "a fatherly friend and counsellor",[48] but Ludlow demanded by his very existence that Maurice should try to explain himself, to make himself clear; consequently Maurice was driven to discover and express the logical conclusions of his thought.

To the extent that a life can be said to have a watershed, the watershed in the life of F. D. Maurice occurred at the time of the Christian Socialist movement. A period which began in 1848, the year of revolution, ended in 1854 after Maurice's dismissal from King's College, London, when he established the Working Men's College. Maurice was never so misunderstood as during the crisis of Christian Socialism. Friend and foe alike found him inconsistent and incomprehensible. Today it would be generally agreed that the difficulty at King's College, London, was not really the result of Maurice's heretical ideas about eternity, perfectly acceptable to twentieth-century theologians.[49] Rather the crisis at King's College was the result of a profound suspicion of Maurice's political opinions by the conservative members of the college council. Maurice's connection with Kingsley was suspect, for example. Dr Jelf wrote to Maurice hoping that Kingsley would "openly disavow" his association "with several notorious infidels, as contributing articles to the *Leader,* a paper, I believe, advocating Socialism and Communism."[50] As an alternative, Jelf suggested to Maurice "that you will openly disavow Mr Kingsley."[51] Maurice himself realized that the real cause of his difficulty with the Council of King's College was not in fact theological but political. Had not the question been raised of how were the working classes to be kept in order if the belief in Hell as a place of eternal punishment be destroyed? He challenged the council

> if they pronounce a theological sentence upon me at all, to declare what Article of our faith condemns my teaching . . . Whether I have unsettled the faith of my pupils by giving an interpretation of the word "eternal", which I maintained to be true . . . before I was asked to join the theological department, the after lives of those pupils must determine.[52]

Maurice also noted in Jelf's letter what he termed, "a rather curious insinuation about the probability of other Anabaptist tenets (promiscuous marriages and confiscations) growing out of my doctrine about eternity."[53] The true grounds of the controversy appeared in a letter from Sir Benjamin Brodie, a member of the council. Reporting the proceedings of the meeting to Archdeacon Hare, Brodie wrote:

> He [Maurice] knew the kind of person with whom he had to deal, and it would have been very much better if he had avoided connecting himself with the Christian Socialists, and discussing questions on which it is plain that persons having great influence in the college would be at variance with him.[54]

The misunderstanding between Maurice and the Council of King's College was minor in comparison with the difficulties of understanding which existed between Maurice and his Christian Socialist friends. The problem was seen most clearly in Maurice's relations with Ludlow, a friendship which served as an anvil upon which Maurice had to forge his ideas. Maurice and Ludlow were attracted and antagonized by one another at the same time, due to elements in the characters of both men. They were aware of the difficulty which neither was ever able to resolve. Many years later Ludlow with profound insight into the relationship as well as into himself was magnanimous in his analysis and judgement. The

Maurice to whom he had been devoted had not been real, he said, but a product, an invention of his own imagination. This had been his own fault, he asserted. He had given in regularly, thinking that the two of them really meant the same thing.[55] But even after he had seen the great gulf fixed between himself, for whom the Christian faith must always be at least in part a "building", and Maurice, who would always only avow himself to be a "digger", Ludlow was bound to Maurice by an unbreakable tie. He supported him doggedly during the ensuing difficult years at the Working Men's College, yet he contested his position in thought as well as in action every step of the way. Maurice regularly sought Ludlow's counsel in working out his thoughts, and always asked his help in matters of personal business. Questions about legal advice prompted many of Maurice's letters to Ludlow, and Maurice entrusted his final affairs to him. Ludlow was executor of Maurice's will and Mrs Maurice gave him her husband's personal copy of *Aids to Reflection*.[56] A hint as to the nature of the bond between the two men was indicated in a farewell speech which Ludlow gave at the Working Men's College on 8 December 1866, after Maurice had been elected Knightbridge Professor at Cambridge. Ludlow said:

> Without in the least admitting or thinking that on the many points in which I have often differed from Mr Maurice I must have been wrong or he right, I yet, as a proof of the reverence which from long and intimate experience of his life I have acquired of him, who, as I never knew a father, is the only man for whom I have ever felt a sense of reverence, wish here and now to ask his pardon for any words or acts of mine which have given him pain, and to offer him the apologies of a man not much wont to bend the knee to any human authority.[57]

Maurice was moved beyond words. Acknowledging the tribute paid to him by the younger man, he wrote: "It was far more than I could well bear to hear all that was said about me by others; but yours was quite overpowering. I will only thank you for it."[58]

Ludlow, like Sterling earlier, made Maurice try to explain himself, and justify himself; nor was Ludlow put off by Maurice's occasional sharpness. The younger expressed an underlying warm support for the older man. Ludlow always returned and Maurice always apologized for being cutting or bitter.

You must forgive me; I am quite sure you will. I know I have said hard words to you which have given you pain. It gives me very great pain to recollect them and to think that I have in any way alienated you. I want to say this before tomorrow that you may know that whatever answer you take or however wrong you may think me it cannot make the least difference in my affection to you. If I have done anything inconsistent with that oh attribute it to myself, or the evil that is in me and not to want of thankfulness [for] your warnings and your faithfulness . . .[59]

The tone of this letter was typical of their correspondence.

Ludlow forgave and made allowances; yet he continued with loving affection to question and to oppose Maurice. It was an anguished relationship. He wrote,

Why do I say these things to you, I your inferior at every point, save perhaps the one bitterest Cassandra-gift of foresight, which I would exchange—O how gladly!—for the very smallest particle of Hughes's blessed power of seeing everything under its fairest and highest aspect.[60]

In spite of the awful revelation of the extent to which he felt he had misunderstood Maurice and made him the projection of his own mind, Ludlow came to see Maurice as clearly as anyone ever did. In 1858 when Maurice proposed to resign from his post at the Working Men's College and leave it to Furnivall, Ludlow showed deep insight into the past and present nature of Maurice's active practical work in life.

Once more I beseech you, by all that is most holy, to drive away from you this devil's temptation which I have seen so often beset you, of tearing to pieces with your own hands whatever God has given you grace to begin . . . You put away from you some years back the work of organizing fellowship of labour among the industrial classes, which I believe the Church of England will have some day to take up, or pass away. You did harm to many in doing so; still, you were no doubt right. The work was not your own originally; you had not measured its responsibilities when you took it. But this work, of organizing the fellowship of education among those classes, *is* your work; all your previous experience has fitted you for it.[61]

All too frequently Maurice was questioned and criticized from what amounted to an impersonal source, from anonymous articles in newspapers or from those who, like Mansel, Maurice had never known personally. Such circumstances were disastrous. Maurice would contain himself as long as he could; then pent up inward pressures would explode. It was said that

> whenever something that he looked upon as morally wrong or mean excited his wrath, he began in a most violent manner to rub together the palms of his two hands . . . . He appeared at such moments to be entirely absorbed in his own reflections, and utterly unconscious of the terrible effect which the fierce look of his face and the wild rubbing of his hands produced on an innocent bystander. A lady who often saw him thus says that she always expected sparks to fly from his hands and to see him bodily on fire. Certainly the effect was very tremendous and by no means pleasant.[62]

His controversy with Mansel was a significant case in which Maurice lost control under attack. Even his closest friends felt he had gone too far. "I have not finished your reply to Mansel," Ludlow wrote. "Crushing as it is for the most part, I still think it is more than was needed,—that a short pamphlet would have embraced all that was required, and more tellingly."[63]

Maurice realized the difficulty he experienced under attack or confronted by something of which he could not approve. He recognized that he was often excessive in his attacks on others. Siding always with the unpopular opinion or the underdog, he appeared to go out of his way to lay himself open to personal humiliation and malicious attack. He seemed pathologically driven. Changing sides from controversy to controversy, he was left early in life, vulnerable from every direction. It was the source of an anguished personal cry:

> Alienation from those whom I love, an impossibility of making them understand what I mean, a continual suspicion of cowardice and dishonesty from one side, of disaffection to the truths which I profess from another; what is far worse that all these, the inward self-accusations of dishonouring God and setting up a way of my own, even when I most disclaim one; the feelings

of pride, of self-exaltation, of division, which are so adverse to all that, after the inner man, I love and aim at; finally, the often recurring hopelessness of ever being able to exert any beneficial influence on any class of my countrymen.[64]

There is an interesting observation in a letter from Maurice's son to Leslie Stephen in which he sought an explanation for Stephen's notorious antagonism to Maurice. John Frederick Maurice cited an attack upon his father in the *Fortnightly Review*.

I confess that I acquired at the time I read it the conviction that the arguments were not put forward to prove what the writer believed to be truth but simply to have the fun of wounding and annoying. It was this that gave me—of course I only speak for myself—the impression of some deep cut wound having been given you as he certainly could at times inflict, and sometimes not quite fairly I think, at all events cutting deeper than the offence warranted . . .[65]

The years of the Christian Socialist movement are important ones in showing Maurice's most distinctive behaviour as a moralist in action. Maurice was threatened and insecure on all sides. He was fighting on the one hand for the integrity of his own ideas among younger men who were attempting to push him farther than he wanted to go along the lines of what they called practical action. He was also involved in a struggle for the security of his position on the staff of King's College, London. There he was suspect, ostensibly on the grounds of his theological teaching, but primarily because of his association with those very same young men who questioned his basic position and tried to force or drag him into another. The period was filled with domestic difficulties for Maurice as well. His second marriage increased his responsibilities by adding an invalid wife to a household which already contained two motherless children. Subject to strong pressures domestically, professionally, and in his association with the Christian Socialists, Maurice carried on a tight daily schedule and produced a prodigious amount of work, weekly sermons, lectures, Bible classes, occasional speeches, and never-ending committee meetings. Maurice was a man conspicuously loving and gentle. In his turn, he required love and gentleness from others.

Perhaps one reason why Maurice has been much more readily heard after his time was that the orthodoxies which he had been so instrumental in demolishing for the young gave way to a new openness, which would accept the things which Maurice said, sift them if need be, and build upon their positive qualities.

3

The Divine Order
The Framework of Morality

————•◆•————

John Malcom Ludlow accused Maurice of being carried away by "Platonistic dreams about an Order, and a Kingdom, and a Beauty," enshrouded though they might be by "the cobwebs of human systems".[1] To what extent does this juxtaposition of reality and appearances represent the framework in which Maurice saw the world, and establish the pattern of his ethical method? There is a remarkable consistency in Maurice's ideas throughout his life and we may expect to find an answer in his earliest mature writings. A. R. Vidler holds that "the germ of nearly all his later thought was contained in a letter of 1831 to his father",[2] and quotes John Tulloch who wrote: "There are few, even of his after controversies, the germs of which cannot be found in these letters."[3] Actually Maurice's ideas are apparent as early as the completion of *Eustace Conway*. The novel appeared in 1834 but it was finished by February 1830, and Maurice had begun the book in 1828.

Eustace Conway, the study of a young man's conversion, is better described as a record of a young man's progress in the orthodox Christian faith. During the time it was being written, Maurice made an abrupt break with the straightforward romantic idealism of his post-Cambridge, early London period.

What remained for him?—He had run the gauntlet of opinions —he had acknowledged Society as God, with the Utilitarians—

47

he had acknowledged Self as God, with the Spiritualists—he now confessed that He is God whose praise is in the Churches; and at each stage, he seemed to have gained more arrogance. He was humbler in his first state than in the second—in the second than in the last.[4]

Torben Christensen dates Maurice's conversion as taking place after a spiritual crisis which occurred toward the end of 1828. He attributes its cause to the profound impression made upon him by his sister Emma during the last months of her life, coupled with financial worry.[5] Maurice did begin *Eustace Conway* "to earn some money".[6] The problem was caused by the failure of his magazine, *The Athenaeum,* and the collapse of his father's investments in the bonds of the Spanish Constitutional party.[7] Maurice returned home from London at the end of May or the beginning of June 1829. Because of the change in the family fortunes, "his second sister, Mary, was about to study the Pestalozzian system prior to setting up her school."[8] The young man planned to take her place in the household, teaching the younger children and attending Emma's bedside. Emma's influence on Maurice must have been important as Christensen implies, though Maurice was well on his way to orthodoxy before his return home. Already writing *Eustace Conway,* his correspondence with Julius Hare makes it evident that he had made up his mind to enter Oxford and had decided upon subscription to the Thirty-nine Articles.[9]

During these months Maurice's relations with Emma were extremely close. The subtitle of his novel was *The Brother and Sister;* at one time he proposed calling the book *Ellen,* if not *Emma.*[10] Like many other nineteenth-century families, the Maurices placed great emphasis on deaths and death-bed scenes. Lucilla Powell's memoirs are full of them, nearly one to a page. The mature theologian distrusted death-bed stories, but the influence of Emma's strong Evangelical piety might have been heightened by the fact that she was "lying on her death-bed".[11] Emma, nevertheless, lived on for another year and a half after Maurice embraced orthodoxy and she had been sick since 1816, if not 1812, "in great pain but with great courage and exemplary faith".[12]

Months before Emma's death on 9 July 1831, Maurice was baptized—actually rebaptized—on 29 March, a sure sign of his conversion.[13] And he had matriculated at Exeter College, Oxford, subscribing to the Articles on 3 December 1829. Two days before, on 1 December, his sister's diary recorded: "Oh! he is safe,—safe for eternity!"[14]

It has already been observed that many of the details of *Eustace Conway* are autobiographical. The very fulcrum of the plot, the abduction of a Quaker heiress, drew heavily from the story of the real abduction of a young Unitarian lady and "heiress" with whom the Maurices were intimately involved.[15] Even if extraneous bits were inserted into *Eustace Conway* from outside his personal experience, the basic movement of the novel described the development of Maurice himself. When *Eustace Conway* was finished, the key was set into the arch of the author's as well as the hero's belief.

Eustace Conway thus presents Maurice's view of orthodox Christian faith. Is there any foundation in the novel for Ludlow's attack on "Platonistic" attitudes?

In *Eustace Conway* Maurice described a young woman, Emmeline, who in early life

> was thrown much into the company of a visionary, (he was a little younger than herself), who for a time infected her with some of his own spirit. But her mind was too practical to dwell long in clouds; land-dreams will not sustain life, and she sighed for something more real, if it were more earthly.[16]

This slightly veiled reference to himself and his sister was more specific in the discussion of the relation between Eustace and Honoria, the novel's hero and heroine.

> Whenever his sister had spoken to him of the Being whom she adored, and to whose glory she wished to live or die, as clothed in human form, sharing man's infirmities, and enduring the punishment of man's sin,—he had recoiled from such a view, as derogatory from the sublime Hebrew idea of God, which he fancied had displaced the vague vision of a great Spirit that had previously possessed his mind . . . it would have been a sufficient answer to his objection—a sufficient proof how merely he dreamed of such an idea without possessing it—that, in the minds of every prophet and sage, (who, supposing Hebrew Theology to be true, ought to be considered the strongest witnesses,) this idea did not precede the feeling of con-

nexion between the worshipper and his lawgiver, but grew out
of it . . .[17]

But something more direct and personal than this was needed
to overthrow a prejudice, to the support of which the passions
and understanding of man equally lend themselves; and he
found it in the practical illustration which all Honoria's actions
furnished of the difference between her real and his imaginary
faith.[18]

Maurice wrote that the sister in her sickness was like a lark, beaten
down by contrary winds, yet finally, after the storm, able to rise and
sing, and that indeed

when she was most possessed with the affections of a higher
world than that in which men are slaving, she seemed to regard
with a kindlier and warmer interest all the objects which
surrounded her; no daily duty, were it never so insignificant,
never so toilsome, looked mean in her eyes, or was tried by any
disadvantageous comparisons with what might be the employ-
ments of another state; . . . [19]

When questioned about her attitude, Honoria's answer provides
a passage of inestimable value in discovering Maurice's own
thoughts.

To me, [she replied] it seems that we begin with thinking too
highly of all the objects around us, and end with thinking far
too angrily of them. That in which I feel the corruption of my
nature most, is that I think of all I see as real—of love and hope,
as only fantastic colourings by which I make outward things
look more beautiful. And then, having given away my soul to
the idols around me, I rail at them as if it were some wickedness
of theirs that I am held fast by them. But, surely, when faith
is called into exercise, which is the first of the beautiful triad
that rises above the degradation of being used merely to brighten
the objects of sense, and we are able by it to contemplate God
as love, we then perceive that these were the realities, and
those the shadows, and that it was ourselves that changed their
relations: and as we approach nearer to heaven, where we shall
never have a doubt of this, where, dwelling in absolute love,
we shall know how real that is, and how the circumstances,

whatever they may be, which surround us, are only the ways of manifesting it, ought not we to begin to think in the same way of ourselves and of our circumstances here? Ought we, when our souls are made alive, to look with aversion on the grave-clothes which once confined them—and not rather to observe how beautifully they are wrought! how fit, when our souls are fitted for them, to become, sometime, our bridal dress! For, surely, there could be no more glorious temple, except the purified soul itself, for the Divine Being to dwell in, than this beautiful world, with its lakes, and skies, and woods, if our eyes were only opened to see his glories in it."[20]

The "Platonistic" overtones of this passage may be compared with Maurice's exposition of Plato in his first major literary effort, *Moral and Metaphysical Philosophy*. It was a common and telling criticism of the *Philosophy* that any man from Aristotle to Acquinas came out sounding like Maurice himself. An explanation of this personal characteristic appeared in Maurice's defence against the charge of holding ideas which he does not hold and imputing to others ideas which he knows they do not hold. He denied being an "Eclectic" who, he said, "chooses bits of theories".[21] He preferred sectarians to eclectics and merely asked the sects to "part with nothing but their pride and self-will and dislike of their brethren".[22] In his desire for unity he said that common truth will be found in men's affirmations, if they abandon only the negative aspects of their faith. Maurice's effort to see and make his own what an author was saying, in spite of, indeed because of, his stated intention to put nothing between himself and the mind of an author, and Maurice's fierce desire for unity made him see and emphasize as positive affirmations those very ideas of a man which corresponded most closely to his own.

His discussion of Plato described "that doctrine of Ideas which constitutes the most native and peculiar portion of his philosophy, that which may not wrongly be called its purely Platonic portion".[23] Maurice continued with a passage important for examining Ludlow's charge.

The Greek word for *appearance* and for *opinion* is the same. An opinion is that which *seems* to each man. Now the whole of the education and discipline of Socrates had been to lead his disciples away from appearances to realities . . . . The essence,

the being of a thing, or of a person, seems shut up in that thing
or person . . . . Must it not be after all some shape or image or
phantom of this thing which I take account of, and not the
very thing itself? Supposing this were admitted, the Socratic
philosophy falls to the ground . . . The sophists had turned the
world into a shadow world.[24]

It was for Plato to deliver men from this world of shadows (Ludlow's cobwebs in another guise?).

There are [he declared] forms permanent and unchangeable
in which that which is manifests itself as it is; in which we
behold it as it is. Are these forms, then, in the beholder, or in
that which he beholds? We answer: the region of pure being,
that in which the inner mind dwells, may be (one might
expect that it would be) under some corresponding law to that
of sensible phenomena.[25]

To do justice to Plato,

if in the minutest thing he believes that there is a reality, and
therefore in some sense an archetypal form or idea, yet he
believes also, just as firmly, that every idea has its ground and
termination in one higher than itself, and that there is a
supreme idea, the foundation and consummation of all these,
even the idea of the absolute and perfect Being, in whose mind
they all dwelt, and in whose eternity alone they can be thought
or dreamed of to be eternal . . . These ideas, being by their
very nature substantial, must be substantially, in him who
perceives them . . . . The idea itself must be considered as with
us and in us.[26]

Maurice wrote this essay in 1835, in his first parish at Bubbenhall. He undertook to write the article at the suggestion of Henry
John Rose, editor of Coleridge's *Encyclopaedia Metropolitana*.[27]
Maurice had just published *Subscription No Bondage*; he was pro-
jecting the first and second *Letter to a Quaker* which developed
into *The Kingdom of Christ*. *Eustace Conway* was fresh in his
mind.

Maurice's analysis of Plato seemed to support Ludlow's
criticism.[28] He was concerned for the relation between appearance

and reality. This relation provided him with a framework for look-ing at the world. But Maurice would have denied that he was so carried away by dreams that an attempt at an earthly realization of an "Order, and a Kingdom, and a Beauty" was but labour lost.

His emphasis on the reality of the Incarnation in the Manhood of Christ, he felt, took the sting out of the criticism of "other-worldliness". Moreover, his emphasis on an underlying divine order established as a consequence of the Incarnation, and the reality and importance of human relations in which the divine order was expressed placed him firmly in the practical world of everyday life. "The hideous blot" on Plato, Maurice wrote, is that "he wishes to supersede all the existing relations of father and child, wife and husband, which lie, as we suppose, at the foundation of all moral apprehensions and all political order".[29] "A person even a person who tells lies, is better than a mere shadow or dream", he wrote about Renan's *Vie de Jésus*.[30]

> Renan's Christ, I said in my article, might seem to him [your friend] a great ascent from the mere picture or doll which he had connected with the name. But he has shown conclusively that an honest person cannot be associated with the name, who is not a divine person; who is not in very deed a Son of God.[31]

The resolution of "an Order, and a Kingdom, and a Beauty", and its earthly realization lay beneath Maurice's explanation to his father of his adoption of the orthodox faith.

> I would beseech you, [he wrote] to observe attentively whether nearly every verse in the Old Testament does not exhibit these two apparently opposite and most contradictory feelings; an acknowledgement of God as incomprehensible and infinite; a desire to see, to understand, to comprehend that same God . . . . If the Infinite, Incomprehensible Jehovah is manifested in the person of a Man, a Man conversing with us, living among us, entering into all our infirmities and temptations, and passing into all our conditions, it is satisfied; if not it remains unsatisfied.[32]

JOSEPH ADAM STEPHENSON, MILLENARIAN
THE KINGDOM ESTABLISHED

If Maurice was concerned somewhat Platonistically about the relation between appearance and reality, he was certain of what was,
for him, the fact of the kingdom of Christ. The kingdom was the
great practical existing reality; it did not need to be "set up" at all;
it was already present. Society and humanity, he said, are divine
realities *"as they stand"*, not as they may become. This belief in a
divine order which was the crux of Maurice's disagreement with
Ludlow had appeared in embryo in *Eustace Conway*. It did not
take its clearest and final form until after 1833 when Maurice
served as curate under his friend Stephenson. Maurice's debt to
Julius Hare, to Coleridge, to Erskine of Linlathen, even to Edward
Irving, has been systematically explored. There has never been,
however, a thorough investigation into Maurice's association with
the Millenarian rector of Lympsham, one of the most important
determinative influences upon Maurice's thought.

It is not too much to say that Maurice owed Stephenson the
characteristic belief that the kingdom of Christ is already and quite
literally established. Maurice paid tribute to what he had received
from the rector of Lympsham and a study of their relations in the
last "formative" years of Maurice's career makes it likely that
Stephenson provided the final touch to what Maurice would never
have called his system, but to the way in which he saw the world.

The first evidence of Stephenson's influence appeared in a letter
in which Maurice thanked him for all that he had learned from him
during his curacy.

> Since I have been engaged in preaching myself, [he said] I
> have found the advantage of your instructions in a degree that
> I could scarcely have believed possible; especially as they have
> led me, almost unawares, into a method of considering many
> subjects, and of setting them forth, which I should not have
> naturally fallen into. I have not hitherto, nor do I intend
> hereafter, for many years at least, to travel much beyond the
> Lord's Prayer and the Creed, and the Gospel and Epistle of
> the day, in addressing the people; but I have found myself in
> all my private meditations, as well as in preaching, drawn to
> speak of Christ as a King, and His Church as a Kingdom; and

whenever I depart from this method I feel much less clearness and satisfaction, much less harmony between my own feelings and the Word of God.[33]

Maurice's *Lectures on the Apocalypse* give us the clearest statement of the literal way in which he understood the establishment of the Kingdom. The *Apocalypse* was one of his favourite books in the Bible. He commended its study to young Edward Strachey in 1837, in order to "learn the sure triumph of order, unity, and love over confusion, divisions, and hatred, . . .".[34] Moreover, in 1859, answering questions about the mystery of "the several persons of the Trinity, and their action on the spirit of man",[35] he wrote, "I believe the Apocalypse to be the book which will at last be found to remove most veils from this mystery, as well as from the meaning of all the previous Bible history, and from the course of God's government of the world from the beginning to the end."[36] His method of explaining the Apocalypse, discovering "the principal historical allusions" to refer "to the state of the Roman world during the years preceding the fall of Jerusalem", he did not pretend to have discovered for himself.[37] "The first hint of it", he wrote, "was given me by a revered friend, a clergyman of the school of Cecil and Venn . . .", a reference to Stephenson.[38]

> I can never be thankful enough for having arrived, through his teaching, at the conviction that the words, "The kingdom of heaven is at hand", were used by the Evangelists in the strictest sense; that the Apostles were not wrong in believing that the end of an age was approaching; that they had no exaggerated anticipations regarding the age which was to succeed it; that if we accepted their statements simply we should understand far better in what state we are living; what are our responsibilities; what are our sins; what we have a right to hope for.[39]

Maurice wrote a *Memoir of Mr Stephenson of Lympsham* about 1838.[40]

> He seemed [declared Maurice] not so much to be carried occasionally into another and higher region as to dwell constantly in it . . . . There was never any wide chasm between his discourse upon earthly and heavenly topics. He liked to

C

clothe what he said of the beauties and glories of the invisible
world in images taken from the things around us . . . . He
never appeared to look upon the earth . . . [except] . . . as the
soil on which the Son of God had walked, and which He had
redeemed from the curse . . . . In the year 1821 he preached a
sermon upon a public occasion, in which he maintained that
the hills and valleys of this earth, redeemed, purified, and
regenerated, were to be the scene of the felicity of the ransomed
children of God.[41]

He was led, as well, to believe that the events about the destruction
of Jerusalem "were nothing less than the actual manifestation of
Christ's kingdom, the actual establishment of a communion
between the two worlds, the creation of a new heaven and a new
earth".[42]

Stephenson's own commentary on the Apocalypse testifies to the
accuracy of Maurice's description of his views.[43] He wrote: "When
Jerusalem was destroyed, with its detested occupants, the mediatorial
throne of Christ was forever established."[44] In the Creeds, the
Church, he said, has "been maintaining that in every successive
generation from Apostolical times, Christ is, and has been coming
and come . . . . The completeness and continuity of the second
advent is a truth that has never lost its anchorage on the immovable
ground of Christian faith, and anchored on that ground will ride
out every storm."[45] The faith of the Church, Stephenson continued, "is the only witness available" for this invisible
"Epiphany".[46] "Faint, indeed, would be the splendour of his Divine
appearance, . . . were it a splendour of which the perception could
be borne, or a lustre of which a glimpse could be caught by any
terrestrial eye."[47]

The argument of Maurice's *Apocalypse* followed Stephenson's
concept that the kingdom of Christ was finally established on earth
in the events which culminated in the Roman destruction of
Jerusalem in A.D. 70. He wrote: "Would not the destruction of
Jerusalem be the winding-up of that series of events—the incarnation, death, resurrection, glorification, of Christ,—which were
themselves that finishing of the mystery of God, which He had
promised to His servants the prophets?"[48] Here is the kingdom
for which the prophets and the apostles hoped, not "the destruction
of the earth, as it came from God's hands, . . . they did not look

for it in any day," . . . not "a kingdom somewhere in the clouds; that they did mean a society of men established upon a principle which does not make society destructive and impossible, a society governed by God and not by the Devil."[49]

> Here [Maurice said] is the true divine order: . . . the Lord God Omnipotent reigneth! . . . He in whom is light and no darkness at all, is proved to be the ground of all things. . . . The Son has claimed humanity for his bride . . . . The Spirit clothes the bride with the graces and beauties of her lord.[50]

The comparison of Maurice and Stephenson reveals startling similarities. Probably the two most distinctive aspects of Maurice's thoughts are his concept of the divine order, that the kingdom of Christ is presently established, and the related concept of eternity. Maurice saw eternity coexisting with the present in a Johannine sense, a qualitative and vertical dimension of present life rather than a quantitative and horizontal extension of time, "not time extended, but time abolished".[51] It is interesting that these ideas were equally distinctive characteristics of Stephenson's thought. What is more, Maurice used the very words which speak of Christ as a king and his Church as a kingdom for the first time in the 1834 letter in which the younger man thanked his former rector for the influence of his instruction.[52] The words attesting to the kingship of Christ and his kingdom (and only indirectly the ideas) do not occur in Maurice's writing before his curacy in Lympsham in 1833. After his curacy, no words or concepts were used more frequently.

Florence Higham mentions the rector of Lympsham in her short biography of Maurice, but little or no reference is made to Stephenson by any of the other major writers on the subject. Mrs Higham says that Stephenson "completed what Erskine had begun, and encouraged Maurice to make the goodness of God not the sin of man the starting-point of his theology."[53] She also suggests close ties between the Maurice and the Stephenson families. A study of the history of the relationships between the two men, and the two families confirms the closeness of the tie and enforces the probability of Stephenson's influence.

In 1838 Maurice began a four year connection with the firm of J. G. and F. Rivington; during this time Rivingtons were Maurice's sole publishers. Each year they brought out one of Maurice's books.

In 1839, *Has The Church, or the State, the Power to Educate the Nation?* appeared, and in 1840 Rivingtons began the publication of the *Encyclopaedia Metropolitana* with Maurice's essay on "Moral and Metaphysical Philosophy". *Reasons for not Joining a Party in the Church* came out in 1841, followed in 1842 by *Three Letters to the Rev. W. Palmer, on the name Protestant*. Also in 1842 Rivingtons brought out the second edition, revised and altered, of *The Kingdom of Christ*. Just before beginning the publication of this long series of Maurice titles, Rivingtons published Stephenson's only major book, the *Christology of the Old and New Testaments*. The posthumous publication was seen through the press by a family friend who also wrote a preface to the two volumes. Beyond question the "friend", and author of the introduction, was F. D. Maurice, just beginning his own connection with the firm of Rivington. The writing has an unmistakable Maurician ring, stylistic as well as circumstantial evidence attesting to his authorship:

> The Rev. Joseph Adam Stephenson, Rector of Lympsham in Somersetshire, was educated at Queen's College, Oxford, took his B.A. degree in the year 1801, and having been successively curate of Beckenham in Kent, and Hatfield Broad Oak in Essex, entered upon the living which he held to his death.[54]

The introduction referred to ". . . early years . . . occupied in pastoral duties . . . later . . . deep interest in the interpretation of the prophetical Scriptures. For a while, his notions . . . seem to have agreed . . . with . . . the moderate Millenarians of our day; but . . . he became dissatisfied with this system of interpretation in all its forms and modifications."

> As he studied the Scriptures more earnestly, he thought he perceived that the Divine scheme which they disclosed was accomplished, when the Church of Christ was established in the world; that the facts which led to this consummation were simple in themselves, grand only in their spiritual meaning and results; that the inspired writers do not speak of events which were to happen long after they had left the world, but rather show what significance lay in the events which were almost immediately to follow the announcement of them; that we are unwilling to consider these prophecies as fulfilled, because we are slow to believe in the actual glory of our position as

members of the body of Christ; lastly, that any future felicity which awaits the Church, can be only the full realization of that which it has, potentially, now; and cannot arise from the establishment of any new order or dynasty in the world . . .[55]

These words were written at precisely the same time as the composition of Maurice's first *Letters to a Member of the Society of Friends*. If the preface is not from Maurice's own hand, it bears an astonishing likeness to it, and contains a concise statement of the nature of the kingdom of Christ as already established, and the quality of eternity as the full realization of that which is, potentially, now.

There are many external indications, as well, that Maurice wrote the introductory passage to Stephenson's *Christology,* not least, the record of a lifelong intimate connection between the two families. It was, in fact, while visiting the Maurice family in Kent that Stephenson's widow died in November 1857. Lucilla Powell recorded that there was just time to telegraph to Lympsham for Mrs Stephenson's only son to come.[56]

The friendship of the Maurice and Stephenson families began with Maurice's sister Emma. Once when the Maurices were living at Frenchay, near Clifton, Emma had gone to Weston-super-Mare to regain her strength after a particularly difficult period of sickness. While she was there she met Stephenson, rector of the neighbouring village.[57] During these years the Maurice ladies went through their greatest religious confusion. Emma's older sisters had been converted and baptized (rebaptized) in Bristol on 23 October 1817.[58] She herself was converted by Stephenson.[59] He became her intimate friend, and later a great source of strength to the whole family.

About this same time, Elizabeth, the eldest of the Maurice daughters, became engaged to a young clergyman, the nephew of one of the Frenchay families. "Curate to Mr Elwin at the Temple Church, Bristol", he was a young man "not serious of his awful responsibility".[60] There were several difficulties. The couple were to wait to be married until the clergyman had a living, but in the meantime Elizabeth developed epilepsy which remained a problem until her death in 1839. Mrs Maurice took her along with Emma once again to Weston-Super-Mare where Elizabeth also became a close friend of Mr Stephenson.[61]

Worse followed. Her fiancé absconded with a former friend of Elizabeth and left England. The clergyman was deposed; Lucilla Powell reported that the "arrangement was tragic".[62] Elizabeth, sick and epileptic, came near to losing her sanity. Florence Higham says that her friendship with Stephenson "enabled her to retain her reason and gave her a new sweetness of nature that deepened every year".[63] One result was that the friendship with Stephenson was more than ever firmly sealed; he became a valued counsellor to all the Maurices.

In July 1825 the family moved to Southampton. Michael Maurice had invested heavily in the bonds of the Constitutional party in Spain. He had already lost a considerable amount of money in the commercial panic of 1825–6, and with the collapse of the Spanish Constitutionalists his bonds became worthless. Ruined, it was necessary for the Maurices to give up their comfortable house in 1829.[64]

The direction of Maurice's thought was apparent at this period; he inclined toward orthodoxy, and generally toward taking orders in the Church of England. But his ordination was not a foregone conclusion. Stephenson justly supposed that Maurice's "intense self-abasement . . . was preventing him from taking a step towards which, in every other way, he felt he was being led, and that without some sympathy and encouragement there was likely to be yet very long delay, even if at all he made up his mind to become a clergyman."[65] Stephenson, who, although "he was not really in want of a second curate, . . . desired to remove every hindrance out of his [Maurice's] way", had urged him "to take Holy Orders at once, and had offered him a title, asking him also to go there [to Lympsham] previous to his Ordination to assist him in his Parish."[66] Maurice accepted Stephenson's offer. He went to Lympsham in January 1833. While he was there William Harding, the Tutor of Wadham, "came to Lympsham Rectory on a visit, and persuaded [Maurice] to take sole charge of his small Parish Bubbenhall in Warwickshire—which he could not reside in himself . . . . His offer was accepted and letters demissory obtained to the Bishop of Lichfield who ordained my brother," wrote Lucilla Powell, "at Eccleshall, and he entered on his duties at Bubbenhall in January 1834."[67]

Doubtless the two men, Maurice and Stephenson, influenced one another during this year of working together. Maurice's biographer emphasized the influence of the younger upon the older man who, while Maurice was with him, "was absolutely at his best, coming out in a way that surprised even those nearest to him and most intimately acquainted with him."[68] But Maurice's son played down Stephenson's influence on his curate.

> My father [he wrote] has left a memoir of the man with whom he then came in contact, which will perhaps give an idea of the special influence on his thought which was thus exercised. But it is necessary to point out here that what can be told of my father's life is in nowise, as has been done in one of the most striking autobiographies of our time, to say, "at that hour, in that field," he was taught this or taught that. His thoughts and character were not in this way built up like rows of neatly ordered bricks. Rather, as each new thread of thought was caught by the shuttle of his ever-working mind, it was dashed in and out through all the warp and woof of what had been laid on before, and one sees it disappearing and reappearing continually affecting all else, having its colour modified by successive juxtapositions, and taking its place in the ever growing pattern.[69]

Nevertheless, the closeness with which Maurice followed Stephenson in his concept of the present establishment of Christ's kingdom, if invisible, yet at the foundation of all society, is too obvious to be denied. It is interesting that Maurice's biographer did not underestimate the other conspicuous influences on his father, Hare, Coleridge, Erskine, or Irving. Perhaps he had a certain half-conscious awareness that Stephenson's contribution was something particularly distinctive of his father's thought, and he was jealous for his father's originality, or perhaps he was self-conscious about the undoubted and unfashionable Millenarian ring of Maurice's emphasis on the kingdom of Christ as a divine order, literally established as the present, if unseen, foundation of society, and wished to place less stress upon it. The similarity of Maurice's view to Stephenson's was illustrated in a letter written by Maurice's pupil, Edward Strachey, to his aunt Lady Louis.

> I think I can give you something more of Maurice's views about the Millennium and the second coming of Christ than when you ask[ed] me before, as I have been lately talking to

him about it. He says we are in the Millennium, and that
Christ's reign upon earth began after the destruction of Jerusalem. At the period, or soon after, the Man-God, the Roman
Emperor, who certainly was in the place of God throughout the
world, was deprived of his real power, though his dominion
was a long while breaking up. All the Book of Revelation
Maurice understands to refer to the dispensation which then
commenced, and which is still going on. He says the Church
is taken into that holy, spiritual state there spoken of, though it
is only after its members pass out of the world and join the
Church triumphant that they realize and fully understand that
state . . .[70] This is pure Stephenson.

Maurice again and again expressed his gratitude to the rector of
Lympsham, indeed to Millenarians generally who

> have done an infinite service to the Church, in fixing our minds
> upon these words . . . "looking for the revelation of our Lord
> Jesus Christ" . . . and so turning them away from the expecta-
> tions of mere personal felicity apart from the establishment of
> Christ's kingdom; from the notion of Heaven which makes us
> indifferent to the future condition of the earth.[71]

The result of the Millenarians' labours "when they bid us think
more of Christ's victory over the earth and redemption of it to its
true purposes, than of any new condition into which we may be
brought when we go out of the earth" is two-fold: "They make all
our feelings and interests social, they connect everything we do and
feel and suffer, with our kind; they give us Christ as the object of
our thoughts, and not ourselves."[72]

1848–1854
CONFLICT AND CLARITY
TO DIG OR TO BUILD?

Maurice said that the words "Behold the kingdom of God is
among you"[73] directed his thoughts first to the victory of Christ
and then toward the everyday world in which he lived. The implica-

tions of a "kingdom already established" appear in 1848–54, the crisis of Christian Socialism. While the "prophet" shared many of his friends' interests, there was an inevitable disagreement between him and his young associates. The controversy weakened and eventually led to the collapse of the whole movement. Maurice's correspondence with John Malcolm Ludlow reveals the difficulty.

In Ludlow's opinion, the eternal brotherhood of the Church was the pattern according to which society was to be reconstituted, not as in Maurice's case, a reality which constituted existing society.

> Surely [Ludlow wrote] the whole work of Christianity is build-ing, and not digging,—just as digging was the work, the only true work of the heathen philosopher, until the Corner Stone should be laid. Surely there is no blessing in Christ's Gospel upon the mere digger, not even the stubble-builder's blessing of being saved as by fire. Dear friend, will you allow me to say that I have often felt that this *was* one of your temptations? I have endeavoured to study you very closely for the last year, both in yourself and thro' your books (I would especially refer to the Moral and Metaphysical philosophy), and it does seem to me that you are liable to be carried away by Platonistic dreams about an Order, and a Kingdom, and a Beauty, self-realized in their own eternity, and which so put to shame all pretended earthly counterparts that it becomes labour lost to attempt anything like an earthly realization of them, and all that one has to do is to shew them, were it only in glimpses, to others, by tearing away the cobwebs of human systems that enshroud them.[74]

Maurice answered Ludlow; he defended his self-definition as a "digger", which he had adopted in order to avoid giving himself the name of theologian. He avoided that title because people usually represented theology as the climax of all studies (Physics, Politics, Economics), not as the foundation upon which they all stand. Even, said Maurice, if he had been able to impress Ludlow with his own conviction that theology is not the climax of all studies, but the foundation upon which they all stand,

> that language would have left my meaning open to a very great, almost an entire, misunderstanding unless I could exchange the name theology for the name GOD, and say that He

C*

Himself is the root from which all human life, and human Society and ultimately, through Man, Nature itself, are derived. I tried to express all in that one phrase that I was a Digger . . . . My business because I am a Theologian and have no vocation except for theology is not to build but to dig; to shew that Economy & Politics (I leave Physics to dear Kingsley who will in that region and in every other carry out my hint in a way I could never dream of and which I admire with trembling hope and joy) must have a ground beneath themselves; that Society is not to be made anew by arrangements of ours but is to be regenerated by finding the law and ground of its Order and Harmony, the only secret of its existence, in God. This may seem to you an unpractical and unchristian method; to me it is the only one which makes action possible and Christianity anything more than an artificial Religion for the use of believers.

I wish very earnestly to be understood on this point, [Maurice asserted] because all my future course must be regulated on this principle or on no principle at all. The Kingdom of Heaven is to me the great practical existing reality which is to renew the earth and make it a habitation for blessed Spirits instead of Demons. To preach the Gospel of that Kingdom; the fact that it is among us and is not to be set up at all, is my calling and business. Because I have preached it so uncertainly—like one beating the air—I have had an easy, quiet life; far too much of the good opinion of my friends; merely a few lumps of, not hard, mud from them who now and then suspect that I have hold of something which might make me their mischievous enemy. But if ever I do any good work and earn any of the hatred which the godly in Christ Jesus receive and have a right to, it must be in the way I have indicated; by proclaiming Society and Humanity to be divine realities, *as they stand* not as they may become and by calling upon the Priests, Kings, Prophets of the world to answer for their sin in having made them unreal by separating them from the living and Eternal God who has established them in Christ for His glory. This is what I call digging; this is what I oppose to building. And the more I read the Epistle to the Corinthians, the more I am convinced that this was St Paul's work, the one by which he hoped to undermine, and to unite, the systematizers of the

Apollos, Cephas, Pauline and Christian (for them who said we are of Christ were the worst canters and dividers of all) schools. Christ the actual foundation of the Universe; not Christ a Messiah to them who received Him and shaped Him according to some notion of theirs; the Head of a Body not the Teacher of a Religion was the Christ of St Paul. And such a Christ I desire to preach and to live in and die in.[75]

The tension which is seen in these two letters existed as long as the Christian Socialist movement continued; it proved destructive rather than dynamic. Maurice was always concerned lest actual associated work should overshadow what he considered the main concern of Christian Socialism, the proclamation of the divine order. His friends repeatedly proposed practical action, always met by the opposition of "the Prophet". Looking back over these years, Ludlow wrote:

I had wished for nothing, as I have said before, but to be his first lieutenant in the campaign, merging my work in his, never coming forward but to ward off from him a blow if I could do so. But I saw that I was myself in fault; that I had wilfully blinded myself; that the Maurice I had devoted myself to was a Maurice of my own imagination, not the real Maurice. He was not to blame. I was.[76]

Successive events in the history of the Christian Socialist movement revealed the "real Maurice" and the nature of the disagreement. In 1849, he blocked his friends' attempt to found a national health league. Their efforts had been aroused by unsanitary conditions among the London poor and an epidemic of cholera.

I should have to go into a long personal history, [he wrote to Ludlow] if I undertook to explain how the dread of Societies, Clubs, Leagues, has grown up in me, how I have fought with it and often wished to overcome it, how it has returned again and again upon me with evidences which I cannot doubt, of being a divine and not a diabolical inspiration.[77]

In January 1852 he refused to allow the Christian Socialists to support the workmen in the first great labour conflict in English history. The Amalgamated Society of Engineers wanted to establish associative workshops to combat a general lock-out, and Maurice adamantly opposed the scheme. His intransigence grew out of his fear that association should be seen as, should in fact become, a new economic and social system. It would then be a man-made construction rather than a testimony of human fellowship and the mutual obligation in co-operation of brothers, in short a denial of the established divine order.

One final example of the breach between Maurice and the other Christian Socialists appeared when he suppressed Lord Goderich's pamphlet, *The Duty of The Age*.[78] Goderich, an aristocrat in the Whig tradition, had joined Maurice's friends because of his liberal ideas. In 1852 he composed a pamphlet which declared that democracy, self-government, is the highest and noblest principle of politics, the essentially Christian political idea. The cause of Democracy, he affirmed was the cause of God. Nothing could have been more calculated to arouse Maurice's indignation and provoke him to a frontal attack. He suppressed the pamphlet which had already been printed, wrote an explanatory letter to Goderich, a memorandum to Kingsley, and sent a defence of his action to John Malcolm Ludlow.[79] Ludlow answered Maurice's explanation by writing:

> You seem to me in it to have done as I have known you do many times before,—glide thro' all my thoughts and arguments, to go and sport yourself in a quiet pool of your own where I cannot follow you at present. All I can do is to fix my stakes closer, and lie in wait for you in the shallows, when the tide runs down again, or when you want to gain once more the real sea of human life.[80]

The passage demonstrates the brilliant clarity with which Ludlow was able to portray Maurice's peculiar elusiveness which baffles, intrigues, and sometimes entertains his readers.

Each incident in its own way laid bare Maurice's views. The divine order was a reality which already constituted existing society rather than a pattern according to which society was to be reconstituted. A moralist's purpose was essentially to proclaim; in due season, his proclamation would lead man to acknowledge and be who he was, a child of God, a member of Christ, and an inheritor of the kingdom of Heaven. The ethical teaching of Frederick Denison Maurice worked out the implications of his concept of the kingdom.

CLARITY OF STATEMENT
ORDER AND ETERNITY

The most straightforward and concise statement of what Maurice meant by the divine order was presented in a series of lectures delivered at Queen's College, Harley Street, in 1849 and 1850. These lectures described the nature of man and his position in the world.[81]

The whole of nature, Maurice declared, is in conformity to a law. "Man", however, "is not a *part* of nature but *above* it." Though man is not in subjection to nature, he himself has an order, the order in which we stand as human beings. The order in which man is placed, Maurice repeated, is "not a natural but a *supernatural* order". "An unseen Being is presiding over it, claiming it as *His* order, as the constitution He has made for man."

The first aspect of the supernatural or divine order is the "family order". We begin with relationships which are "fixed *for us,* and which we ourselves do not create". "I am a son, a husband, a brother." We find ourselves surrounded by things; then we are led to discover that we are in fact surrounded by persons, natural relations and natural affections.[82]

Maurice asserted that there is also another society to which we belong. "As being born on the same soil, we are members of a *nation.*" This too is settled for us "part of *human* order, and not of nature." It is "not possible for a man to be a man in the true sense of the word if he has not the feeling of being a member of a nation, if there is not a national order for him." Maurice said that "the conscience corresponds to national order in the same way as the affections correspond to family order". The second part of our moral history is the awakening of the conscience by which an individual is enabled to say "I am myself a man", just as the first part of our moral history is the acknowledgement that "I am a son, a husband, a brother". Common locality, common law, the bond of language, and government, are characteristics of a nation. Nor does a nation extinguish family life; it adopts it.[83]

But Maurice asked if there may not be another aspect of the divine order, if "some human fellowship, some condition for man as man, if a universal society cannot exist?" There is indeed a universal society which grows out of the nation as that did out of the family, and "that it was all the while lying at the root of that . . .", i.e. the family. Both the family and the nation are included in this larger society which "must be in some sense a Kingdom of Heaven, tho' a kingdom upon earth".

There must, too, be a divine foundation for the universal society which "must be a living one, a living Being at the root of it, and it must be the righteous Being, the source and root of all order and fellowship". That Being cannot be a mere man, yet he must have human sympathies; he must be "perfect righteousness". "A universal society without this foundation is lower than family or national society instead of being a more perfect society." It is necessary as well that the Divine Being must reveal himself to man, not for man to find him. One "must look above man for a foundation, and yet it must be in man."

There is such a universal society, said Maurice, witnessed in the life, death, and resurrection of Jesus.

> When the world was ripe for it, in due time it was declared to be the true society for men, sustaining all that existed before, containing deliverance for men from their selfishness and self will. And the conditions are laid in *sacrifice,* in the giving up of self, in shewing that this is not the proper law for humanity, but the destruction of it. It must be in some higher sacrifice than any man could offer, and be connected with the evidence that society has a divine ground, and fulfilled itself in bringing the nature of man into connection with the nature of God.

Each aspect of the divine order, family, nation, and universal society is composed of relations. Maurice spoke of the primary family relations, fathers and sons, husbands and wives, brothers and sisters. Within the nation there are also relations corresponding to the primary types of the domestic order. Monarchy, aristocracy, and socialism (a word Maurice preferred to timocracy) correspond in the nation to paternal, conjugal, and fraternal relations in the family.[84]

Maurice's discussion of orders composed of relations is made easier by understanding the way in which he used the word "institution". In 1834, in a letter to W. E. Gladstone, Thomas Acland mentioned Maurice and his distinctive institutionalism. " 'Men up to institutions, not institutions down to the level of men.' —Maurice says this, and wants to hear people say that they are supporters of institutions *and therefore* (not *and yet,* or *on the other hand,* the formula of shuffling trimming conservatives) reformers of abuses."[85] There was for Maurice a divine "givenness" about institutions which was applicable to each aspect of what he termed the divine order. His concept of the "givenness" of societies, domestic, national, and universal, allowed him to be seen as a straightforward institutionalist by his opponents. Some critics accuse him of the most chauvinistic type of mid-nineteenth-century English nationalism. Still, Maurice's analysis of domestic relations, parental, conjugal, and fraternal, and the development of these primary forms of relation in national monarchy, aristocracy, and "socialism" does have a certain objectivity.

Indeed it seems fair to say that beneath Maurice's arguments about reforms and institutions was a profoundly philosophical, or rather theological, juxtaposition of appearance and reality; and that beneath this juxtaposition there was a doctrine about time and eternity. To Maurice time and eternity were coexistent dimensions of a vertical experience of reality rather than mutually exclusive sectors of reality seen as horizontal. Eternity, we may say, was always beneath time; time was not followed by eternity. Time was the appearance of eternity. Such an understanding of the nature of the eternal, which led directly to his dismissal from two professorial chairs at King's College, was a lifelong facet of his thought dating back certainly to his association with Stephenson. His ideas were set forth in 1845 when Maurice wrote:

> I take the words "aeterna vita", not as they are explained by any Doctor of the Church, by any Council, provincial or oecumenical, but as they are explained by our Lord Himself in His last awful prayer, "This is life eternal, that they may know Thee the only true God, and Jesus Christ". Now that the knowledge of God and of Jesus Christ was offered to men in the Old Testament, as well as in the New; . . . all this I steadfastly believe . . . And it would be an outrage upon my conscience to express assent or consent to any article which did put "future state" in the Article for "eternal life".[86]

The clearest discussion of the relation between time and eternity appeared in a letter to a young clergyman named Dangerfield. The letter is similar to but not identical with one that Maurice wrote on the same day and which was published in the *Life of F. D. Maurice.*

You are quite right in your interpretation of my words. I never dreamed of merging Time in Eternity. The phrases which suggest such a thought belong to the popular Theology and seem to me most unsatisfactory. I maintain that Time and Eternity coexist here. The difficulty is to recognize the Eternal State under our temporal conditions; not to lose Eternity in Time. This difficulty which we all feel and confess and to which preachers so continually allude has been illustrated I think in my recent controversy with Dr Jelf. I cannot perceive that he has ever, even for a moment, contemplated Eternity as anything but the future state contrasted with the present.[87]

The happy blending of the logically exclusive dimensions, time and eternity, appeared several times in Maurice's correspondence where he was always more at ease than in his public statements. Then he was enabled to enter that illogical, extravagant world, the world of poetry. Wrestling with the dual dimensions of eternity and the present, the realm of the underlying divine order, the idea of the kingdom, just before they were married he wrote to Georgina Hare:

We may find eternity in every hour. The more we know of love the less will time have to do with us; the better we shall understand that our life does not consist of successive instants, but that there is a wholeness and unity in it which it derives from its connection with the life of God. I am sure you have felt how many years there may be gathered up in a few minutes. Did we not learn something of it last week?—past, present and future seemed to be wonderfully blended, and so indeed they were; and God has, I am sure, various ways of teaching us that they are.[88]

4

The Law of Sacrifice
The Principle of Morality

SACRIFICE
THE NATURE OF GOD

Maurice declared that the conditions of the true divine order which
constituted human relations are laid in *sacrifice*. Sacrifice, he said
is the cardinal principle of human morality because it is involved in
the very character and being of God himself. It is a matter of living
experience. Undeniable overtones of this view appeared in Maurice's
exposition of Plato. The doctrine which lies at the root of Socratic
teaching, he said, is

> that the selfish self-seeking principle leading men to animal
> gratification is the source of disorder and confusion in the life of
> man, not really the moving spring of it; that there is in man
> something higher which is not satisfied with itself, but which
> seeks after converse with the good.[1]

Discussing Platonic ideas, he wrote that they are "witnesses in our
inmost being that there is something beyond us and above us".
Every idea had its ground and termination in one higher than itself,
and finally in one supreme "Idea", the absolute and perfect Being,
the foundation and consummation of all. It is for us

> to abdicate our own pretensions to be authors or creators, to
> become mere acknowledgers of that which is. And to enter into
> that deepest and ultimate idea, which is the ground of our
> being, must be in the deepest sense an abdication of our own

71

notions and imaginations, an act of submission to, and reception of, the Truth.[2]

When asked for a definition of sacrifice Maurice turned to the First Epistle of St John. The author, he said would give us "an answer, though I doubted whether it would take the form of a definition."[3] The quality of sacrifice which is the ethos of God was manifested in the whole incarnate life of Christ, the total event of his life, death, and resurrection.[4]

Unlike Coleridge, however, Maurice emphasized the particularity of the Gospel; not for him any abstract idea of a diffused incarnation.[5] There was a moment of eloquence in the crucifixion. The cross is our definition of sacrifice, an adequate definition, showing both what love is, and what love is not. Stated simply, taking away the life of a brother is the result of departure from the law of sacrifice; the laying down of a life for others is the very principle of that law.

Maurice could not compartmentalize the life of our Lord into separate unconnected actions. Every aspect of his life was interrelated and formed a unity with the wholeness of God. Neither could Maurice speak of Jesus as an "individual," only and always as a "person" with all the dynamic overtones which the word person held for him. And the person of Jesus could never be considered a static thing; rather Jesus' life and Jesus' person are the same, set for a moment in a specific spatial and temporal context, but equally transcending space and time in what for Maurice was the coexisting dimension of eternity. Maurice's concept is made clearer by the insight of the contemporary American theologian, Schubert Ogden.

> Maurice [he wrote] may help us to understand that the responsibility of contemporary theology is to make clear that the hidden power, the inner meaning, the real substance, of *all* human happenings is the event of Christ. What faith means by "Christ", he rightly tells us, is not one historical event alongside others, but rather the *eschatological* event, or *eternal* word of God's unconditional love, which is the ground and end of all historical events whatsoever.[6]

Maurice developed his teaching about sacrifice by comparing subjective and personal religion. "Subjective religion", the study of religious experiences, states of mind, feelings, and emotions in order to discover our identity and the nature of our relation to God was essentially self-centred and resulted in a "conscience of bondage".[7] By "personal religion", Maurice meant "what has to do with us as *persons,* that in fact which ascertains in what sense we are persons and how we can realise our privilege of being such".[8] The resolution of the crisis of personal religion, as Maurice saw it, was the renunciation of self-dependence and the acknowledgement and appropriation of the living sacrifice of Christ. It was Luther's experience of justification by faith which resolved the torment of his subjectiveness. The faith which justifies a man, Maurice declared, "is the act of going out of himself; . . . faith has no meaning than this; that a man is converted to renunciation of self and acknowledgement of another."[9]

> It is not a fine thing to give up self, [Maurice wrote] to renounce all self-dependence, it is not a high flight of celestial saintship; it is simply a person confessing himself to be that which he is; not something which he is not . . . self-repudiation being that conscious act which is required of him. And why demanded of him but because the self-assertion is an untruth; the being in Christ the true state.[10]

Abel's "mute expression of . . . helplessness, dependence, and confidence", Maurice said, demonstrated one primary aspect of the nature of sacrifice.[11]

From Noah, we learn " something more of the social nature of these offerings"[12] . . . "how the social and the individual sacrifice are connected, how they may be separated to the peril of the community and its members."[13]

Moreover, Abraham

> found sacrifice to be no one solitary act, no sudden expression of joy, no violent effort to make a return for blessings which we can only return by accepting; but that it lies at the very root of our being; that our lives stand upon it; that society is held together by it; that all power to be right, and to do right, begins with the offering up of ourselves, because it is thus that the righteous Lord makes us like Himself.[14]

Maurice stressed that sacrifice is not to make God do man's will. Rather sacrifice "proceeds from God, . . . accomplishes the purposes

of God . . . enables those creatures to become like their Father in
Heaven by offering up themselves . . .".[15] The pettiest events provide
occasion for sacrifice, a law not just for the crises of our existence.

> You may have very exstatic feelings about the Christian brother-
> hood at large; but are you ready to help that particular brother,
> who is lying destitute there, not with feelings, but with a little
> of the actual food and raiment that he is in need of?[16]

Some men submit reluctantly to the law of sacrifice.

> They try to set up another law, the law of self-pleasing . . . .
> They cannot succeed. They do *not* please themselves. Earth and
> Heaven are at war with them. For the mind of the Ruler of
> Heaven and Earth is a mind of self-sacrifice; it is revealed in
> the Cross of Christ. Some submit to the law of sacrifice cheer-
> fully . . . They allow it to shape their acts. These are consciously
> or unconsciously yielding to Christ, confessing Him as their
> king, bearing His Cross.[17]

Such men are freed from self-consciouness about their acts. They
need not glorify themselves upon the giving up of themselves, "for
they look upon no sacrifice as satisfactory but His; every other
derives its virtue from His".[18]

Maurice's problem was to connect the sacrifice of Christ in which
the nature of the Being of God is manifested and the reflection of
that sacrifice in the innumerable sacrifices by which mankind
acknowledges and expresses that it is created in God's image. For
Maurice saw the divine and human action as inextricably linked,
the latter finding its true source in the other.

He wrote of "the Union of Godhead and Manhood in Christ, and
the Sacrifice which followed on that Union"[19] as both the manward
manifestation of "a Universal and Absolute Morality . . . [and] . . .
the Human Manifestation of Morality . . . which yet, in the fullest
and most perfect sense, is the Morality of Man, the ground of all
which is moral in each particular man."[20] This, for Maurice, was
the foundation of Christian Ethics. If there is such a manifestation
as this, he could understand the words that man is made in the
image of God, and could understand how it is possible for men to
show forth that image.

Men "could keep alive brotherly kindness, hospitality to strangers, the purity of the marriage bed, compassion to the afflicted . . . acceptable sacrifices"[21] remembering the sacrifice of Jesus, a reconciliation "grounded on a perfect union of the *will* of God and the *will* of man".[22] Maurice saw the sacrifice of Christ in all these homely human actions. "He who by the Eternal Spirit offered Himself to God . . . could alone give that Spirit by which all creatures united in Him might offer themselves as sacrifices well pleasing to the Father."[23] Maurice asked:

> Must not the presentation of the one real perfect Sacrifice to the Father, the continual thanksgiving for that sacrifice, be the central act of all worship to God—of all fellowship among men? Must not the offering of the worshipper's soul and body as living sacrifices to God be the necessary fruit and accompaniment of this act, that which gives meaning to all the greatest and meanest services—to the most transcendent and the commonest acts of life.[24]

SIN, SEPARATION
THE CONSCIENCE OF BONDAGE

Sin and forgiveness, Maurice felt, could only be considered in connection with sacrifice. They were best thought of as different dimensions of a single fact of experience, never separated as if they were set in an horizontal line of temporal continuity. He liked Coleridge's image of a tree being contained in the seed all at once in a moment in time.

Sin was the opposite of all that Maurice meant when he spoke of relations as found in the Name of God or in the reflection of the divine relation in human society, domestic, national, or universal. Sin, for Maurice, was separation. It was making myself the centre rather than acknowledging that God is my centre, making myself the source rather than recognizing that God is the source, finally attempting to be dependent only on myself, rather than to acknowledge my dependence upon God. And "all sin", Maurice said, "is contradiction; if you speak of it, you must denote it by words that cross and seem to confute each other. Unless men were spirits, you could not complain of them for acting as beasts; unless they proved every moment that they were framed for fellowship and mutual dependence, you could not blame their selfishness."[25]

The mark of a man's self-conscious identity was his ability to examine his relationships or to look within his own inner self. Such "digging", to use Maurice's own word, is God-inspired; it is for the purpose of discovering God. Unfortunately the movement toward personal awareness most often reveals an "utterly unsocial condition", domestic discord, national disunity, sectarianism. Within himself a man discovers what can best be described in St Paul's words, "The good that I would that I do not, but the evil that I would not, that I practice. Oh wretched man that I am; who shall deliver me from the body of this death?"[26] Maurice's consciousness of sin is a "conscience of bondage", an overall sense of powerlessness connected with the condition of separation.

Nevertheless—and here is Maurice at his positive and hopeful best—a man does not feel the power of sin, his disposition to be false, or to be at war with his fellow creatures, until he believes that God is true and has created men to be one. Maurice was, as always, God-centred, making God, not man the source. He even said that it was because of sin that man was moved to seek for, to find, to be found by God. The insights "that I am not what I am meant to be" may be dispelled certainly. There are many ways of dispelling them. If, however, they are listened to they may be God's messengers. Man's position could be denied or violated, but never completely destroyed. We may say that to be aware of the condition of separation, of the disposition to self-centredness, is itself a sign of hope.

There was an apparent dichotomy in Maurice's statement that the awareness and acknowledgement of sin, the state of separation from God, is concurrent with the awareness of and acknowledgement of the presence of God himself. No doubt his wrestling with the thorny nature of such a paradox caused him at times to despair of the structure of logic in which opposite affirmations could not exist. Maurice was, and is, regularly accused of being a muddled thinker; and this would seem a case in point. But he was desperately concerned to say as strongly as possible things that he knew to be true, even if he could not fit them together into an orderly, logical structure. He disliked systems, not least because they prevented men from seeing that contradictory facts of experience could be true at the same time.

How did Maurice explain this situation of moral evil, or shattered relationships? How is it that a man, being in a relation, does not acknowledge his position? And what is there to be done about a restoration of the proper condition of relations reflecting the one primary, underlying relation between God and man, yes, but founded upon the nature of the being of God himself, in the relation of Father, Son, and Holy Spirit?

Maurice said that he discovered within himself both an inclination and an influence. This experience, he declared, is undeniable. He knew, he said, *"my inclination, my tendency, my disposition"*[27] to rebel against relations, to become attracted toward objects which are presented to the senses as objects, or in fact to become attracted toward persons, not in fact as toward persons, but as if they were objects as well, units, individuals, things which stand over against me as thing to thing, not in the proper mutual inter-relation of person with person. Maurice admitted that it was not a concept in which he had been brought up as a Unitarian, but the source of such inclinations to make the self the centre is simply an "Evil One", "a Tempter", "a Devil".[28] He used what he called a distinctive concept of the New Testament. "For once that the Devil is introduced into the Law, the Psalms, and the Prophets, he is spoken of twenty times in any single Gospel or Epistle."[29]

Maurice seemed either not to know or not to care about the development of historical or textual Biblical "higher criticism". While he developed his concept of the source of evil beyond this bald statement of a personal (objective?) "evil one", in a sense he required the opposite of what he meant by a person to be the source of the disunity or chaos which is the opposite of what he meant by a relation.

Because of his insistence on the underlying givenness of the divine order, of relations which can be denied, distorted or violated, but as God given, never completely destroyed, as well as because of his imputed "universalism", Maurice has been accused of denying the reality of sin. Many of his contemporaries were wary of his concept and claimed that he made light of it even if he stopped short of disputing sin altogether.[30]

One of the reasons why Maurice was criticized for giving too little importance to the meaning of sin and the fact of sin was because he began his theology with the being of God, never with man or the sin of man. He was severely critical of the popular

theology of his day for failing to do as he did. Few of Maurice's
statements are better known than his accusation that the Calvinists
started theology not with the goodness of God himself, but with the
sin of man, fallen human nature.

The charge that Maurice failed to give proper importance to sin
was met among others by Maurice's biographer. John Frederick
Maurice appealed to his father's own deep personal consciousness
of sin and to innumerable passages in Maurice's works which
illustrate the profound depths of sin's reality to him. No one who
has read Maurice for long, or who has taken the time to try to
understand him as a person in his own right, can fail to see the
terrible power which sin held in his ethical thinking, or the terrible
weight which the sense of sin bore on his own life, and in his own
psychological awareness.[31]

Maurice attempted to explain himself in a letter to F. J. A. Hort.
"The more I have thought and felt, . . . the more have I been sure
that I was meant to trust this Being (God in Christ, reconciling the
world to himself, exhibited to me in the Scripture),—that my sin
was *not* trusting Him."[32] This failure to trust, this refusal to
acknowledge my position, and God's centrality, this choosing of self
amounts to

> a rebel state of will, at war with God, . . . the highest, com-
> pletest misery . . . All will admit that damnation is in some
> sense loss of God's presence, that the curse lies in the rejection
> of love, separation from love, abandonment to self. . . . I know
> that we may struggle with the Light, that we may choose
> death. But I know also that Love does overcome this rebellion.
> I know that I am bound to believe that its power is greater than
> any other. I am sure that Christ's death proves that death, hell,
> hatred, are not so strong as their opposites. How can I reconcile
> these contradictory discoveries? I cannot reconcile them. I know
> no theory which can. But I can trust in Him who has reconciled
> the world to Himself.[33]

Maurice refused to place limits on the human potential of denying
God and his order; this agnosticism is his defence against the
universalist charge. But he did affirm, for him an undeniable if
poetic truth, that "the abyss of Love" is deeper than the "abyss of
Death".[34]

FORGIVENESS
AND THE CONSCIENCE OF FREEDOM

Forgiveness was the crucial stage which lay between sin, character-
ized by the conscience of bondage, and the conscience of freedom.
The connection of forgiveness with freedom, and the way in which
freedom is expressed in obedience, indeed makes obedience possible,
marks an important progression in Maurice's ethics. Several elements
sustain his discussion. Maurice could not separate forgiveness from
a serious consideration of judgement. Moreover the freedom wrought
by forgiveness was integrally related to what Maurice meant by
worship.

The words "Forgive us our trespasses as we forgive them that
trespass against us" provided Maurice with a textbook. There was an
indication in our Lord's own prayer of "that forgiveness which men
had been most imperfectly exercising towards each other,"[35] as well
as an acknowledgement of the fact that human forgiveness had its
ground in the divine forgiveness. "The forgiveness which came
forth in the cry upon the Cross" manifested and fulfilled both these
aspects of forgiveness.

It goes without saying that there must be a recognition of that
which needs to be forgiven, although Maurice placed forgiveness,
divine and human, prior to judgement, human and divine. Maurice
chose words of Milton to describe God's judgement upon man's
refusal to acknowledge who he is, and his proper relation. God had
been resisting the Evil Spirit in a war with Evil, and the Spirit of
Evil. Maurice saw the divine judgement as a state of war "with
sickness and sorrow".[36] On the Cross, Maurice saw the judgement
of Christ, judgement from the throne of God, and he declared that
God's judgement lay behind or beneath all the "imperfect judgements which had been proceeding against the like evils from the
consciences of men in all times".[37] But if Maurice saw divine judgement working through human judgements no matter how imperfect,
how much more does the divine forgiveness lie beneath human
forgiveness! He quoted words of Jesus, "If ye forgive not men
their trespasses, neither will your Father forgive your trespasses."[38]

> Our Lord's sentence about forgiveness meets us [affirmed
> Maurice] and we make an exception for it. The most difficult
> of righteous acts must be done *before* we can receive the grace

of Christ! But suppose the gift of Divine forgiveness to be that which works in us the forgiveness of our brother; suppose it is His Spirit and not ours which sheds abroad forgiveness in our hearts; *then* clearly we reject God's forgiveness when we refuse to forgive one another.[39]

Maurice knew intimately the experience of forgiveness as well as judgement in his own personal life. He also knew the creative strength which arose from that experience, and he responded with a profound sense of gratitude. It was a matter of freedom, the only freedom he had ever known. The quality of thanksgiving in freedom illustrates best what Maurice meant by obedience. He touched on the question over and over again in his correspondence.[40] Thanksgiving, he felt, is simply a man being "himself" in his domestic relation, in his nation, and in that universal family or "kind" which Maurice called the kingdom of Christ. Each of the three divisions of Maurice's Cambridge lectures on social morality concluded with a discussion of "thanksgiving" in which Maurice outlined family, national, and universal "worship." "Worship", as much as any word, expresses what Maurice meant by ethics, the response whereby a man in freedom accepts divine and human forgiveness. Worship, the life of freedom and obedience, is founded upon the being of God as its source, expressed in his self revelation in the Living Word whose character is that of self-sacrifice. The Holy Spirit, Maurice felt, moves in this living experience in which a man both acknowledges who he is and becomes who he is. Finally, the word worship captures the dimension in which man's individuality is held in dynamic tension with his participation through relationships in a universal society. It takes into consideration "those truths which belong to us not as individuals but as *men*".[41] There is no sense of limitation of worship, or thanksgiving to prescribed areas. It is a matter of the daily life of every man, of all men, in a moment in time and in the whole context of history.

An intimate connection exists between Maurice's word "acknowledgement", a word he used repeatedly, and "worship". Writing to Sara Coleridge who had complained that his use of the word acknowledgement was cold, he said:

I meant to translate St. Paul's "epignosis"—which answers, if I am not mistaken in his language, to "prognosis" and implies the knowledge taken of the Creator by the Creature, in answer to the knowledge which the Creator has first taken of the Creature. How should such knowledge be taken? I answer fully and perfectly only in the highest and most heavenly acts of adoration and thanksgiving. Self-sacrifice in everything is implied in the idea of the Eucharist, secondly in every act of confessing, faith, hope, prayer, gentleness, kindness, and forgiveness. All these are (just) ways of acknowledging ourselves to be nothing and God to be all in all, ways by which the spirit casts off its chrysalis coat of selfishness and ascends where its Lord has himself ascended.[42]

The force which invigorates life, personal and corporate, which Maurice calls worship, is the Spirit. The force can only be likened to a dynamic encounter between persons in relationship. In such a way only can we defend the mutual integrity of the moving Spirit, and the person upon whom, and in whom, the Spirit is active. Maurice appreciating the dangers of confusion, still, characteristically, took the risk and plunged ahead to say in the simple straightforward way he reserved for children: "The Spirit of the Father and the Son, *has* made men good and true, *has* fought against what is bad and untrue in them, ever since there were men on the earth. But they did not know who it was who was leading them to choose goodness and truth . . . till Christ came."[43] "When we are bitter against each other; . . . when we are suspicious of each other, . . . when we think ourselves wiser or better than one another . . . the Spirit of God would take away these hindrances from us. Those from whom He takes them away are made saints or holy."[44]

That human worship is in a real sense the activity of the Spirit, and that human worship is essentially a fulfilment or a reflection in freedom of Divine self-sacrifice, Maurice was sure. "The oblation which He enables us to make that we may be like Him, is the oblation of ourselves." This is the idea of "Christian Worship",

an acknowledgement of a Fatherly Will—a Will to redeem and restore Humanity, a Will which is expressed in Sacrifice; . . . it is an offering to that Will of the men themselves that they may be what He would have them be, may do what He would have them do.[45]

5

The "I"
The Subject of Morality

———◆———

"WHAT AM I?"

Maurice's analysis of human nature is shown in his answer to the question "What am I?" His emphasis on man as a social being, and his true position as a member of an order made it difficult for this theologian of relations to speak of one man apart from others. He felt compelled, nevertheless, to speak of the "I". As elsewhere, he was often forced into the use of such quaint phrases to avoid "abstractions." Some men who heard his first lecture as Knightbridge professor supposedly thought he talked about "the eye."

The "I", he asserted, is not to be examined where "things" are examined, or covered over with such words as individuality or personality. "I" points not to a thing, nor to an abstraction. "I" points to a man himself, what he *is* rather than what he possesses. Hearing, seeing, handling "brought me in contact with the outside of a man, . . . but he was within".[1] Not "outside manner," Maurice repeated but something inward "makyth man", the life which is in him. That life is different from the outward manifestations but I can converse with it, and it is the seat of goodness, wisdom, and power. The words inward and outward had value for Maurice and he was interested in the inward, but he was careful not to partition human nature. Here he agreed with Mansel.

Man, as a Person, is one, yet composed of many elements;— not identical with any one of them, nor yet with the aggregate of them all; and yet not separable from them by any effort of abstraction. Man is one in his thoughts, in his actions, and in

82

the responsibilities which these involve. It is *I* who think, *I* who act, *I* who feel; yet I am not thought, nor action, nor feeling, nor a combination of thoughts and actions and feelings heaped together.[2]

Although he protested bitterly that such words were only theories and opinions torn out of systems, Maurice did use various terminologies or psychological mythologies. The classic words "reason", "affection", and "will" appeared in his writing along with such phrases as "pure reason", "speculative reason", and "the understanding". Maurice also attempted to express the "social" aspects of the "I", that dynamic engagement which he knew to be going on within himself, and within the "I" of every man. He referred to "the problem of the Many and the One, which is thus forced upon us by our earliest domestic experience", and which "becomes again the problem of our life as citizens of a State".[3]

As we examine the "I", Maurice declared, we are to seek "not merely certain outward acts, but an internal habit, a something which would give to all their (men's) doings, words, gestures, evenness and order."[4] Some might call this disposition or habit or character "an *artificial* disposition or habit or character. But it is by some means or other wrought into the man or woman. It becomes his or hers."[5] These habits are characteristic of our "selves". "They cannot come to us from without. They must be internal. And yet they do not spring up in men without education."[6]

The study of the proper human condition "lies in the discovery of a certain character or ethos first doubtless in some individual, but in him as connected with a Society smaller or larger, in him as showing what character makes the Society harmonious or discordant, tenable or untenable."[7]

ETHOS

CREATIVE RELATION

"What am I?" led Maurice on to a discussion of "ethos", a Greek word chosen intentionally rather than the Latin "morals". "Ethos" expresses the underlying character which produces outward behaviour or "manners". Sometimes Maurice spoke of the character of a single person, referring to a certain condition of being with

overtones of habitual quality. Normally he used "ethos" in terms
of a relation between persons. He asserted that the Name, the
Being, of God is best described in terms of "ethos", of a relation.
Occasionally Maurice spoke of the principle, or the disposition, or
the law of sacrifice, but Love as Sacrifice, or Self-Sacrifice, a matter
of relation, was the underlying nature of God the Holy Trinity.
"The most pure and perfect state we can conceive, is the state of
which sacrifice is the Law."[8]

"My desire", he declared, "is to ground all theology upon the
Name of God the Father, the Son, and the Holy Ghost."[9] Such a
theology could not fail to be a description of relations. Aristotle,
Maurice affirmed,

> in his apprehensions respecting the nature of relationships . . .
> surpassed Plato . . . while he fell so far short of him in every-
> thing that concerns the absolute. He discovers in the relation-
> ships of father to son, of husband to wife, of brother to sister,
> three primary forms as it were of friendship; and the grounds
> of the three kinds of government to which all others may be
> reduced, Monarchy, Aristocracy, Timocracy, and of which the
> three corruptions are, tyranny, oligarchy, democracy, . . .
> Friendship . . . will take its peculiar form from the form of
> the society. It will be the friendship of patronage and reverence
> in a monarchy. It will have the conjugal model in aristocracy,
> one party being respected as the superior in worth, and retain-
> ing that respect only while he asserts dominion on that ground.
> The fraternal type of equality will be preserved in all friend-
> ships under a timocracy.[10]

Maurice expanded Aristotelian friendship in accordance with
what he felt to be the demands of the Christian revelation, asserting
that the underlying "ethos" of each of the three forms of human
relations had its foundation in the character or "ethos" of God.

The character of the relation of father and son, Maurice said,
was *authority* and *obedience,* as opposed to dominion and submission; Maurice closely identified authority with "education."[11]
The quality of the relation of husband and wife he found to be
trust.[12] His lectures on marriage at Cambridge echoed the words of
Annie Barton shortly after their engagement. Her letter reflected
the conversation of courtship between two earnest, self-conscious
young persons.

I can well believe what you say that our new relation to each other must bring us nearer to God for I feel that it would require less faith in him to resign myself to him in death than to trust myself so entirely to you as I now must . . . I may be able to sympathise with you as you desire but I feel perfectly awestricken at the thought of your trusting to me as a means of raising your character unless indeed the constant forbearance I should require of you might be of use to you.[13]

Finally *co-operation* was the form in which divine sacrifice was manifested in the relation between brother and sister.[14]

His mother would have approved of this. In a letter which she wrote in 1819 when she thought she was dying, Mrs Maurice counselled her daughter Emma to "obey" her elder sisters, and to "co-operate with them in all that is useful and good, and in teaching the young ones in what is right".[15] Indeed his mother's influence may well be reflected in Maurice's concept of the underlying quality of a relation. The forms in which the divine character of sacrifice appeared in specific relations were not mutually exclusive, but could be and were apparent in each kind of relation. Mrs Maurice's counsel to her daughter involved not only fraternal co-operation but parental authority in teaching the younger, and filial obedience in her behaviour to the elder members of the family.

Different forms of sacrifice are found in the different relations, however—and one person could share various forms of relations with others, not simply the one generic relationship in which they had ostensibly been placed.

This fact was brought out in Maurice's argument for women's education. Women must have sound educations, he said, particularly because they fulfilled the role of parents to so many children, their own, their charges, their pupils and others.[16] The topic of domestic education, Maurice stated, "has especially called forth the quicker and more delicate observation of women, whether mothers themselves, or those who like Miss Edgeworth have performed the part of mothers to sisters, brothers, or strangers."[17] Maurice's elder sisters, Elizabeth, Mary, and Anne, were commissioned to function essentially as mothers to the younger children. Elizabeth did the mending and darning for the family. Mrs Maurice declared Mary "to be the one who can most take my place with her father".[18]

Maurice himself wrote to his children shortly after the death of their mother. The letter, typical of early Victorian domestic sentiment, showed how he had to be both father and mother to his little boys.

> My very dear Boys,
>   Frances will read this note to you and will tell Freddy the letters in it if he will look at them. I want very much to see you both and to hear you speak to me and say "Dear Papa". But I am very glad that you should be with your Freddy's dear Godpapa and with Mrs Trench and the little boys and Mina who are so kind to you. And I like to think that you are running about the nice garden. There is nothing like it here at Guy's. And yet this is a good place too and I hope you will like it very much and that Freddy will remember it and who was in it with him once. Let me hear that you are good boys, very obedient and very loving to each other; you cannot tell how that will please me. May God bless you my dear Freddy and Edmund. Tell Frances how much I thank her for being so kind to you. You must kiss all the children for me and each other too.
>   Your own Papa.
> Your dear aunt Priscilla is very ill.[19]

AFFECTION
THE DYNAMICS OF A RELATION

So Maurice turned from his analysis of the "ethos" which expresses the relations in which the "I" develops to examine the process of that development. Before the child came to the self-consciousness which underlies "I am", and before the child learned to know what duty is which underlies "I ought or I ought not", the child was already surrounded by affection. According to Maurice, affection forms the sinews which bind the relations of a family together, strong yet supple, supportive yet always allowing, even creating, freedom. And affection is called forth by affection. All that Maurice had to say broadly about family, or nation, or universal society, and all that he had to say about isolated specific matters of education, for example the question of punishment or the more complex question of rewards, is seen to be the interaction of loves, spontaneous and responsive, writ large. The dynamic energy of love, of self-sacrifice, comes from outside, God's love towards man enabling man to respond; a parent's love for his child, husbands' and wives' love for one another, brotherly love for brother, enabling the response of love. Loving sacrifice in relations, Maurice felt, is not only the image of God's work, but the very means by which God draws men nearer to himself, and consequently nearer to each other.

An example of the way love enables the response of love appeared in Maurice's correspondence with his mother. Mrs Maurice was unable to accept the fact of her own "election". Maurice sensed the intricate complexity of relationships in which the roles of parent and child were interchangeable. His attempt to reassure his mother essentially reversed that relation. He used the facts of her everyday life to calm his mother's anxiety. Her experience of loving and being loved should convince her of her "heavenly relation".

> I have been myself, I think, learning one truth in the other; and I never should have understood so much even as I do of the necessity of taking our heavenly Father's love to us for granted, in order to be the ground and parent of love to Him in us, if I had not by a series of painful, almost agonising, discoveries been led to feel that I must acquiesce in the delightful feeling of others loving me, in order to enjoy and realise the belief that I love them.[20]

These words record the testimony of the child awakened to love and obedience, and enabled to love in the context of being loved and accepting love.

Maurice's point of view caused him to react strongly against the contrary opinion that parents or schoolmasters were able to call forth responsive obedience by the use of force. He was outraged by those who taught that "the imposition of penalties begets at once the sense and avoidance of the *forbidden* and the awe of authority, . . . retained through life as the basis of the individual Conscience, the foremost motive to abstain from actions designated as wrong."[21] This was exactly opposite to what Maurice meant by conscience.

Personal development was illustrated in Maurice's discussion of education, not simply *"the giving of Information,"*[22] nor *"the development of the faculties"* as taught by Pestalozzi.[23] Nor was

D

"restraint" the end of education. Each of these notions was important; each contained certain truth, but the truth lay beneath the
truth in all of them. For education, a "Deliverer" was needed to
loose not man's faculties, but man himself, from bondage "to an
evil nature which was holding him down".[24] The external
authority, the educator, must appeal to that which is within the
child, to call it forth.

It is all too easy for us acting carelessly to discover that we are
bringing up "not citizens, but slaves". Maurice said that we must
first of all remember that we have "living spirits to deal with", to
be brought "to trust, to think, to hope, to know".[25] They must be
led to regard themselves as human beings made in the image of
God, as such, "social beings bound to each other by the ties of
family, neighbourhood, country, and by a common humanity".[26]
Men, said Maurice, have, all of them, a craving for *"freedom and
for order"*, and "all education is intended to excite these cravings,
and to meet them".[27] We must show men their shackles and
deliver them from them, that is, make them "understand that they
are Persons, and not Things".[28] Education is not only to make us
free, but able "to perceive an *order* in all that we do, and in all that
we think".[29] "The great problem of all, then, is how to make men
know that they are persons, and therefore that freedom and order
are their necessary and rightful inheritance."[30]

Parental treatment, by which attitude is expressed, must neither
be indulgent, apt to destroy family life, nor crushing which tends
to dwarf the child, and instead of creating true freedom brings about
the response not of obedience but submission. Submission, Maurice
clearly saw, is only the other side of the coin of latent or active
rebellion. The proper parental attitude in this crucial period of
liberation within order was seen in a conversation in *Eustace Conway,* in which Lady Edward, Eustace, and Mrs Franklin, an elderly
Quakeress, discussed the education of children. "I do not doubt
thou wouldst be kind to the young as thou art to the old," Mrs
Franklin said to Eustace. "I think thou wouldst not have sufficient
reverence for children!"[31] "Certainly there is a respect due to
children", continued Lady Edward who mentioned with disapproval
a former tutor who advocated making remarks about children's
behaviour in front of other people as a device of instructing them.[32]
This was tantamount to treating the child as a "thing". Eustace
agreed: "If we abstained from acts of ill breeding because they are

cruel, and not because they are forbidden, we should perhaps remember that the outrage is greater in proportion to the weakness of the object."[33] There is a delicate balance between dominance and permissiveness on the part of the educating parental authority in which the child comes to awareness of himself.

CONSCIENCE
THE TOTAL RESPONSE OF A MAN

Having described the "I", the concept of relations in which the "I" develops, and having analysed the process of development, Maurice following his own advice, made it clear what he meant by a person by making it clear what he meant by a conscience. He spoke of conscience, not as being a part of a man, or a thing which a man may be said to possess, but rather the whole of a man in his total response to the primary expression toward him of God's love.

As we study his teaching about the conscience, we remember the undeniable sense in which Maurice was a Platonist according to Coleridge's dictum, "Every man is born either a Platonist or an Aristotelian."[34] Indeed we may well remember his statement to Edward Strachey: ". . . all little children are Platonists, and it is their education which makes men Aristotelians."[35]

Whether his Platonism is traced through Coleridge or Hare to the disciple of Socrates, Maurice always had one foot planted firmly in the tradition of the Fourth Gospel and the Johannine Epistles. Beneath many of the controversies of his life lay his loyalty to Coleridge's Platonic affirmation. "The outward world of sense is but the appropriate clothing and manifestation of an invisible and spiritual world."[36] He shared with all idealists the problem of knowledge in such a view of reality. It was primarily from Coleridge that Maurice derived his own solution of the problem. Sara Coleridge, commending Maurice's *Kingdom of Christ* to Mrs Arabella Brooks, said that it was important to read the book as a balancing qualification of the Tractarians generally and John Henry Newman in particular. She wrote

> Maurice is a profound thinker, a vigorous though rough writer; and I trust you would not like him the worse for sharing my father's spirit. His divinity seems based on the Aids

to Reflection, and though no servile imitator, he has certainly
borrowed his mode of writing and turn of thought very much
from S.T.C.[37]

Maurice acknowledged his debt to Coleridge. Dedicating the
second edition of the *Kingdom of Christ* to Derwent Coleridge,
Maurice underlined what he owed to his father. He also paid
tribute in a letter to Sara Coleridge, mentioning her father's "faith;
from which if in any point I can venture to dissent it is with
caution and trembling; attributing the very power of doing so in a
great measure to his own instructions, and the love of truth with
which he has been the instrument of inspiring me."[38] Maurice
spoke of Coleridge as "the writer whom I honour most" even if
on many points he disagreed with him.

Maurice nowhere showed his indebtedness to Coleridge more
than in his own affirmation, often emphasized, of "that spiritual
organ which takes in actual things as the sensual eye takes in the
forms and images of things".[39] He enlisted Coleridge's support to
say

> that Reason is a Universal faculty; secondly that it *constitutes*
> the man; thirdly that we are to predicate of it not conscious-
> ness but that which is higher than consciousness, *intuition*;
> fourthly, that the Reason may never come into exercise, may
> be quenched, is quenched if it do not enter into communion
> with the divine Reason. Add to this the clear physical convic-
> tion that which is the necessary complement of it the theological
> truth of Him who is perfect Reason entering into fellowship
> with manhood, bringing the Infinite into union with the
> Finite, declaring man to be constituted in him before all
> worlds; to have no life or light but in him, to be in an
> anomalous condition out of him and you have, it seems to me,
> that idea of which Baptism is the beautifully simple and divine
> expression.[40]

For Maurice, this baptismal declaration of man "to be constituted in him" provided the gospel which he was able regularly
to proclaim at this particular time to the patients in his care at
Guy's hospital, whether he was enabled "to look upon the broken
legged, broken backed, drunken portion of humanity whom I have
to speak to day after day, as portions of humanity or only as that

which they *seem* to be fragments torn from it, perishing sinners as the language is."[41]

He is not to "look at them merely as creatures who have some potentiality of grace, . . . [but] . . . as creatures who are bound to look upon themselves as redeemed and as members of Christ."[42]

Maurice, in his own mind, was far from saying that baptism is simply the affirmation of that which is already true, and, as his antagonists, both Evangelicals and Tractarians, understood him, practically unnecessary.

> But then how can *Baptism* have anything to do with conferring upon man his true state? [Maurice wrote] The word "conferring" is far from a happy one, one which I should never considerately use. But the character of the state itself is an answer to the question why it cannot be spoken of as a birth state; why it *must*—I would desire to use the word reverently—be devoted to us by some divine token and testimony. For what have we just been saying; what has every good man been saying all his life through? That this state though the only true one; though man's proper state must be felt to be God's gift . . . Let the man say it is mine by my right as a man and he utters either the greatest truth or the greatest falsehood . . . the greatest falsehood, if he supposes it in any respect an independent matter of course, a possession—a state of nature.[43]

Maurice returned again and again to this truth which he said lay beneath the sacrament of baptism, the affirmation of a real state of communion between God and man, and consequently between man and man.

> The deepest conviction in my mind, [he wrote to Sara Coleridge] (greatly strengthened and called forth by those passages in your father's writings which speak of the truths of the Reason as necessarily embodied, if expressed in minds at all, in two contradictory propositions) is that there is some organ for the higher spiritual realities and apprehensions answering the purpose which verbal forms and propositions answer for the facts of the understanding.[44]

Maurice believed that there is a right state belonging to man as man, the proper human condition, and that knowledge of such a "constitution" is given to him by means of "an organ in man for conversing with the infinite".[45] Maurice objected to Locke because he taught that "man derives no knowledge except from his senses".[46] He attacked those philosophers who, like Locke, said "that there is no knowledge but that which comes to us through the senses. The idea of a communion between the divine Word and the heart and conscience and reason of men has been of course rejected."[47]

Loyalty to the "light that lightened all men" had contributed to his uncertainty about taking orders. In a letter to Richard Trench, he expressed "the strong conviction that my call is to remain at Oxford". He had been offered a "title and all the formalities. . . . But my conscience still sticks, and the more because I almost feel as if I ought to undertake the semi-secular work of writing a diatribe against Locke. I am so overwhelmed with an impression of the mischief he has done and is doing; . . . I feel mightily tempted to take a stone out of the brook for the head of this Philistine."[48]

Wrestling to bring out clearly what he meant by the "spiritual organ", Maurice followed Coleridge's objection to Bishop Leighton's statement, "It is a fruitless verbal debate, whether Conscience be a faculty or a habit. . . . Conscience will be found to be no other than the mind of a man, under the notion of a particular reference to himself and his own actions."[49] Coleridge attacked any view which did not see conscience as antecedent to, as underlying, anything which could be spoken of other than as the most profound depths of a man.[50] No matter how reticent he was about naming names and attaching labels, Maurice regularly spoke of "that spiritual organ" as "conscience", which he equated with the whole of a man in himself. "First make it clear what you mean by a Person," he asserted, concluding his Cambridge lectures on the conscience; "that you will do when you make it clear what you mean by a Conscience."[51] Butler was correct, Maurice said, when he abandoned all attempt to speak of conscience as faculty, or habit, or indeed as a moral sense. "Man has not merely a moral sense, he has a CONSCIENCE."[52] Because Butler had to speak to his age, Maurice asserted, he was compelled to write with little reference to revelation. Furthermore he was obliged by his mode of argument to speak of the conscience "as being simply *in* man", something which a man "has" when it is "a connecting link with that which is above him".[53]

Maurice developed his understanding of conscience in his distinction between "personal" and "subjective" religion. Conscience was not so much a matter of an individual as it is a matter of relation; in a sense "conscience" is social. We may say, too, that conscience is not so much a "thing" as it is a "being", rather a "becoming", with all the dynamic overtones of the word.

6

The Family
The Discovery of Morality

FATHERS AND SONS
EDUCATION IN FREEDOM

The belief that the family was sacred was, of course, characteristic of the Victorian middle classes, and Maurice's attitudes often parallel, if not reflect, the views of that society. Indeed his stand on many social and national issues was frequently so similar to that "mirror of English popular opinion" as to explain his biographer's statement: "*Punch* more than once struck in vigorously on my father's side of questions".[1] Nevertheless, Maurice provided his own peculiarly "theological" basis for any position which he held. In the Sabbatarian controversy at the time of the Great Exhibition of 1851, during the war in the Crimea, or in his observations on the French political scene, Maurice gave "theological" grounds for his point of view, shared, though for quite different reasons, by others of the British public. However, there were times, for example during the Indian mutinies, when popular opinion could not be reconciled with his belief in an established divine order manifested in history and contemporary life.[2] Then Maurice could not stand aloof; no one ever feared less than he to enter the lists, and he was even more combative when he felt that majority opinion implied "an acknowledgement of Society as God".[3] It is therefore important to examine Maurice's teaching about the family, as on other matters, from his "theological" basis.

Maurice placed the father at the centre of the family. This followed from the divine origin of human society. The father's authority was supported by the role which God had appointed Abraham, but even the Romans, Maurice said, "held that the authority of the father was at the root of all their life. All their Institutions stood upon that authority; and they had stronger Institutions than all other people that have been in the world."[4] What is more, "they confessed that the authority of particular human fathers rested upon the authority of a Divine Father."[5] Likewise the Scots, whose patriarchal domestic life Maurice admired, found their domestic life "grounded first on the authority of the father, . . . the example of righteousness which he afforded to his children, has its ultimate root in the belief that God was the righteous Father, and that each head of a household was to present Him in that character through his own acts."[6] Maurice felt that there were defects in the Scottish system but they sprang from other sources. He found the Scots "complaining of that idea of the Trinity which makes it the ground of human relations; and insisting that the idea of Persons who perform certain acts of creation, redemption, sanctification (which, subject to the other, I accept also), is the only orthodox one."[7]

Maurice had of course learned the relation of human to divine fatherhood in his early Unitarian upbringing and his relations with his own father. But "the idea of the Trinity which makes it the ground of human relations" was the determining factor for him. Because of that idea, he took refuge in Trinitarian orthodoxy, in the Church of England, "a fraternity", he said, "not founded on opinion", unlike those societies founded on opinions which consequently "are always changing, never growing".[8] "The Church of England confesses a Father, who has revealed Himself in a Son; a son, who took our nature and became Man, and has redeemed men to be His Children; a Spirit who raises men to be Spirits." And that Church "tells all . . . that they have no less right to claim their places in her as members of Christ, than they have to claim their places in the nation as subjects of the Queen, and in their families as children of an earthly father and mother."[9]

Commonplace experience will not allow us to accept a view of society in which a man regards himself as a unit, indeed as the centre about which all events and persons revolve. "We are sons." It cannot be escaped. "I cannot be the centre of the circle in which I find myself, be it as small as it may. I refer myself to another. There is a root below me. There is an Author of my existence."[10]

There is a relation, and "there is a manner which answers to the relation."[11] As soon as I refer myself to another, as soon as I acknowledge a root below me, as soon as I admit an "Author" of my existence, I must recognize an authority over me. "In the very fact of Fatherhood Authority is involved. . . . I learn what it is through my filial relation . . .".[12]

Maurice compared authority with a similar word, dominion. He said that dominion was a battle of physical force against physical force without the possibility of a relation. Dominion was essentially the extension of a man's brute power over things external to himself. A man had dominion over all manner of physical objects, instruments for the exercise of his will. Thus a man used acres of land and ploughs. But he discovers a difference between these "things" and the men who hold the plough. Words may be used with them; there is a bond between men which cannot exist with things. I give them orders, Maurice said, of authority and not of dominion. Maurice observed, too, that when words are used with animals rather than sheer force I become "humane" to them.[13] I cannot refer this sense of fellowship with men or "humane" rule over animals to my "separate nature," as a unit among units. "But I am related to a Father, he is related to me. I cannot destroy this relation though I try. It brings forth a manner in me."[14]

Any relation springs from a source beyond itself as created by God. The sheer existence of a relation sets up a tension between the persons of whom it is formed. Consequently a relation can never remain static; it is dynamic, and is itself creative. The living quality of a relation is like Maurice's idea of the peace of God, not so much the frozen inactivity of an icy mass as it is the quiet calmness of a constantly moving stream within which are strong tensions, currents of ebb and flow. For example, the mutual interaction between father and son produces an ethos, Maurice asserted. Engendered by collision and sympathy of forces, authority and obedience are manifested in outward acts, words, or behaviour which Maurice called "manners". It is a matter of "education". "The father *must* educate his child; so far as he has any authority over him that must be an Education."[15] "How to temper punishment so that it may be a witness for authority, and may never express mere dominion—so that it may foster obedience and not stimulate disobedience—is one of the hardest problems of practical education upon which we cannot too earnestly seek for light."[16]

The light which came to Maurice was passed on by him in these words:

> Suppose parental authority, as I have maintained, the very ground of Education, we must believe that through it all the faculties and energies which belong to a child are developed, that without it they would lie dormant. The obedience of a son is shewn in receiving those influences and impressions from a father's authority which most tend to quicken his own activity. No true father wishes his son to present an image of his opinions. He knows that the copy will be probably a caricature; that an echo conveys the sound not the sense of the original voice. On the other hand, the son whose opinions are most unlike the father's has often learnt most from him; in his latest years he probably discovers how much the father's authority has helped to mould the very convictions which appear to separate them.[17]

Maurice elsewhere laid bare the basis of this understanding of the parent's role. He said that in the first relations of which we are aware, of "a mother at all events, a father; perhaps brothers and sisters," the child

> sees their faces, he hears their voices, as he sees the curtains of the bed and hears the noise in the streets. But his relation to them must be something different from this. . . . All the seeing and hearing in the world do not fulfil that relation. We speak of affections. Evidently a man's relation to his fellow-men fails utterly, is not fulfilled, unless he has these affections. They are as necessary to it as seeing and hearing are to his intercourse with any thing that is not human.[18]

Maurice was certain that the creation or genesis of character was the work of God, the Holy Spirit; men are appointed to work with him. The collision and sympathy of forces to which Maurice often alluded was moreover a question of affections. Affirmation marked the creation of an ethos, never negation, the quality of punishment.

Letters from Maurice to his son, Edmund, indicate how this combination of conventional with theological views about fatherhood worked out in practice. Maurice was pre-eminently careful that his son's own individual integrity was never crushed and that his son's obedience was always able to take the form of "receiving those influences and impressions from a father's authority which most tend to quicken his own activity."[19]

Maurice himself was not an over-indulgent father. His gentle firmness provided support as well as a guide for his son's development. Occasionally he even displayed a trace of irritation, perhaps an impetuous attempt to enforce will upon will, which Maurice felt distorted authority into dominion and violated the relationship.

"How is it that we have heard nothing of you this week?" one letter began. "We have been expecting a letter every day and have always been disappointed." The note of rebuke was lightened. "Is it that you want to get mine about Homer?"[20] Letters were a matter of great importance in the family and caried the weight and importance of conversation in the cultivation of a relation. They were exchanged at least on a weekly basis, reminiscent of the "box" which Maurice regularly received from his parents during his own student days.[21] Maurice was conscientious about his own responsibility in the correspondence. He wrote on one occasion: "I am sorry we did not write last week. I have been occupied, but not with anything to hinder my writing to you. I hope it will not happen again."[22] On the other hand, any lack of punctuality on the part of his sons in answering letters was noticed. "Freddy has not written to us for some weeks. I suppose he is very busy."[23] Once when Freddy did not arrive in London when he had been expected, a telegram was dispatched to discover the reason. Maurice did not hide a note of concern. It later appeared that Freddy's absence was due to a "stupid blunder" on the part of "his General".[24] Maurice expected his own sense of responsibility to be met by responsibility on the part of his sons.

Edmund was thought to be careless about finances and money was frequently mentioned in the letters. Once when Edmund was offended because he had not received an acknowledgement for a toy sent to his brother's new baby, Maurice explained that the child's mother had not been well. "Say nothing about it," he wrote. "I mention it as you were surprised at her not thanking you." This was the occasion for a gentle personal reminder. "Your mother finds that you have not presented the £10 cheque to Drummon. I suppose it is all right."[25] Obviously more than one domestic transaction had gone unacknowledged. Maurice needed to say nothing more.

Positive encouragement, however, always accompanied parental correction or advice.

> I wish to tell you that both Mamma and I were much pleased with what you say about Dr Moberly's remarks on the [   ]. I have seen that a steady manly purpose in that and in every other temptation is God's own gift and will bear you through. Apply the same resolution whenever you are disposed to spend money recklessly and bear the punishment if you have done so. I wish I had been made to feel in a number of the like cases that I could not both have my cake and eat it.[26]

Maurice's relation with his son was seen best in connection with academic matters. Here he came closest to being a dominant parent, yet the way he handled the question of Edmund's academic career and eventual "vocation" shows better than any other way how Maurice put the principle of authority and obedience to work in his own household.

Maurice had great expectations and firm intentions for his younger son. He expressed his wishes in his usual self-effacing manner though they were all the more telling for that.

> I do not wish to force the Goddard upon you if it would be considered unusual for you to sit. I think you want some stimulus to application. I do not like to hear of your being sent down in Class. Now you are a Prefect you should feel that is part of your function to set an example of stedfastness and application as well as to rule wisely and justly. I am sure you will try to do this. I should like you very much to get some Scholarship at Oxford and Cambridge. . . . I know you say that you do not have a chance; but I think if you proposed resolutely to do it you will find that God gives you strength. And I think success would not puff you up but would do you good. Of course if you failed I should hope for good from that also.[27]

Later on, positive direction was given with the same negative introduction.

> I do not wish to trouble you about the Studentship as you say you would rather not hear more of it. I dare say you did what you could. I fondly hope we may succeed another time. If you

should be advised to try for any scholarship in another College and should be inclined to do so, I should make no objections; but I do not at all urge it."[28]

There was always a warm supportive tone about Maurice's correspondence with his younger son even though Edmund was never to win academic distinction.

Don't trouble yourself about Moderations. We shall not expect any great success for you; *whatever* comes we shall receive as a gift. And a quiet and [   ] mind is a gift which I desire for you more than success and which I am sure God will bestow. Like you I have to be educated for it, through an experience of my own haste and restlessness."[29]

He attempted to give advice in the gentlest of ways. Once when Edmund was preparing for an examination, his father wrote

You have been very good indeed in complying with my wishes about the Motion. I would have willingly accepted your judgement about the matter if I had not known from bitter and repeated experience of my own how difficult it is to be thoroughly interested in one subject without becoming confused about another which is less interesting but is pressing on us at the moment.

You are good also in not liking me to spend my money on you. But that is a mere trifle to the security of your passing and of your not being overdone by useless labours of your own brain . . . I should like you to get someone who thoroughly knows what is done in the schools and could give you just the help which is needful for the next fortnight. You might ask Mr Dodgson who knows me to recommend you such a person. Never mind the terms. I will settle it with the other expenses of the Degree. I shall count it a blessed [   ] [   ] if it enables you to have done with Examinations and to begin work fairly in London.[30]

Edmund took a third class in moderations in 1863, and an ordinary B.A. degree in 1865.[31] Maurice never failed to encourage him. He was always ready to point out some excellence which he saw in his son. At the same time, he always tried to show some way in which he himself had experienced "that particular difficulty" and was able to identify with Edmund. Ultimately he met his son's "failure" by looking forward positively to a valued vocation, not in spite of but because of his academic record.

If you knew what delight you have given us by your courage by going in and by all the spirit you have shown during the vacation and since [Maurice wrote after one disappointment], you could not think that our grief at your failure—much as we feel it for your sake—was unmixed. Looking back at my own life I think I reckon my University failures amongst my greatest trials and greatest blessings.

(Maurice had actually taken a first class in the civil law classes at Cambridge but, unable to subscribe to the Thirty-nine Articles, he went down without a degree. Later at Oxford he received a second class. The story is preserved that Dr Jacobson—and others—expected Maurice to get a "first". They believed that he had in fact done so and congratulated him accordingly. When the class list appeared with Maurice's second, "there was not the slightest symptom of disappointment shown", demonstrating, says Jacobson, "his unaffectedly lowly estimate of himself."[32]) The letter continues:

I know I should have got at quite a false position if I had succeeded. I know therefore that God is guiding you and will make these things to work out for your good also.

Let us hear nothing about Scholarships. You are just as you are; work as well as you can; profit by experience; do not be the least restless about my means. [This letter was written at the time of Maurice's proposed resignation from St Peter's, Vere Street, which would greatly have diminished his income]. If you can do with a little less than the £200 I know it will comfort you and therefore I shall be content. But if you cannot I shall be quite able to supply you.[33]

Maurice even supported Edmund when, somewhat daunted, he proposed to give up working toward the honours degree.

I do not the least wish to hold you pledged to the honours examination if you see your way to something more practical and more suitable for you [wrote his father]. I never have been a passionate lover of Triposses, and if young men would work without them I had much rather they did. It is only because of deference to the order and habits of the place in which we are receiving our education that I would accept that doubtful stimulus to engage in study and that not always trustworthy warrant of its soundness. . . . But you must consider your new scheme seriously before you desert the old love for it. I have run after a good many will o'the wisps in my day and I would rather you were saved from the weariness of such chaces, if it is possible. I will not discourage you, however; for when I know what you mean I may see the desirableness of that course. At all counts I am always glad that you should tell us whatever is in your mind; the confidence is very pleasant if nothing else comes of it.[34]

Maurice continued with reassurance, self-identification, and practical suggestions. "You have been calm and wise about the business whatever happens." "I quite agree with you in your opinion of the importance of the time on which you are now entering", he wrote after Edmund had finished the moderations examination.

It may, as you say, properly be the beginning of your University career with the advantage of not starting as a Freshman. I believe that you are much more likely to take an interest in your new course than in your old one. And I am not at all sure that you may not obtain or recover some of the scholarship which you have wanted while you did not exactly appreciate the worth of it in the act of studying books for the sake of their scientific worth.[35]

Maurice acknowledged his own debt to the books his son was studying. Aristotle, he said, gave him an appreciation of "the beauty of accurate definitions". Plato made "me impatient of mere definitions". He sympathized with Edmund's difficulties over the *Gorgias*. Yet, there, "you may find that the difference between what seems good to us and what we will, is radical and immense. And you will be grateful to the man who was permitted to point it out. When you have the dream you will ask for the interpretation; till then you need not trouble yourself about it."[36]

Finally in this letter to Edmund beginning a new term at Oxford, his father wrote: "I do not know whether you have done wisely in going into lodgings. They may answer better than College; some of my saddest and perhaps also my best hours were spent in lodgings. But I like the fellowship of a College even if I am in solitude."[37] Nevertheless Maurice acquiesced in his son's plans, providing advice rather than dominance (authority rather than dominion?). He was laying the foundation of future emotional strength when the son's steps towards his own integrity, his own identity, would be made safer and surer, aware that his way had already been covered by a parent who knew from experience its pitfalls.

There was, as we have seen, help about the choice of a tutor, help about the choice of a plan which did not lead to an honour's degree, counsel about not cluttering his studies with extraneous matters, all given in such a way as not to be peremptory, by a parent who left the door open for a full expression of freedom.

Small bits of homely advice appeared in letter after letter. "I think you are quite right about breakfasts. I always found them very inconvenient for study. The longer I live the more I prize the morning hours. To resolve that you will use those, will be the best moral effort you can make."[38] This from a man who was notorious for filling up his house at breakfast, of becoming so involved with conversations at breakfast that he sometimes filled up the pot completely with tea leaves. To drink his tea was said to be a labour of love.[39]

Despite early morning working hours, chosen tutors, uncluttered pursuits, Edmund's university career was not to be a great success. Examinations over, a letter waited.

> I know you will have been feeling the trend of an Examination of this week and perhaps will now be feeling disappointment at the close of it. We have not expected success for you and will be delighted to hear that you have done reasonably well. You worked diligently during the vacation and I dare say have been not idle since. Do not be less steady when you have not the stimulus of a contest.
>
> You will experience the blank of being without Mr Luke's lessons and kind words. But keep up the memory of him and be sure that he and all your old friends will be helping you.[40]

Or "I rejoice very much that you think you got through the paper work satisfactorily. Your last note was much better written than the former one; *that* I hope was your school writing. I do hope you will have heart and strength for the vivâ voce. Thank you for proposing to send the Telegraph. I shall be particularly thankful for it."

"Let me hear what the expenses of the degree will be and of your leaving—and I will send a cheque for you to take to the Bank. By no means take your name off the books. I have always repented doing it."[41]

Edmund read law privately after he left Oxford, and spent some time in Germany. Maurice entered into all of his son's interests. Their correspondence covered Edmund's enthusiasm for Mazzini, a long discussion of democracy, and the desirability of educational qualifications for suffrage. Maurice's younger son entered the Inner Temple in 1866, but he only began his life's work after his father died. Maurice even agreed to a proposal Edmund made to remain in Germany.

> I should be very sorry not to have you at home—it would be a great loss to an old man; but it is one which should not be thought of if you could be sure of a healthful life and steady occupation, and one which would in due time allow you to marry. I think Emily Hill might be a valuable help meet. . .".[42]

It had already been determined that there was no question of either son continuing the Maurices' clerical tradition. In support of that decision, the father had written a birthday letter to the son for St Peter's Day, 1866.

> May you always know the rock at your feet on which the Church stands! *I* do not wish, if I ever did wish, that you should claim a place among the pastors of the Church of which the Collect for tomorrow speaks. I know too much of the perils of that office and of the terrible failures in our fulfillment of it, to be the least anxious that those whom I most care for should grasp eagerly at it. If it grasps them; if they feel that they must speak a word which is burning within them and must be [   ] to speak it; well and good. But I would far rather you took any place in the household than the one which I am serving. That should be the highest and may become the lowest and basest of all. But one of the household you are and must always be. You have a calling as much as I have, being a man and a baptised

man besides. And you will have a distinct calling to serve with as much as I have to mine.[43]

Edmund was to be lawyer. After he left Oxford, his father wrote:

I was very glad to get your pleasant letter. It encourages me much to hear what you say about Mr Hill. I have often feared that I might not be doing the right thing for you; but I hope it was not a mistake. I had a strong feeling that you wanted help in reading. I am sure it is in you to understand anything to which you will apply yourself and that the habit of application is to be cultivated. The reward of cultivating is very great indeed. And since Law is your calling it is on that you must exercise the gift, even that you may be useful in any other way. I do not the least despair of seeing you a good lawyer, whether a successful one or not in the pecuniary sense of the word signifies little comparatively. Really to know what your profession is and what your capacities for pursuing it are is a great object; if Mr Hill helps you to see your way, and tests the soundness of your previous apprehensions you may be very thankful for his scoldings. I wish I had had more of them.[44]

There were still doubts about Edmund's chosen profession, his "vocation" as his father always called it. If he were not to be a clergyman instead of a lawyer, should he be a teacher? His German studies looked very much like it. But again there were doubts, doubts relieved by his father's encouragement.

I never, however, set my own mind upon this as your vocation. I think there may be many difficulties in the way and the dependence upon official men for appointments has always seemed to me wearisome if not ignominious. . . . Hughes' kindness is very great as I know by long experience. But the better course is to work steadily at something without feverishness and restlessness. It has struck me this morning that perhaps a year or two of quiet study at a German University—say at Jurisprudence—might fit you for work in England and that you might perhaps have some literary employment there which would fill up a portion of your time usefully. . . . But do not fret about things; that destroys the power of work.[45]

Edmund was admitted to the Bar in 1871. Like his older brother's military life, Edmund's legal career was to be a "vocation"; Maurice could have written Edmund similar words to those he had used when his older son was about to be posted to India.

> That prospect I do not much like to face; though if it is appointed for him it will be the best thing. He will have to encounter a strange world. He will see the worship of strange gods which you only read of. I wish much to be thinking of that Eastern World that I may live in it with him even if ever so many miles separate us. Perhaps he may be allowed to do the people there some good. A soldier, I sometimes fear, might be often as good a witness of God as a Clergyman, and that without setting about to teach principles. By justice and fair dealing and kindness he might teach them what Being he serves and lead to feel the difference between a righteous God and unrighteous.[46]

Edmund married Emily Hill in the autumn of 1872. After his marriage, he "left his chambers in the Temple to live in the country, merely pursuing literary work and giving lectures at different colleges."[47] An interesting study might be made of the careers of Maurice's diametrically different sons each of whom witnessed to the creative force of his father's authority, in his own way responding to that authority with an obedience appropriate to himself.

HUSBANDS AND WIVES
OUT OF DIFFERENCES, TRUST

Husband and wife constitute the second basic relation which comprised Maurice's family "order". Marriage illustrates three important aspects of any relation; that it is "given", that it is composed of persons rather than things, and that its purpose is to enable man to know and acknowledge his primary relation with God.

Accepting the fact that God himself is the source of marriage as of any true relationship, Maurice asserted that the union of the sexes was derived from the very nature of man. He asked in Jesus' words: "Have ye not read, that he which made them from the beginning made them male and female?"[48] Maurice felt that Genesis referred to this relation when it declared that "God created man in his own image . . . male and female created he them." The social implications of the text were not lost on the theologian of relationships. Man stood in relation with other men inasmuch as he was created in God's image to reflect the inward divine nature. The personal relations within the Trinity extended to the direct relation between God as personal and man created to be in communion with himself, thus with other men who shared the divine relation.

While Maurice was loyal to the biblical declaration of the mighty acts of God, his discussion of marriage underlines the fact that he was no biblicist. Though he never entered into the spirit of nine-teenth-century criticism, and though he was always faithful to the scriptures as received, Maurice felt that men were idolators if they substituted the veneration of a Book for faith in a person. The Scriptures, he said, do not contain codes or tables for us to copy "slavishly". Scriptural records are in reality "lesson-books for mankind, teaching by experiment what is incompatible with the order of human existence, gradually discovering the principles which are at the root of it."[49]

Monogamous marriage, he emphasized for example, was neither of biblical nor of Christian origin. Milton, a true biblicist, Maurice observed, was loyal to his authority and "scandalised his puritan contemporaries by the consistency with which he accepted [Old Testament narratives of the patriarchal order] as warrants for polygamy in the Christian Church."[50] The patriarchal narratives are, in fact, records of polygamy. Genesis, however, shows us its mischiefs and enables us "to perceive by what unseen processes, and under what living teacher, Greece must have attained to her exemption of its curses."[51]

Maurice discovered the historical origins of monogamous marriage in classical Greece. The Homeric epic poems and the Greek drama-tists both proclaimed that the union of husband and wife was the ground of Greek society. Greek manners were created by the con-jugal relation and any weakness of their manners may be traced to the violation of it. Maurice discovered a faculty in the Greek mind combining the masculine and feminine qualities; aiming at a perfect balance between the passive and receptive, the active or creative temper, which constitutes the complete artist.

In this respect he compared Greek society to the Roman Patria Potestas in which the relation of father to son was dominant. Maurice observed that when marriage was regarded as merely a legal bond, and the husband began to look down upon the wife, a rapid deterioration destroyed the whole political order of Greece.

The relationship between husband and wife manifests in a special way "the sacred distinction between things and persons"[52] which Maurice took from Coleridge. As with Coleridge, "personality and the rights and obligations of persons . . . are to be found somewhere in the heart of all his philosophy and all his theology."[53] The differences which are essential in marriage focus the need for personal integrity. The wife must be distinct, and not the creature of her husband, Maurice wrote to Georgina Hare just before their marriage. The husband

> does not come in to set aside any of his wife's previous education, or to put himself in place of all other influences, past or future, but only, when he does best, to gather them up, direct, and harmonise them. I am sure exclusiveness in him is a special sin and one which draws a number of others after it. I conceive much of the alienation and bitterness which one reads of in the stories of married life, and of which one sees far more than in books, and the roots of which lie in ourselves, arise in a great measure from the incapacity of the husband to recognise the earlier habits and tendencies of her mind, and his determination that she shall be cast, whether she will or not, into his mould; so she does not really reflect the image of his higher and inner life, but only of his tastes, prejudices, likings, antipathies. A man must either do as Day, the author of *Sandford and Merton* did, take a child and bring her up for himself—which did not answer in his case or any other I ever heard of—and could only produce a miserable dwarf product of his own narrow understanding; or he must take a living creature whom God has formed, and believe that He has managed the matter more wisely than any of His wise servants could. God forbid that I should have anything to do with anyone who was my handiwork.[54]

Husband and wife, indeed, are meant to be mutually dependent and mutually sustaining. "The man cannot be without the woman nor the woman without the man if there is a Lord in whom they are one."[55] "The relation of man and woman which is expressed in marriage, the dependence of each upon the other," is lost, Maurice asserted, in "the attempt to exalt either at the expense of the other".[56]

Such exaltation amounts to what he called idolatry. In every instance the idolater degrades the object of his idolatry and is himself degraded. Maurice found many examples of this tendency. It appeared nowhere more strongly than in the abuses of the medieval Courts of Love in which, because of a perversion of chivalric reverence, the superiority of the feminine sex was asserted but its dignity was lowered.

On the other hand, the tendency to treat women as things was not counteracted by proclaiming their independence. In fact, no person can be independent. The assertion of the "independence" of women is but another form of that idolatrous exaltation of sex by which both male and female are degraded. "There will be perpetual alternations of slavery on both sides . . . until we look upon the relation of Marriage as that which expresses and embodies the principle of the union of the sexes, their necessary dependence upon each other."[57]

Marriage, however, was not the only manifestation of the relationship between the sexes. There are many reasons, Maurice admitted, which might make it the duty of numbers of men and women to prefer a single life to a married, not only the preponderance of one sex to another in a given society. That there might be the preference of a single life to a married emphasized the element of personal choice, of personal response, and responsibility by which a man and a woman entered *into* the conjugal relation. Single men and single women are also found in relationship, the basic quality which underlies all social order. Though not necessarily defined by marriage, the relations of single persons to one another are illuminated by truths expressed in the relationship between husband and wife. According to Maurice,

> There will be in the single man the habit of reverence, of chivalry, the desire to learn from women what they can teach much better than men; there will be in the single woman the grace and dignity which belong to the wife, most of the gifts and qualities which are seen in the highest form in the mother; always a willingness to receive from men what they better than women can impart.[58]

Single life, in fact is the reflection of the married life.

Finally, for Maurice, the end of the whole relationship between the sexes was in its beginning. Marriage was not something new

created by human efforts. It had a divine source and its purpose was
to bring men and women to God. Maurice spoke of a "spiritual
principle which adds a sacredness, and only not sacramental dignity
to marriage."[59]

God has created the relation; the man and woman enter into it.
Maurice was specific. "They *enter into it.*"[60] Maurice's emphasis
upon givenness seemed almost to imply the pre-existence of the
relation. Indeed God had been preparing the husband and wife for
marriage all their lives to share his creative work. The man and the
woman had been brought to maturity and freedom as children,
obedient to parents, and in fraternal co-operation with their brothers.

Aware of themselves and free in their responses, husband and
wife were enabled to be God's conscious, willing instruments. Yet

> All the inward feelings which attract them to [marriage] do
> not determine its nature; that is determined before. But without
> the attraction they cannot in any degree understand the relation;
> it is for them as though it were not. There must be in each the
> sense of incompleteness without the other; the belief of each in
> the other; the dependence of each upon the other; not of the
> weak upon the strong more than of the strong upon the weak.
> So that Trust is engendered, which becomes as essential a part
> of the domestic ethos as the Authority and Obedience which are
> demanded by the relation of father and child, without which
> the Family can not subsist.[61]

Like the underlying bond between God and man, no basic
relation between men could ever be completely destroyed, but
Maurice felt that there was always the possibility of denial or violation. This was true of the relationship between the sexes. Such a
violation occurred whenever a person used another as a thing.
Maurice was sensitive to this disorder when he attacked "slavery as
a domestic institution".[62] In the assumption of the "negro as the
chattel of his Master . . . all relations of father and child, of husband
and wife, of brother and sister, were thrown into the wildest
confusion."[63] The white was more degraded by the presence of this
anomaly in his household than the black. In such a way, the denial
of any relationship was an infection which proved disruptive in every
area of human life.

How did Maurice's doctrines of marriage and womanhood work out in practice? His response to the Contagious Diseases Acts is a vivid example. These acts provided for the registration and compulsory medical examination of prostitutes. The government by these measures gave its tacit approval to prostitution. On 1 January 1870, Mrs George Butler issued *Women's Protest* in an attempt to bring about the act's repeal. Maurice's younger son was deeply interested in Mrs Butler's efforts and wrote to his father. Maurice answered,

> At the request of some Medical friends on whose judgements I relied—too hastily perhaps—I signed a petition in favour of extending the act; being influenced by the thought of the innocent persons who suffered for the guilty and by the general consideration that all kinds of disease should be dealt with, as well as they can be, medically; though the springs of them must have another treatment altogether. But I suspect that I did not take enough into consideration the injury which might be done to the woman by recognising, in any degree, her degradation as part of a System. That recognition seems to me very shocking and if I have in any degree assented to it, I am bound to consider earnestly what I can do for the object which Mrs Butler has at heart. Whether it should be in the form of opposition to the Contagious Diseases Act, I feel doubtful, as you seem to do. But if not in that way, then in some more positive and efficient way. I am sure men and women ought to be striving against Prostitution with the same kind of energy and the same hope, in the midst of despair, with which Clarkson and Garrison fought against slavery.[64]

Prostitution, Maurice said, clearly violated the sacred distinction between things and persons. Economic pressure, no less "brute" force than sheer physical coercion, reduced persons to objects. The man himself was degraded by treating a woman as a thing.

The basic abuse of prostitution was far down at the roots of society—beyond law. The answer was not simply law, nor, as Maurice again wrote to his son, "the camel hair about the loins." "We want Society to be leavened, not dissected or even denounced. The process may be more difficult, but I believe God's Spirit will go with it and in time make the fruits of it manifest."[65] The remedy against this social evil which, as much as any other, represented the distortion which Maurice called the atomic theory of society, was to be found in the assertion of, or the reassertion of who men and women really are, persons, inviolable, with integrity, created by God in his own image, and created in relation with him, and for relation with one another.

Maurice was always "positive" in his attempts to apply "underlying moral principles" to social problems. His method appeared in the effort to eliminate prostitution. Dangers of disease were of secondary importance, nor did the dangers of illegitimacy take precedence in his argument. Rather he felt that any argument in a matter of social concern must rest upon what he felt to be the essential truth which lay at the foundation of society, the divine origin and existence of true relations between persons, rising out of the original and ultimate relation between God and man which reflected the nature of God as Sacrificial Love. That which asserted the underlying relation, that which supported the inviolable integrity of persons as distinct from things, must be emphasized. Threats would never suffice. Punishments were only another form of inserting the use of force into that which force had already violated, and could only violate. It was important to proclaim to men who they were, created by God in his own image, consequently created for communion with him, and with one another, a relation which arose from the fact that, and which required that, man, like God, have those qualities which Maurice called personal. "If the tone of young men's thoughts about women can be raised", Maurice wrote to his son, "—if the thoughts of the young women about themselves and their relation with men can be raised, the effect will come more completely, even more rapidly, than if a vain effort were made to put it [prostitution] down openly."[66]

As a member of the Royal Commission on Contagious Diseases, Maurice ultimately voted against the Act. His behaviour represented a change or at least a development in his point of view. Nevertheless it was an example of his persistent, underlying consistency, loyal to a divine order which needed only to be proclaimed and acknowledged. Maurice admitted that he had signed a petition in favour of extending the former legislation dealing with contagious diseases. In 1870 when he was appointed to the Royal Commission, he went up to London regularly each week to attend its meetings. Josephine Butler recorded, however, that when she appeared before the Commission in March 1871, "Frederick Maurice was not present, I am sorry to say."[67] The Commission eventually supported the Contagious Diseases Act. Maurice sided openly with Mrs Butler.

Some critics maintain that Maurice was reluctant to take a decided stand on social issues lest he tamper with the underlying divine order. On the contrary, his belief in an order founded upon relations between persons frequently compelled him to break with his conservative support of the status quo. This was true in many issues which confronted Victorian English society, particularly true in questions concerning women. In the case for woman's rights of ownership, that there was a cry for legislation was an indication that the true ethos of trust in marriage did not prevail. Maurice warned those "who oppose any measures for protecting the distinct property of women . . . When Trust vanishes from the Family, commercial men may feel their need of it—may seek for it eagerly—but they will not find it."[68]

Maurice whole-heartedly supported the cause of female suffrage. Giving women the vote would make them more responsible in exercising the undoubted political power which, because of their place in the family, they already possessed.[69] Moreover, the consistency with which he affirmed a divine order made Maurice concede that institutions themselves must constantly be examined in accordance with the basic principle of the divine sacrificial nature reflected in human relations. From age to age, or culture to culture, there might be a difference or even a reversal in the provision of institutions. Maurice's discussion of divorce demonstrated this development of his thought. At first sight a straightforward conservative, he had dismissed the question of divorce briefly with an earnest protest against that licence "which some European countries have sanctioned".[70] It was necessary, however, to remember Milton's lenient attitude toward polygamy, the marital pattern, certainly, of patriarchal society. The question was related to divorce, according to Maurice, who maintained that a marriage must be judged as it brings men and women to the ordered freedom of mature persons, nearer to God.

BROTHERS
ONE BLOOD, ONE WORK

The third of the primary, underlying relations, that of brothers, occupied Maurice's thoughts throughout his life. Indeed the subtitle of *Eustace Conway* is "The Brother and Sister". Looking "for some quality which shall be distinctive of this relation as Authority is of the paternal, as Trust is of the conjugal, some quality which shall be its contribution to the domestic life, and through the domestic life to the life of the most expanded Societies," he selected what he called the "ethos of *Consanguinity*".[71] While authority, obedience, and trust are found in the fraternal relation, the distinctive quality of brotherhood is consanguinity. That the brotherly ethos is worked out in co-operation shows how important a place it held in Maurice's thought. Few words are more closely identified with him than co-operation, the watchword of the whole Christian Socialist movement. Maurice wrestled with the tension between co-operation and competition in lectures, sermons, and publications all during that productive period which led to the foundation of the Working Men's College. The college is a tangible, lasting contribution made by the Christian Socialists. Equally tangible was the work of Thomas Hughes and Vansittart Neale, Christian Socialists, whose efforts in the establishment of the Co-operative movement arose directly out of Maurice's analysis of the fraternal relationship.

There was a certain cloudiness in Maurice's assertion that consanguinity is the distinctive quality of brotherhood. He himself was embarrassed by his choice of word; it has too much of "Latinity" about it, a legal and technical term, the sort of word which he did not normally like to use. He used it because of "what it means".[72] Consanguinity does not really point to an abstraction, but to a physical fact, the acknowledgement of a common origin. Maurice feared lest fraternity should become a mere metaphor. He felt that speaking too easily about trade "brotherhoods", or "religious fraternities", weakened the sense in which brotherhood referred to a real underlying relationship among men, their real consanguinity as children of God.[73] The concept might be expanded to include cousins, or adoption, but there must be an inescapable reference to common physical origin which could not be destroyed.

How often, Maurice said, there has been a confusion between

fraternity and equality! He felt that equality, like such words as imperial and empire, tended to blot out important differences between persons or nations. Those very differences give persons or nations their own distinct identity and integrity. Within the bonds of brotherhood were legitimately found all distinctions of temper, taste, or intellect. One brother had this claim, another that, to superiority. It was important that as the child grew he should become aware not only of the common origin which he shared with his brothers, but also of his own special powers. Maurice felt that awareness of personal differences was an integral part of the way in which a member of the family came to know that he was a member of a family, as well as a member of a nation.[74]

An intimate and valuable insight into what Maurice thought about the fraternal relation was given in some of the unpublished letters written to his own sons. Edmund, more than Frederick, inherited his father's "morbid sensitivity".[75] Maurice mentioned this fact in discussing a possible or an imaginary slight which Edmund had received from Frederick. He wrote a paragraph which brought out the whole creative aspect of relationships in which co-operation is made possible because of differences. Maurice said to his younger, sensitive, slighted son,

> The very difference in your characters which has acted as an estrangement since you have grown up and been aware of it, will ultimately be found to be a bond between you. God makes us different that we may fill our different place, and can do what the other cannot do. He will make you understand this by degrees if you will try to believe it on the testimony of a father to whom you must both be equally dear and whose greatest conceivable joy it would be to see you thoroughly and inwardly united as he believes you will one day be. Your mother in Earth is I am sure helping to bring about that union and so I doubt not is your mother in heaven. And God's Spirit is working with them both . . . .[76]

Maurice welcomed that form of competition which developed when members of a family tried to express their different powers just as he welcomed the wholesome inclination to break the relation between parent and child. Competition was properly connected with the consciousness of a distinct life and distinct differences of temper, taste, and intellect. However, certain forms of competition could threaten society. Timocracy, the danger, Maurice felt, of democratic systems of government was the result of self-centred competition. A simple balance of competitive interests against one another led to anarchy. Moreover, when a dominant and domineering individual crushed the interests of others there was dictatorship. Maurice was afraid that any attempt at pure democracy led inevitably to dictatorship. Too often majority rule was distorted public opinion.

It was possible, however, for a balance to arise naturally between competition and the sense of the unbreakable relationship of consanguinity. The balance was the result of positive, gentle, but firm guidance by parents. They must encourage distinct differences on the part of their children at the same time as they cultivated the fraternal relation. The feeling of distinct powers must be put forward for the help not the overthrow of the others. A sense of special vocation must grow so that the total "destiny" of the whole family was more complete. If the craving for independence was merely indulged, family life was destroyed; if it is peremptorily crushed, the child would never become more than a child, essentially a slave under circumstances of abject submission.[77]

Maurice felt that there was an active power among men operating against socially destructive powers. It was important to discover and to be open to such an influence, a view which made Maurice appear to shun any effort toward "shaping human life, individually, socially, and politically". Not so much bound by "the hypnotic spell of Platonic idealism", Maurice was reticent because of his profound distrust of force when it was introduced into human relations. All too often, he believed, practical efforts to shape human life were little more than compulsory manipulation by which relationships were distorted. A society produced by "brutalization" did not reflect the image of God but the opposite of reality, "no-thing". Maurice wrote to Edmund,

> I have had to learn—by what experiences none but God knows —that love is His gift and His highest gift and that there is a perpetual struggle against it, an influence which is always at work to divide us from those who are nearest to us. It is thus, I think, I have been taught what Evil is, taught to regard it not as an abstraction but as an actual Power working upon me at every moment.[78]

Maurice implied that evil was not so much an abstraction as an actual power, an idea reminiscent of a remarkable passage in *Eustace Conway*. In a conversation between the hero and Fanny Rumbold, brought up by her "brother" with methods of "anti-education", Eustace, to comfort the frightened child, said that she had "seen nothing".

> "Oh, how horrible!" she said, shrieking, and springing into his arms. "Then it *was* nothing that I saw."
>
> "And does not that comfort you?"
>
> "Oh, to think that I can see nothing! The other day, when I read about Nothing to my brother, it seemed so horrible. But to have seen it!"[79]

Maurice found in the "law of sacrifice" a power acting against this destructive force. It was the power of co-operation.

> Co-operation in its largest sense is what all good and true men have been fighting for in all parts of the world, because they felt it to be that which was most contrary to the destructive principle which is undermining families and nations and churches and our humankind, and because they felt that being this it has its root and foundation in that which is divine and eternal.[80]
>
> Any association, however small which is a fellowship among men for work, and not a mere arrangement between money and hands, is I believe carrying out the true principle of English society, that which has been asserting itself from age to age in our history . . . that which has had to encounter manifold opposition in the selfishness of each class. . . .[81]

That principle, co-operation, "has been the real source of national growth and prosperity, that which has been upheld by all the best and bravest defenders of moral order against confusion and anarchy, of whom England has had to boast."[82]

His confidence in and loyalty to the principle of co-operation allowed Maurice to go far towards what is now called the celebration of the society in which he lived. Speaking to men in Leeds, he referred to that "power which has created Manufacturers", and declared it to be worthy of our "reverence". "Some might be afraid of your rating such a power and such a law too highly; they might think it needful to warn you that there are things more precious than these with which you are familiar."[83] Maurice would not take that tone, he said. "I would not go into the country to persuade an Agriculturist that he should not dwell too much on ploughs and oxens."[84] "I believe," Maurice declared, "that when we rightly estimate of any work whatever in which it has pleased God that we shall be engaged, when we see what the real meaning of it is, we understand better the worth of all things else and the relation in which they stand to it."[85]

Men rightly estimating and eagerly engaged in their specific work, Maurice said, were following a divine vocation. As each pursued his differnt occupation, the destiny of the whole was furthered. Such co-operation "is grounded upon a fellowship and relation between men as men, not merely as workers or producers," and "this co-operation may be carried yet further . . . into the interchange and disposal of articles as well as to the production of them."[86]

Maurice admitted the existence of competition, rivalry, and self seeking which express the selfish principle by which society was undermined and destroyed. Nevertheless, people in all ages "have been striving to resist those tendencies to separation and selfishness which they knew to exist as well as we do. Churches, nations, families, have existed in the midst of them and in spite of them."[87] And something had kept them together, Maurice asserted, "something against which selfishness has been always trying to make head, and which it has not yet vanquished."[88]

It is significant that co-operation in which the fraternal ethos of consanguinity expressed itself in the active relations of men provided a point of transition between the immediate relationships of domestic family life and the all-encompassing relationships of what Maurice called the universal family. Co-operation in effect was man's acknowledgement that he was a "kind". Such positive and active acknowledgement provided Maurice with the means of understanding and setting forth the implications of what he spoke of as worship. Worship was essentially the acknowledgement and active fulfilment of all human relationships, domestic, national, ultimately on that level which was both the foundation and culmination of human society, the kingdom of Christ.

7

The Nation
The Cultivation of Morality

———— • • ————

THE EMERGENCE OF A NATION

Any examination of Maurice's ethical teaching must consider the
nation, the second of the three institutions which composed the
underlying divine order of human society. The history of any
nation was its own Old Testament, and Maurice felt that the story
of Israel provided him with a model with which he could understand that history. Contemporary events simply disclosed principles
apparent in Exodus; they revealed the ethos of a nation.

Consequently Maurice could enter nineteenth-century nationalism
with sympathy and support and he hailed the emergence of Germany and Italy. The events of their history were like Israel's passage
through the Red Sea, from bondage in Egypt to conscious national
identity in the promised land. At the outbreak of the Franco-
Prussian War, he wrote to his younger son in Germany:

> You will learn to realize something of what a people at war
> means,—our imagination is too weak, our insular confidence
> too vain. I feel with you that the nation of Germany may be
> learning more than before that it is a nation; a *nation*, not I
> trust an *Empire*, which seems to me a vain and dangerous
> ambition. It is struggling against an Empire, why should it
> dream of being one? I dread the phrase when I hear it applied
> to England, as it is so frequently nowadays; especially by
> Gladstone.[1]

A nation's identity existed even before it became aware of itself.
It emerged as it came to acknowledge its existence. Its source lay

outside itself; its authorship was discovered in the nature and being of God. And it was in the context of crisis, a divine instrument, that a nation became self-conscious.

The crisis at the Red Sea and the wanderings in the wilderness, Maurice felt, proclaimed that God was the deliverer of any people. His covenant was at the root of national society as it had been at the root of the patriarchal family society. Maurice contrasted the institutions of Israel and the institutions of Egypt, "grounded upon man's conceptions of God: the Israelites upon God's declaration of Himself to man".[2] Israel assumed that it was established by the living God himself, the result of his guidance or education; the Egyptians assumed that man must construct the sanctions by which a society is upheld.

The one characteristic function of the nation was to be the witness of the truth and permanence of God, and to protest against every attempt to confound God with visible objects.

> It is a witness of a perpetual battle that is going on between order and disorder, right and wrong, the invisible God who is the Lord of man, and the visible things which are claiming lordship over him. The Israelite, the covenant servant of God, is to take part in this fight; he is to go forth as God's instrument in putting down corruption and oppression. When he has a commission to destroy, he is to destroy.[3]

The moment when any people learns that it is a nation is marked by the commencement of "Song and Written Law." The song, said Maurice, is that of an individual man who feels himself to be the spokesman of the people. He speaks God's praise, yet feels that he is inspired by God. "The flame of the song, like that of the sacrifice, has been first kindled by Him to whom it ascends."[4] The code was exactly the opposite of the song; it came from the lips of God, and was simply His utterance. Moral obligation could never be of human origin; it depended upon divine authority. The law, in the form of the code, Maurice declared, is addressed to the covenant people and can only come to them because "it . . . comes forth from a Deliverer".[5]

Maurice distinguished between the code and the statutes of the Jews which have not commended themselves to other nations. A "Wisdom which adapted a certain class of commands to the peculiarities of one locality and age must intend a different one for another."[6] Each of the nations of modern Europe, he said, recognize the essential ground of the Jewish polity. They acknowledge, as applying to themselves in their national character, the covenant, calling, and actual government of an unseen Lord. In this, Maurice emphasized "his two-fold conviction that the unseen kingdom is the ground of every other, that it is the true substantial kingdom, and that man is intended to be the image of God in his royalty."[7]

Two principles constitute what Maurice called the character or ethos of a nation, "contiguity in place", and "individual distinctness", terms which referred to the experience described by the Anglo-Saxon words "thy neighbour and thyself".[8] Men progressed from domestic to national relations as they acknowledged their own individual distinctness and the implications of their neighbour. It was not an absolute break; family and nation must always be closely interwoven. "The formation of a manner which shall not be utterly unsocial, utterly destructive of Society, depends upon their fellowship."[9] "Never for a moment let us try to separate, or dream that we can separate, our individual life from our national. Our vocation is the same in the most private occupations, and when we are fulfilling what are called our duties as citizens. Every duty is a civic duty."[10] While then there can never be a real separation between family and nation, there comes a time when man must pass out of the condition of a family into that of law. Maurice's whole development of the nature of law, and in fact the nature of the human response to law, conscience, is set in the context of this progression from domestic to national relations.

Maurice found the seed of national development in the tendency which appears in every man to break the underlying relations into which he is born, parent and child, brother and sister. It was characteristic of Maurice to affirm that the source of unity and the source of disunity were the same. He felt that the striving to be separate, to be a unit, to break the relation, if misdirected caused the destruction of society; at the same time, this striving is the divinely ordered instrument by which the social order developed out of the family into a national society. "We strive to be units," he said, "though by the order in which we are placed we cannot be."[11] This striving becomes a blessing as it introduces us to other parts of our social order, specifically as it contributes to the energy whereby we move from domestic to national life, from the realm of affection to the realm of duty and law, of reason and will.

It was in the school that a child finds himself for the first time among equals other than brothers or perhaps cousins. He begins to experience relations with his contemporaries who have brought with them different recollections, traditions, and instincts. Maurice was fond of quoting George Herbert: "Then Schoolmasters deliver us to Laws."[12] He felt that the schoolmaster functions as the midwife to deliver a child out of the intimate relations of the family into the wider relations of neighbourhood. It must be remembered that Michael Maurice maintained a school; for Maurice, schoolmaster and father were one. Apart from the experience expressed by "thy neighbour", school provided opportunity for a child to learn the meaning of "thy self," that other experience which constituted a nation. For it was in school that a child first realizes that he is a distinct person. "I am not merely the son or brother of such a man; but I am myself a man."[13]

It is the law which "takes each man apart from his fellows; it addresses him with a 'Thou'; it makes him feel that he is under obligations to his fellow-citizens because he is under obligations to an invisible Lord,—his Lord and theirs."[14] Maurice's fascination by the distinction between the words "thou" and "you" goes back to Julius Hare, one of the first men to introduce nineteenth-century German theology and philosophy into England. In a letter to Hare in 1838, Maurice thanked him for the gift of some of his books and hoped to make an extract from a passage about "thou". "I seem to perceive a real worth in the 'you', which the 'thou', does not possess, though it undoubtedly expresses a truth of its own which is most important to remember. The 'you' strikes me as the *Catholic,* the 'thou' as the *'Ethnic'* symbol."[15] Julius Hare answered: "Your finding the *Catholic* spirit in *you* amuses me much. One might have been sure that you would do so."[16]

"Thou shalt and thou shalt not," as well as "Thy neighbour and thyself" are created by man's need to respond to a demand from outside himself, and are expressed in his response. Maurice discovers what he calls the "secondary" characteristics of a nation in the context of these basic principles, the underlying ethos of a nation. Law, language, and government are the essential "secondary" characteristics of a nation emerging out of "contiguity in place and individual distinctness".

LAW
GOD'S SELF-REVELATION

Maurice's discussion of law is a good example of his whole style of
ethical teaching. There is no co-ordinated statement about law in
any of his writings. At times he appeared to say that ethics and law
are opposed to one another. Ethics, he repeatedly affirmed, was
concerned with an underlying character and only with overt acts
as they manifest that character. Law, he asserted at times, on the
other hand, was only concerned with outward acts. The last sermon
Maurice preached declared that St Paul "did not leave Morality to
the threats or promises of the Lawgiver. He knew that the Lawgiver
had never been able to make men moral—to keep them from lying,
from corrupt communication, or from stealing. He knew that the
lawgiver could not reach the evil until it comes forth in crimes."[17]

In no sense, then, could law be said to undertake the task of
forming the character from which outward actions proceed. Law
cannot make men just, or charitable, the results of inward dis-
positions. Such habits arise, for example, out of relations as between
parents and children. Love is shown and affection is returned in
personal encounter. It is this interplay of affections by which a
relation is made alive and justice and charity arise.

Maurice once referred to what he called universal laws which we
do not make for ourselves and which are shared with all the peoples
under heaven, even if we or they do not know about them. For
example, the phenomenon of the Thugs, he said, does not make
murder lawful. Such universal laws Maurice found based on the
Ten Commandments given by the Deliverer to Israel. On the other
hand, he said, "there are laws which are not of this universal
character; laws which suit one people and not another; laws which
have been partly formed by their character, and their language, and
their circumstances, and partly have helped to form these."[18] These
laws are not so sacred, Maurice declared, but they too are sacred,
although we are not to enforce our laws on Frenchmen, or our
institutions on Spaniards.

While Maurice did use the word law in different ways, as universal, and non-universal precepts, he preferred to say that law is not
a matter of statutes and codes at all. Law is a matter of revelation,
a matter of personal disclosure, the outward manifestation of the
inward character of God. It is thus possible to speak of the Law of

Sacrifice arising out of the inward nature of sacrifice in the relations of Father, Son, and Holy Spirit.

"Law has its root in the mind of God", Maurice said. "It is one great utterance of His mind."[19] Law is the self revelation of the righteous lawgiver. While, Maurice wrote, "an announcement about this or that act which it behoves a man to do or to leave undone is called a *statute* or an *ordinance*, . . . a *revelation* is a discovery of Himself to a creature whom He has formed to know Him."[20] Inasmuch as the purpose of the law is the disclosure or the revelation of the being of God, it makes it more correct, in Maurice's sense, to speak of our Lord as the Law rather than to speak of "laws". Christ the Son, as the Revelation of the Father, is "the Law". Maurice emphasized the purpose of law as personal revelation both in his lectures on the Commandments and on the Johannine Epistles. "Simple people", he asserted, by keeping God's commandments "acquire a knowledge of His character and of His ways, of what He is in Himself and of what He is to them, which can be reached in no other method."[21]

It is only to be expected that Maurice would use the analogy of human relationships to illustrate what he meant by law as a matter of divine revelation. Is it not by human relationships that we are led to God, and do we not see who God is in our relations with one another? Maurice observed how we come to know fathers, schoolmasters, commanding officers, and friends. In just such ways God is made known to us. How do we know a friend (an equal); how does a youth know an old man, or a son know a father?[22] Maurice said that we come to know a friend by keeping a thing or a request. "*Kept* . . . and cherished as the commandments of a friend; . . . they will give us an acquaintance with Him which we can have in no other way."[23] Consider, he said, some indulgent and inconsistent fathers and compare them with a father who lays down rules firmly but gently, with the feeling that he is just and cares for us as much when he punishes as when he commends. In this relation we learn the man's principles, we know him. St John, declared Maurice, says that we can know God even more than men who are uncertain and capricious.

Law, considered as a matter of personal self-disclosure, works in two ways. God's law, for example, tells me both who God is and who I am. A parent's command introduces me to the knowledge of myself as well as of him. There is revelation on both sides. Indeed law had four functions according to Maurice. It revealed to man the meaning of, and reverence for, human life.[24] It also showed the meaning of character in the sense of personal reputation.[25] The nature and the foundation of property as an expression of personal identity was disclosed by law.[26]

Finally, and most important, law revealed to a man that which was in him. Law's enactments have only intimations of an inward "spiritual" process, but they make a man realize that he is not merely an outward creature but that he is subject to strange invisible influences. "This law is his education into the feeling, that there is a light within him, which he is meant to follow, and which will guide him on to truth and righteousness; and that there is a power within him, which is resisting that light, and preventing him from walking in it."[27] Law treating man as an individual, "brings him to perceive what there is in that very individuality which leads him to struggle with it, to be at war with Society."[28] Law brings to a man "the conviction that there is something wrong in him; something very close to him, a part of himself, if not his very self, from which he needs to be emancipated."[29] "Anything is better than the presence of this dark self", cried Maurice in the *Theological Essays*.[30]

"Man's own dissatisfaction and despair," revealed by the working of law, "come from his inability to be satisfied with the temporal and his slavery to selfish objects."[31] But if law makes a man see in himself something which is wrong, something from which he needs to be emancipated, that is not all the law does. While indeed law cannot be the agent of man's emancipation, nor can it undertake the task of forming the character from which acts proceed, the mere realization by a man of that which is wrong makes him realize another truth. "There can be no Wrong if there is not a Right." Maurice said a man "cannot be unjust to his neighbour or his neighbour to him, if there is not some justice which is over them both. The sense of being under a Law forces that belief upon us."[32]

The final conviction that there is something very close to a man, a part of himself, if not his very self, from which he needs to be emancipated may be seen on another level. Maurice did at times actually speak of the "conscience" of a social group. This seemed to imply that a family or a nation itself became aware of its distinct identity because of the function of law. Did such a conviction on the part of the family of Abraham mark its passage into its nationhood? Was it possible that a nation's conviction of that from which it too needed to be delivered was the crucial moment of self-recognition that occured at its passage, retaining a distinct identity, led by the Deliverer to acknowledge its position among other distinct nations in the kingdom of Christ?

LANGUAGE
BOND OF PEOPLES

For Maurice the immediate function of language like law, was educative. By the expression of his inward convictions and beliefs, language revealed a man's identity to himself as well as to others. But language has two functions. It draws men together and bridges distinctions. Maurice felt that language "ought to be the bond of intercourse and communion between citizens."[33] It is a "contract" subsequent to the birth of society, the outward and visible manifestation of that contract of trust and faithfulness which underlies any real society. "A Nation . . . is held together by words."[34]

Words indeed have a sacred character because they express bonds between persons which cannot exist between things or between persons and things. At one stage in the development of a language, words may be identified with things. This has value but words acquire a new force, they become more sacred than things when a man becomes aware of the distinction between "thy neighbour and thyself." The discovery that words are freighted with personal responsibility is the great sign that men are beginning to look upon themselves as a nation.

The cultivation of language is one of the most important aspects of the relation between parent and child, one in which the ethos of authority and obedience (as education) and the mutual trust of husband and wife are joined. In learning a language, the individual becomes a person. He is not only addressed by "thou", but is drawn into society, is united to the catholic "you". Nor was language simply a matter of words in spite of the sacredness which Maurice attached to them. The whole set of a parent's life instructed the child in the knowledge of a language. "Only a resolute sincerity in his own acts, a punctual observance of his own promises even in trivial points to his children, can cause them to appreciate veracity", can instil in them that quality of trust which it is the purpose of language to express.[35] Children learn respect for a parent's words first, not for words as such. Words at first are playthings to be twisted, and broken, used how they will. To cultivate respect for words should be a primary object, said Maurice, but the cultivation will proceed slowly with many obstacles.

The concept of parliament as a "speaking place" had tremendous appeal for Maurice. He found in the dynamic energy of those deliberations a manifestation on the national level of that dialogue which goes on continually in a man's inner self, and which is seen outwardly as he participates in society.

Just as, for Maurice, a nation is not a static thing, neither is a language static. It is necessary for languages to grow by adopting new words and abandoning outworn usages, but Maurice deplored the careless use of words which debased a language. In borrowing words from one language by another, instead of being a matter for enrichment, all too often words were borrowed from the wrong sources. Languages, like nations needed to have their own integrity. A healthy language can send out new shoots, still retaining its past integrity. Then it serves as the bond of contemporary society; but it is also a vital link with the past. Connecting the present with the past heritage of a nation, invigorating the present with strength drawn from a people's underlying and mutual trust in one another, language provides a stimulus, a guide, and a safeguard for the nation's future advance, in its self-conscious acknowledgement of its identity, and its position among other nations, and other languages out of which mankind as a universal family is formed.

LOYALTY
A PERSON, A RIGHT, AND AN ORDER

In speaking of law and language Maurice was led to speak of loyalty. Law and language make me know that I am an individual, and "to feel myself an individual—a distinct living person—is to feel myself responsible for my acts".[36] But to whom am I responsible? Responsibility and obedience formed the quality or ethos which Maurice called loyalty. To what am I loyal? Not, certainly, we would expect Maurice to exclaim, to an abstraction, but to a person. There are, he said, certain persons whom loyalty associates with law, who represent law to it. But loyalty is not merely personal. "In all

E*

cases Loyalty implies the union of a Person with an order or a Right."[37] In this context Maurice entered upon his discussion of government.

The best insight into Maurice's concept of loyalty is contained in his memorandum to Kingsley and in his explanatory letters to Ludlow after he had suppressed Lord Goderich's *The Duty of The Age*. Goderich maintained that all barriers were broken down by the Christian "proclamation of a universal brotherhood".[38] Democracy's cause, he declared, was the cause of God. Maurice disagreed. First of all, he said, Christianity proclaimed "an invisible and righteous *King,* a King taking the nature of His subjects, sympathizing with them, dying for them."[39] The voice of the Deliverer must come as the voice of the King."[40]

Goderich and Ludlow, Maurice said, differed from himself in method. They began with democracy, the sovereignty or government of the people, and developed something like a monarchy out of it. "Twist the word as you will it must imply a right on the part of the people to choose, cashier, and depose their rulers. It must imply that power proceeds from them that it does not find them . . . Do they make Christ their King? Might they choose another if they liked?"[41] This idea could never be the Christian polity, Maurice declared. "I must have Monarchy, Aristocracy and Socialism, or rather Humanity, recognised as necessary elements and conditions of an organic Christian Society."[42]

Monarchy, asserted Maurice, pointed beyond itself to a law, to a source of authority by which it is itself governed, the kingship of Christ. "This is the principle upon which the monarchy of every European nation has stood, contradicted of course every year and day in practice, but vindicating itself by the crimes and falls of kings as much as by the brave acts which they did, and the dynasties which they established."[43]

A monarch is governed always by a power higher than himself, a corollory of the affirmation of Christ's kingship. But Maurice did say that "the King being the Person who represented and embodied the Law could not be treated as if there were some power in the State superior to him; i.e., to the Law".[44] This was acknowledged, Maurice declared, "more distinctly than ever before, by Pym, Coke, Eliot when they were asserting the dignity, permanence, sacredness, of Law against the invasions of Prerogative."[45]

Maurice continued: "The function of an Aristocracy is . . . to maintain the existence of Law and Order against the efforts of the Sovereign to set up a power independent of Law; against the efforts of any mob to set up a power independent of Law."[46]

"I joyfully admit", Maurice wrote, "that Christianity has a third side, that it asserts a universal brotherhood, and that this principle is implicitly contained in both the others, though in the order of development they are I believe meant to precede it."[47] "Socialism", he had written to Goderich, "or the acknowledgement of Brotherhood in heart and Fellowship in work seemed to me the thing you were aiming at, the special craving of this time; the necessary fulfillment of the principle of the Gospel."[48] "I look upon Socialism as the antagonist power to Democracy, just as I look upon Aristocracy as the antagonist power to Plutocracy, and Monarchy to Despotism."[49]

The democratic principle had an advantage for Maurice, inasmuch as it expressed the worth of each single man, counteracting "the monarchial and aristocratical tendency to set up either certain persons in authority or any formulaes and decrees against living beings who form the Nation."[50] But Maurice had no use for a democracy which implied that the power of law, the power of sovereignty, is from the people rather than derived from a higher power. Reconstitute society upon that democratic basis and Maurice anticipated "nothing but a most accursed Sacerdotal rule or a Military Despotism with the great body of the population in either case morally politically physically serfs more than they are at present or have ever been".[51] No, rather than democracy, Maurice preferred "Socialism".

> The gift of a Spirit, to dwell with men, to lift the beggar out of his dunghill, that he may be an heir with princes, is in some sort the peculiarly Christian truth, and this is as I conceive the ground of the *Socialism* of the modern world, that Socialism which was proclaimed by St Paul when he spoke of a body with many members, each having distinct functions and offices.[52]

Maurice unquestionably felt that monarchy best represented the kingdom of Christ to men, and his antipathy towards democracy did not dispose him towards the United States. Nevertheless, his correspondence during the American War of 1861–65 implied that other forms of government might point beyond themselves to Christ's kingship. He wrote to Ludlow,

I regard Lincoln's inauguration speech as the grandest return from the Democracy of the Declaration of Independence to the Theocracy of the Pilgrim Fathers that I have seen anywhere . . . . And it was not merely the old Calvinistical Theocracy—the divinity *minus* humanity. In so far as it recognised the divine vengeance for the wrongs of the coloured race, it implied a Christ as Head of the Human race.[53]

Maurice's characteristic and sometimes maddening view of the English Establishment, on the surface simply Tory conservatism, has been attributed partly to the influence of Coleridge. It cannot have been learned from his liberal, Unitarian background. There is an indication, here again, that Joseph Adam Stephenson made Maurice's "Monarchy, Aristocracy, and Socialism" possible. In 1834, Stephenson issued a pamphlet comparing the Church of England with other "polities". Congregationalism, he said was a "spiritual democracy" which vests "the ultimate power in the congregation or body of communicants", rather than "the subordination of the congregation and all its members to higher powers", the polity he discovered in St Paul's text, Romans 13 1-8.[54] Presbyterianism was a "spiritual aristocracy [Maurice would have preferred "oligarchy"], the government of the Church by coequal presbyters to the exclusion of individual authority". In St Paul, he said, individual authority was "graduated and systematized", "the superior dependent upon the higher".[55] Finally, Stephenson was opposed to papal government of which the principle was spiritual tyranny, "the lodgement of all power in a supposititious representative, or rather an entire superseder of Jesus Christ".[56] Stephenson examined the three estates of the realm, the clergy, the nobles, and the people, all distinct yet all united. Over them the law-governed king was supreme, to whom the obedience of the nation, a nation of free men, was not so much a civil as a spiritual obligation. The similarity of this view to that of Maurice requires more than may be left to chance.

WAR
CRISIS OF NATIONAL IDENTITY

National identity, then, was established through law, language, and loyalty. The crisis of this identity, Maurice asserted, is war.

If War is said to be the relic of an uncivilized age, we ask ourselves why it has called forth most enthusiasm amongst the people of Europe, which boasts to be the most civilized, most to have outgrown old superstitions? If it is pronounced irreligious, the question suggests itself why religion has produced so many wars?[57]

Nor was Maurice's statement about war unconsidered. He defended military action often in his correspondence with his elder son before and during the future general's Indian service. And he wrote to Kingsley that the Crimean War "is more like the commencement of a battle between God in His absoluteness and the Czar in his than 1848 was . . .".[58] And in the *Apocalypse,* Maurice asked bluntly, "who can make war but He who has been striving with each man, with each family, with each nation—but He, against whom every idolatrous, malicious, foul thought, and desire, and word, and deed that has corrupted societies or individuals, has been striving?"[59]

Maurice's militarism was distinctively his own; in no way did it reflect his heritage or his family upbringing. He wrote to his son, then an officer: "Of your profession I heard little in my early years, except in the way of protest. The Peninsular war was filling the land with its excitements and triumphs during the years I passed at Normanstone; but I cannot recall any allusions to it or to its English hero. And this was not because politics were not much discussed in our house . . .".[60] Maurice's father "became ultimately a member of the Peace Society, and I should fancy had a dislike to all fighting at this time . . .".[61]

Maurice delivered a lecture on war to Cambridge undergraduates each year from 1867 until 1870.[62] He declared that it would be easy to speak "of war as essentially and inevitably immoral", of the profession of a soldier as not "right and honest".[63] "I mean therefore to show you what I deem to be the morality of War, what its immorality."[64] He identified his own stand immediately: "We do speak of it as good for both", that is, "for the Nation or the Individual".[65]

Maurice asserted that he had no use for arguments which support war as a necessary evil or "merely as a necessary indulgence to the weakness of human nature".[66] To say it is a necessary evil is "an immoral phrase. . . . No natural instinct, nothing less than a moral obligation, can be an excuse for risking the lives of our own citizens, for threatening the lives of other men".[67] War, to be acceptable, must be a matter of duty.

Maurice had already acknowledged that God reveals himself in carrying on a war against evil, "sweeping away by pestilence and famine whole multitudes; vindicating the truth and order, which are the only happiness of mankind, at the expense of the lives of individual men".[68] Consequently a nation is "not to scruple the sacrifice of individual life, sacred and awful as it is, for the sake of maintaining that, without which life is a mere miserable lie".[69] A nation must regard as its enemies "the enemies of God, all who invade the order which he has established, all who would set up power against righteousness".[70] Maurice saw the Mahometan Conquest of Eastern Christendom as a divine judgement which forced the reformation of society.[71] Indeed, he said: "War may be— so far as we know has been—the only means of reforming [Civilization]."[72] In all wars, he continued,

> some beastly power, some lie which has deceived the world has been thrown down. . . . Something has been done for the purification of the earth, for the fuller manifestation of the sons of God. . . . One more step is gained in the triumph of the Perfect Will over rebellious wills; one step more toward that restitution of all things which God . . . has promised.[73]

Maurice gave short shrift to "religious wars", or to what he termed the "trade wars of the last three centuries". Religious wars arose when loyalty to a doctrine or notion took precedence over loyalty to a person. On the other hand, in trade wars, "men agreed to treat convictions about the invisible world with indifference, only to busy themselves with visible interests".[74] Maurice's objection to his pacifist father was because "I never found . . . that he distinguished accurately between the first French war [a "trade war"] and the one which was connected with the freedom of Spain, Germany, Europe."[75] In this latter "war of principle", England at first questioned Burke's direction but at length "she heartily plunged into the war as one for the liberty and distinctness of the Nations".[76]

Maurice said that the creation and preservation of national identity were important criteria for determining a "moral war", as well as the punishment of evil and the reformation of society. God used military crisis to create nations.

In such a way England had been transformed from a province. The Saxon wars were in fact a blessing bringing about a truer, wholesome family life, developing a strong sense of neighbourhood, personal existence capable of law, government, and a vital native speech. "What is true of England", Maurice observed, "is true *mutatis mutandis* of every state of Europe".[77] Maurice's justification of war on the basis of national identity and integrity continued in his argument that Christ came into the world to establish a "Kingdom of Peace for all Nations".[78] "Unless there are Nations, distinct Nations", he observed, "this Kingdom loses its character; it becomes a world Empire".[79]

Writing to his son, Maurice affirmed that a soldier had a "calling" or "vocation" like all other men, lawyers, physicians, tradesmen, not least clergymen. Apart from his general calling to that state than which there is none more glorious, "obedience to Law is the soldier's characteristic".[80] Soldiers are "witnesses for Law against the brute force of Numbers".[81] The endurance which springs from obedience is admirable in soldiers. Maurice wrote: "I find a spirit of order and obedience in them which I scarcely find elsewhere, and which I wish civilians could imitate. I find justice, gentleness, tenderness not merely mixing with such qualities in military men, but eminently characteristic of some among them."[82] Just as the distinctive characteristics of a tradesman, industry, forethought, fidelity may simply be regarded as means to the great end of success, the soldier may lose the value of his obedience in ferocity. Referring to Roger Bacon who trembled at the invention of gunpowder, Maurice declared, "No gift of Science is itself a curse, though every one may become a curse."[83] The danger is not in machines, but in the soldier becoming a machine. Both tradesmen and soldiers need a greater reverence for their calling, and Maurice urged the members of the company of volunteers at the Working Men's College to think of themselves as defenders of a life and a nation which had endured for generations. In his soldiering, the military man manifests his humanity.

It is important to remember that the elder son of this theologian of war became a distinguished military figure, Major-General Sir John Frederick Maurice. Edmund, the younger son, lived in Germany for some time after his years at Oxford and was a keen supporter of emerging German nationalism. Eventually he became a deeply committed pacifist. The story is told that during the Great

War of 1914–18, Edmund agreed to active service on a mine sweeper provided he was allowed to sweep the mines of both sides.[84]

THE STATE, I THINK,
CANNOT BE COMMUNIST . . .
BUT THE CHURCH, I HOLD,
IS COMMUNIST IN PRINCIPLE[85]

The ethical question of property could not be avoided in nineteenth-century England, and Maurice turned his thoughts to personal possessions when he considered the underlying national order.

"England", he said, "is a greater laboratory than all other countries in the world; there are more hands busy in making up the materials which nature supplies into articles for the necessity, comfort, or luxury of men. There are more machines assisting these hands in their operations; there are more heads inventing, directing, perfecting these machines . . . more poverty . . . more inherited lands . . . more wealth"[86] than ever before or anywhere else. It is taken for granted that capital or property "is the great moving power in the world, the great object to be sought, that which society exists to preserve and augment".[87]

Maurice opposed those who "assumed individual property to be the basis of a nation" or who "affirmed that the chief use of a nation is to uphold property".[88] He questioned whether society exists for the sake of property, or property for the sake of society.[89] He asked of "the relations in which men exist to each other, whether these relations are not antecedent to its [society's] existence, and must not be first recognized, as well for much higher aims, as because they are the only security for property itself".[90]

Maurice began his study of the nature of property with the family. "Property in its strict sense", he said, "does not exist in the Family, . . . there is a common stock, which is vested in the father".[91] Nevertheless, "A craving for separate possession may be always traced among the members of a family and is the chief interruption of their fellowship."[92] Maurice quoted H. S. Maine who felt that the "most important passage in the history of Private

Property is its gradual elimination from the co-ownership of kinsmen".[93]

Personal ownership emerged in the context of the nation. In the feudal order "the King who represents the whole Society is possessor of the Soil, we hold it of him and under him", and he "held it subject to conditions which a divine ruler" supplied.[94] Later, trade guilds, craft guilds, civil corporations were "fraternities," Maurice declared, emphasizing the "direct personal relation to the other", the "superiority of persons over things".[95] Both of these historic developments support the "proposition that the relations between man and man are not determined by the relations of property, but that the arrangements of property are dependent on human relations".[96]

Property, accordingly, is holy and established, but its tenure is under God and has obligations. It is subordinate to many other national institutions, for example, the order of the week, the honour of parents, the sacredness of life, the sanctity of marriage. More than any others, laws governing property have upon them the stamp of a particular time, or place, or accident. Maurice noted that certain laws "bewilder the conscience respecting the weight and authority of the Eighth Commandment; . . . they do very often touch that point where the claims of property become robbery; where the individual privilege invades the common justice of the nation."[97]

" 'Law after all wants some support besides its own authority; whence must the support come?' The most popular answer has been, 'It must come from a sense in the holders of Property and the seekers of Property, of that which is for their own interest.' "[98] Maurice would have none of it. He found a court of appeal, higher than the law, Christ's kingship, by which law and separate possession are both judged. The acceptance of a higher authority enabled him to say that "property exists for the sake of great common interests, and must perish if it is exalted above them".[99] Maurice spoke of the Church which, unlike the nation, but like the family, must be communist. The Church cannot make laws but it must zealously bear witness to the great common interests for which property exists. The principle of separate possession must not be exalted above these common interests, lest it perish.

8

The Universal Society
The Fulfilment of Morality

―――――――◆―――――――

THE CHURCH
FAMILY AND KINGDOM

There is within every man a longing for communion with God
and with his fellows. The need to be delivered out of his own
aloneness was never far from the centre of Maurice's deepest feelings.[1] "Anything is better than the presence of this dark self",
reflects the cry of Eustace Conway; "what I want is a strong man,
one whom I may meet and grapple with in a death embrace."[2]
These words express years of moral confusion and contradiction,
tensions apparent in the unfinished sentence, "I had none of the
freedom . . .".[3]

Maurice knew that freedom and unity, a universal craving, were
not to be found in the immediate family. His own domestic life
was proof enough. Nor could a man find wholeness as a member
of a nation. Is there not some human fellowship, this apostle of
freedom and unity asked, a society in which unity and freedom
could be found? The need of Maurice's "bed-ridden old woman",
the need of every man who ever lived, could not be met by any
doctrine of "individual salvation". Man's spiritual necessity demands
a community which is inclusive and which is able to connect itself
with all the ordinary circumstances and transactions of life.
Maurice felt that God led man to apprehend his need; that awareness enabled a man to discover that he was in fact a member of a
human "kind".

Man's longing for fellowship with God corresponded in

136

Maurice's mind to the possibility of communion between God and man; there is a relation between them. Maurice shared the Quakers' belief in the principle of an inner light. George Fox perceived, he said, "that man is a twofold creature; that there is a power always drawing him down, to which he is naturally subject, and to be subject to which is death; but that there is also a power drawing him up, a light shining in darkness, and that to yield to that power, to dwell in that light, is life and peace."[4]

"My brother", Maurice affirmed, "there is a light shining in the darkness of your heart—the darkness has not comprehended it,—Oh believe in that light, follow in that light, and be happy."[5] It was his "object to show", Maurice wrote to his Quaker friend, Samuel Clark, that "a body constituted by Baptism, upheld and united by the Eucharist, instructed by the written Word, preserved alive in each age by a succession of ministers, expressing its united will in acts of worship, does embody that principle, for which your Society is the witness, does connect it with those facts, for the sake of which the other sects have rejected this principle, does fulfil the idea of a Church Catholic."[6] Such a body existed, Maurice said, the family of man as man.

Maurice found this universal society beginning in the most exclusive of nations, affirming that it was meant for all nations. The men and women who formed the society were divided from each other in place, often even in language, but they were united by a secret bond of fellowship; they acknowledged an invisible Head, the Lord of all. The society of which he spoke, Maurice asserted was not a religion; it described itself as a Kingdom, and it had all the characteristics of a kingdom. Its Law, its Language, its Government were the ground of every law, and language, and government; and it waged, certainly throughout time, a war against every disorder among men.

Maurice called this inclusive community the Church, at times the kingdom of Christ. But it is not a visible kingdom. Only the heart and mind of man can take cognizance of it; it is within us.

> The words *Visible Church* [he wrote to Sara Coleridge] I confess I have never rightly understood. You seem to think that I have somewhere used them; I do not recollect *ever* to have done so—except in the preface to the first edition of my Kingdom of Christ wherein I protested against the whole

method of considering the subject which is involved in the adoption of the words Visible and Invisible—I left out the passage in the later edition because I had taken so much more pains to bring out my idea of the Church as a spiritual constitution that I thought the formal announcement of my objection to the other [mode] of speaking unnecessary and perhaps exasperating.[7]

Tracing the development of society from its divine source, Maurice said that men are born in families; as being born on the same soil, they are members of a nation; the national order grows out of the domestic order; it adopts, but does not extinguish family life. Finally, there is a universal society which grows out of the nation as that did out of the family and "that it was all the while lying at the root of that . . .".[8] Like Stephenson before him, Maurice asserted that the universal family was proclaimed at and by the Fall of Jerusalem. "Just at the commencement of our era, at the moment when Octavius Caesar became lord of the World, did the age of Nations pass away with a great noise, did the universal age begin."[9]

"When the world was ripe for it," Maurice said, in due time, that universal society "was declared to be the true society for men". The conditions of the society of which a man is a member simply as man, "are laid in *sacrifice*", Maurice affirmed, "in the giving up of self", in shewing that selfishness and self-will, "is not the proper law for humanity, but the destruction of it".[10]

The universal society, Maurice said, was an order for all time, abiding from generation to generation. God, entering into a relation with his creatures, prepared a perpetual bond of fellowship between him and mankind which time and circumstances cannot break.

THE SIGNS OF THE KINGDOM

In no way could man be said to erect the kingdom established by God and based upon principles which cannot be affected or undermined by the inconsistency of those who belong to it, or the unwillingness of any to partake of its privileges. Like any society, however, this kingdom must have some actual signs of the *bond* by which it is constituted, and there are indeed certain distinctive outward marks or badges by which the Church is known. These signs are intimately related to its inward character which would disappear if they were removed. Maurice pointed to the distinctive law, language, and loyalty of the kingdom of Christ. Sacraments, the Written Word, the Ministry, outward Worship, and its constant warfare against disorder among men are the outward signs of the kingdom.

The law of the kingdom of Christ, Maurice said, is the outward manifestation of the inward character of God. It is a matter of personal self-disclosure, "the one great utterance of His mind".[11] The Sacraments, divine ordinances, tell me both who God is and who I am. In Baptism, the "sacrament of constant union",[12] there is the "strongest and plainest assertion, that the baptized child is regenerate; that it is a child of God".[13] In no way a "natural" state, though man's proper state, it is God's gift. It is distinctly brought out "that the child is taken into covenant with God, that it is really and truly a spiritual creature, redeemed by Christ, and adopted into union with Himself".[14] Maurice made no attempt to explain the mystery. The need for explanation, he felt was superseded by the fact that the child's reception into the Church "*is* its deliverance from the evil of a fallen world".[15] Maurice felt that his view did justice to what he called this High Church "idea", as well as to the Evangelical belief that we are holy only in Christ, that all individual holiness is contradiction.

The divine ordinance of the Lord's Supper communicates and preserves to men that regenerate life. In the context of the Eucharist, Maurice said, our earthy bonds make the heavenly bonds intelligible and the heavenly bonds glorify the earthly. "What an Eucharistical song must have risen from all creation—from the world seen and unseen! . . . He desires communion with you . . . and we speak of the Eucharist as a religious duty which must be performed if we would escape perdition—not as the celebration of a wedding which the Son of God has made with our race!"[16]

The Written Word and the Creeds, like language, are the bond of the universal society. They revealed a man's identity to himself and drew men together. The concept of language as covenant makes it easier to understand Maurice's enthusiasm for the Thirty-nine Articles. In defence of the Articles, Maurice wrote that "in all Schools and Universities there is a contract expressed or implied between teacher and learner, as to the principles on which the one agrees to teach and the other to learn—and that to state the terms of this contract is at once the most honest method, and the most serviceable to education".[17] Mutual affirmation about God and man provided a guide in all the "Branches of Academical Education"; the Creeds provide a common ground for daily life in their mutual affirmation of faith. Moreover, the Creed, "a common and united form of utterance" by the people of God, "is a safeguard against the identification of the Gospel with any of the particular interpretations of it that have been or are held by different individuals or schools of thought".[18] Most important of all, the Books of the Covenant, Old and New, declare the nature of the being of God, and the relations in which the divine image is mirrored in the family of man.

In a nation, loyalty was always to a person; it implies the union of a person with an order or a right. This was true, as well, in the Church. Christ is the great Bishop to whom the Church is loyal. Episcopacy, Maurice asserted, a ministry connecting one generation to another, sets forth the Head of the Church in all his great relations to it. "Episcopacy", Maurice insisted, "is the *universal* element in the constitution of the Church, and . . . without it a Church may be a collection of individual units, it cannot have any expansive, comprehensive, harmonizing principle."[19]

The fourth of the outward badges of the Church Maurice believed to be worship. For him, worship was never "suggested by the wish to account for natural phenomena or to produce some change in them".[20] Worship is founded upon the being of God as its source, and is fulfilled in the freedom of obedience. In worship a man acknowledges his essential nature and becomes who he is; it was primarily marked with the spirit of thanksgiving. In various acts of allegiance and offices of thanksgiving, intercession, and communion, worship is simply a man being "himself" in his domestic relation, in his nation, and in the human "kind" which Maurice called the kingdom of Christ.

Over against the universal family, the kingdom of Christ, Maurice set what he called the "world". The world, he said, is that portion of men who reject the idea of a relation between man and God, and the fact that men are brothers. Contempt of human relationships, indifference to marriage, loss of filial reverence, carelessness of their children, all these characterize such men. The "world", Maurice felt, is based on selfishness and the exaltation of individual man; it leads to the indulgence of tastes, tempers, and opinions. The wordly man lives in the present, aware neither of past nor of future. Biblical language, with a happy insight, speaks of the world in terms of this "present age", an apt expression. The world can only know that which is of a single age. It confesses only that which is seen. It has fear, said Maurice, but no reverence; it has affections, but no love; system, but no order.

Against the world the kingdom of Christ wages a ceaseless warfare; indeed, like crisis in national life, conflict between the Church and the world brings the Church to the knowledge of its identity. Nevertheless the world, for Maurice, does not denote a society or an organization separate from the Church. "It denotes a principle", A. R. Vidler observes

> on which men are naturally inclined to organize their lives, a principle which is opposed to, and a contradiction of, the order which has been prepared for them by God. This false principle is at work everywhere and always, in the Church itself as well as in the nation and the family, but it is the special office of the Church to witness against it by witnessing to the truth.[21]

"The Church is, therefore, human society in its normal state; the world, that same society irregular and abnormal. The world is the Church without God; the Church is the world restored to its relation with God, taken back by Him into the state for which he created it."[22]

The Truths of the Trinity, the Atonement, and the Incarnation are expressed then in Sacraments; their relation to the constitution of the Church and of Society is expressed in the Written Word; their meaning is interpreted to the people by a ministry which connects one generation to another, and is expressed in various acts of allegiance and offices of thanksgiving, intercession, and communion.

What is the purpose of the Church, Maurice asked—the universal society of man as man? He felt that God had not made man a brother or a son in order to cultivate certain good and graceful qualities in him. Nor had God made man a citizen for the sake of bringing out certain other qualities such as patriotism.

> As then I must affirm the Family and Nation to be certain real States into which I am brought, [Maurice wrote] and which exist for me only in the same sense as the Sun now

6000 years old exists to give me light and warmth who at the most, shall not look upon him for more than three score years and less; so I, in the deep feeling that I need a universal Society more adapted to my spiritual life and, more universal than either the Family or the Nation . . . nevertheless dare not believe that such a Society can have been constructed for my education or salvation or glorification. I must believe that it could not effectuate these ends, unless it were a great, permanent reality, not a platform erected for certain temporary purposes; nay unless it were the reality (the highest and the greatest *end* conceivable) next to that in respect of which it may indeed be looked upon *only* as a mirror—(like the outward universe yet infinitely more divine and glorious than that can ever become even when there is a new Heaven and a new Earth)—the manifestation of his Being and Unity for whose glory all men and all things have been created and in glorifying whom they obtain their own perfection.

That there is such a Society, that it is in the highest sense a reality, unseen by outward eyes, but distinctly cognizable by faith; that it is a Society belonging to man as man; to man, that is to say, considered in those relations out of which he cannot be what he is created to be; that man living according to sense and nature renounces his position in it, that man living according to God only assumes a position which has been given him, and to which he has the same right with all his fellows, and that this Society stands in the Name of God and sets it forth, these truths Baptism preaches to me;—these I believe it preaches to the world.[23]

CHURCH AND STATE

Having described a universal kingdom which, though invisible, is manifested by certain outward signs, setting forth the very law under which mankind exists, Maurice continued by saying that there must be an unbreakable relation between the family of man and individual nations. Just as Maurice felt that the nation grew out of the family and that the two could not be separated, so the universal society grew out of, and could not be separated from, the nation. Coleridge influenced Maurice strongly in this belief that Church and State must be joined, two bodies, one governing the other for the purpose of education. Maurice asserted that in any nation the Church must be the foundation and upholder of all political institutions, an absolute necessity, he said, lest these same political institutions become instruments of internal oppression or external aggrandisement.

Maurice observed that the United States, "the land in which Church and State were to exist in joyful separation," may be the one which shall establish beyond all others, the proof that by God's law, they are necessarily united.[24] The task of the American Episcopal Church was this:

> Preserving the model of an orderly and perfect polity in the midst of a society which recognizes only a polity framed out of circumstances and dependent on the will of the people, it may be the means of first averting threatened convulsions from that unstable edifice, and then of silently working out in the mind of the nation, the idea of one far more readily adapted to circumstances, because it has a permanence which circumstance cannot affect, far more really expressive of the will of the people, because it is not at the mercy of their caprices.[25]

Maurice expected two valuable consequences from the union of Church and State. It is their privilege to look upon laymen in all their different offices as subjects of Christ's kingdom, as having a vocation from him. It is possible to say: "God has called you to your office, and is enabling you to fulfil the duties of it honestly and wisely."[26] Equally Maurice believed that the State ties the hands of ecclesiastical despots "in lawn or in crape, in Synods or in newspapers . . . so that they cannot hinder the expression of thought in any direction. The State protects the Evangelical, the High Churchman, the Romanist, the Protestant Dissenter, the Secularist, from spiritual tribunals and from religious mobs."[27]

Maurice expected the Colonies to teach the Church in England many "lessons which we had learned only imperfectly". He deplored the movement toward separation of Church from State in any part of the world. He hoped, he said, that bishops overseas "would feel the advantage of leaving the functions, jurisdiction, and formal legislation to the representatives of the State, and would recognize their own high calling as guides of a spiritual society. . . . The name of father we trusted would have become a real name, . . . indicating the relation of men to a more comprehensive fellowship, a family in heaven and earth."[28]

"Were the voice that [Christ] is indeed . . . the actual King of Kings and Lord of Lords" to go through your land, he wrote to churchmen in Australia, "you would find that you had a Church and a State both; that one as much as the other is a divine work; that the Church is not more exclusive than the State but is the all embracing Society, while the State's business is to assert the dignity and distinctness of each people and race."[29]

CHURCH AND WORLD

Maurice connected Church and State so closely that he was accused of identifying the kingdom of Christ with the Church of England. Samuel Clark mentioned the problem. No one was likely to confuse the two, he said, but they might suppose that the English Church aspired to be the Church of Christ in a similar manner to that in which the Church of Rome aspires. Clark, following Maurice, felt that the American Episcopalians might show the way. They used the English Liturgy and adopted the whole ecclesiastical constitution, but they were staunch republicans. Their actions pointed beyond any merely national connection to a true universal society which, maintaining unity of fellowship, made possible local and national differences.

Maurice's own defence against the charge that he confused the Church of England with the Catholic Church laid him open to the charge of universalism. He affirmed the "idea of the Church as of a body circumscribed by no laws of space and time, binding together all nations and all ages".[30] The State must assert the dignity and distinctness of each people and race; but the Church is the all embracing society and Maurice was unwilling to define its boundaries. "I cannot answer the question", he exclaimed; "I believe only one can answer it; I am content to leave it with him."[31] When he wrote "the history of the Church, I had nearly said of mankind since the coming of Christ," it requires a subtle distinction indeed to determine the difference in Maurice's thought between mankind and the Church. "Maurice", wrote A. M. Ramsey, "viewed the Church not only as the home of the redeemed, but as the sign that God had redeemed the whole human race and that the whole human race was potentially in Christ."[32]

This identification of the Church with the world has deeply influenced English-speaking theology, often with a direct tribute to Maurice. We may note incidentally that similar identification has been made by Karl Rahner. The contemporary Jesuit theologian says that "since the incarnation and the resurrection of Christ, the whole of humanity is the people of God; God deals with the whole of mankind as a single unit, so that, since the time of Christ, every human being in the world has been born as a member of a race which in the sight of God is actually redeemed."[33] Stephen Neill, commenting upon Rahner, observes that "Anglican readers will at once be reminded of the teaching of Frederick Denison Maurice concerning Christ as the Lord of the whole human race, and not only of that part of it which happens to be included in the visible Church."[34] Another twentieth-century parallel with Maurice is to be found in Bonhoeffer's *Ethics*:

> There is no part of the world . . . which is not accepted by God and reconciled with God in Jesus Christ.[35]

> All men are taken up, enclosed and borne within the body of Christ. . . . This is just what the congregation of the faithful are to make known to the world by their words and by their lives, . . . The Church is divided from the world solely by the fact that she affirms in faith the reality of God's acceptance of man, a reality which is the property of the whole world. . . . God and the world are thus at one in Christ in a way which means that although the Church and the world are different from each other, yet there cannot be a static, spatial borderline between them."[36]

Ethics after Christ can have but one purpose, "the achievement of participation in the reality of the fulfilled will of God. But this participation, too, is possible only in virtue of the fact that I myself am already included in the fulfilment of the will of God in Christ, which means that I am reconciled with God."[37]

Maurice's understanding of a universal family, a race redeemed in the sight of God, appeared at times even more comprehensive than "mankind since the coming of Christ"; it included men from the very beginning of time. He wrote a charming series of letters about Homer when his son Edmund was at Winchester. "You know I have always told you that Homer may be made a Christian

book to us. I am sure it may be."[38] And during the Crimean War
he wrote:

> Let the good conquer, as that orthodox Christian and true
> Gospel preacher Aeschylus said some thousand years ago. Oh,
> that my lips were unstopped to preach that gospel in the
> strength of a manifested and crucified and risen Christ, which
> he preached in the belief of Him before His incarnation![39]

While Maurice's intuitive sense of the cosmic importance of the
life and work of Christ made it possible to see the whole of human
history transformed by the eschatological event, his loyalty to
historic fact gave another dimension to his discussion of the
universal society. There was, he said, as he looked around him at
the ninetheenth century, admittedly a crisis approaching. "Whether
there is a universal society or no, in which men may claim fellowship with one another, will be debated. . . . Schemes of universal
government, fellowships cemented upon principles inconsistent with
national society, subversive of family life, are arising all around
us."[40] The last peculiarity of the age was seen in "the disposition
to combine, not on a family or national basis, but in one that aims
at being universal."[41] The crisis in general history corresponded to
the earlier crises in individual history. Maurice hailed internal
impatience on the national level as he hailed internal impatience on
the domestic level. Man learned to address his neighbour as "thou"
in the context of the nation; in the context of universal society, man
is addressed and learns to address his neighbour with "the *Catholic*
you".

But Maurice was wary of any scheme of world government which
would destroy differences. The universal society must not be an
empire but a family in which the vocation to wholeness is enriched
by distinct personal and national characteristics. Maurice's son
indicates the way in which the various social groups that composed
the underlying divine order were inter-related in his father's mind.

> I have often wanted to ask you whether you were aware that
> my father's dream always was that the Jew, as at once the
> most cosmopolitan, in spread, of all races, yet absorbed in the
> nationality of each might be the means designed in that supreme
> government of the world, which he was always studying, to

bring mankind back to the worship of Righteousness out of the worship, into which he believed that Christendom had sunk, of the Evil Spirit seating himself in the place of the Most High. He was during his last years engaged on a novel which he never completed. The title was "The Jewess", the model for the heroine my own mother—not Mrs Maurice his second wife, and I am pretty certain it was this aspect of the question which he meant to bring out.[42]

Within the universal family, Maurice said, "there is a living power for the union of all races, and at the same time a security for the distinguishing characteristic of each race". None "will lose any of its distinctive characteristics; each will be found to have its own place in the Divine polity, its own appointed vocation."[43] This fact was also true in the case of sects, each of whom may touch some chord in the heart of the nation. For example, the Unitarian shaking off his negations will never cease to feel that he is bound more than ever to maintain the divine unity, and to see in it the ground of all unity for men. "Each is entrusted with a special trust, not apprehended with the same distinctness by others. That he will cherish more devoutly, he will proclaim more effectually, when he understands that it blends with those of his brethren, and brings them out into greater clearness."[44]

The full realization of the universal kingdom which was the culmination of Maurice's thought was not "the substitution of a new universal society for all the separate organizations of men, but rather the participation of all these [families, nations, etc.] in the one universal kingdom of which Christ is the head."[45] Each man and each society has been given its own particular, necessary work in service to the head of the body and to all its other members. Maurice was no more interested in the eradication of national identity than of self. He placed real value on varieties of national cultures. Each nation, each school of philosophy, each religious or political opinion had particular value. Disorder only arose because men mistook their partial contributions to the truth for the whole truth, and it was the work of God the Holy Spirit to bring men out of their partial understanding into the knowledge of the whole truth.

THE SPIRIT WHICH ALL THE WHILE
HAS BEEN WORKING

During his last year Maurice's life entered an autumn period. "The rush of his start for a walk had gone." He still made his way across the street to Addenbrooke's Hospital, visited the almshouses, and taught the children in his parish, but often university notices announced that Professor Maurice's lectures had been cancelled; students gathered for conversation at 3, St Peter's Terrace. These conversations were not so much "about" ethics as they were, Maurice felt, a matter of becoming open to the work of God the Holy Spirit. Maurice was increasingly aware of the Spirit of God. His final sermon in St Edward's Church spoke of the Spirit, a living power for the union of all races. Not so much a power, "I can never think of the Holy Spirit as some sudden emotion, some casual impulse, which may be here today and gone tomorrow. I must think of Him as an abiding Counsellor, Redeemer, Friend . . .".[46] Not only were his final words from St Edward's pulpit words of the Spirit; exactly a year but for one day before his death, in the same pulpit, he had asked:

> Can we be brought to desire fellowship with men not superiority to them? Can we be that taught we are *not* superior to them; that we are made to be one with them? If the Son of Man is One with God; if the tender love of the Father was manifested in giving Him up His Son for all, then we can understand how this may be; then we may look upon the [   ] cares of the world, upon all the events of our lives as discipline to fashion us to humility; the humility of Him who is our Head and Prince; then we may believe that there is a Spirit proceeding from God which can act upon these minds and hearts of ours and subdue them to that likeness.[47]

> Are we not to learn that, at every moment of the day, the Spirit of the eternal God is moving around us, speaking to us, acting upon us; but that His mightiest operation, that which alone fulfils His purpose towards us, is when He enables us to become the willing servants and children of our Father in heaven?[48]

Maurice's lifelong desire for unity and freedom was closely bound up with the expectation that God the Holy Spirit could bring wholeness. Both desire and expectation were voiced in that "apologia pro vita sua" of Maurice's youth, the revealing 1832 letter to his father.[49] Forty years had not changed the inward longing which he had known in all his earlier relationships. "Though all outward impediments to intercourse were removed, there was still an inward impediment,—the same kind of impediment which exists between two men who, though they see one another and may be outward friends, are not one in heart."[50] That impediment the Spirit of God would remove, making a man aware that he is separated from other men, divided in his inner being, bound in his own spirit; bringing repentance, God's Spirit teaches a man who he really is. But "The Spirit of truth is also the Spirit of liberty," Maurice cried, "the Deliverer of the conscience from its bondage."[51]

However, "we need the Spirit to regenerate social life as well as individual life . . .".[52] And Maurice fully believed that the light of God's Spirit shining in men's hearts would lead mankind out of aloneness into fellowship.

> I believe [he declared] in a Spirit who is at work on the inner life of human society, who is contending with all that makes it brutal or effeminate, slavish or anarchical. I believe in a Spirit who is not content with the semblances of civility and manliness, of freedom or order, who seeks to deliver us from whatever makes us ungracious to each other, cowardly in our resolutions and acts, from whatever leads us to crouch to any tyrant, or to set up any form of self-will in our own hearts. I believe in a Spirit who can never be satisfied till He awakens real energies: till those energies bring forth fruit in action.[53]

Everything that he meant when he spoke of ethics is the result of the dynamic energy of God the Holy Spirit. Where is that dynamic energy tending? The question was presented to Maurice no less in his last years at Cambridge than in his early years, writing *Eustace Conway*. Torben Christensen saw his answer lying beneath the Master's craggy contribution to the Christian Socialist movement. Maurice's mind turned toward the universal order which, he felt, lay at the foundation of human society, toward fellowship, unity, and freedom. In a poignant statement at the end of *Lectures on the Apocalypse*, speaking of the heavenly city, the New Jerusalem descending as a bride out of heaven, he declared: "Let us attach

ourselves to that polity which has a Centre. Or rather let us believe
that we are attached to it already."[54]

Maurice never really solved the problem of the difference between
what he saw in the world around him and what he believed to be the
true underlying state of things. He was forced to admit the existence
of those aspects of human society which made it "brutal, or
effeminate, slavish or anarchical . . . But there is forgiveness among
enemies," he said, "reconciliation of friends; the wars of nations
end at last."[55] Such facts of experience were signs of a new heaven
and a new earth to come—or rather, these facts proclaimed a heaven
and earth already joined, God with man, and men brothers of one
another. Maurice's whole being proclaimed that, in spite of
appearances, in spite of apparent outward contradictions, the kingdom had been established; the universal family lay at the foundation
of human society. "The end of our life", he declared, "is the ground
of all,"[56] the ground which is lying beneath all the time.

Maurice following his Millenarian mentor, Stephenson, discovered
in the Fall of Jerusalem the proclamation of Christ's kingdom; but
Christ's work in his Life, Death, and Resurrection brought the
kingdom into reality. If the Resurrection of Christ proclaimed that
a new life is to be conferred upon men, Resurrection did not refer
to the future more than to the present. "He whom [the Resurrec-
tion] announced as the Son of God was the Head of every man."[57]
And the Resurrection announced "that there was in man, in human
beings, a spirit which His Spirit had come to bring out of its prison-
house, to claim as the child of God, the inheritor of a Divine Life."[58]

Maurice found "the establishment of sacrifice as the bond between
the divine and human nature, between the divine and human life".[59]
Like pure light through a prism, sacrifice was refracted into each
specific relationship among men. It was apparent in that freedom
which characterizes a son's obedience to a father's authority, never
the bondage of slavish submission. Spiritual freedom was seen in
the mutual trust of husbands and wives, real trust not mere semb-
lance. There was sacrificial freedom in brother's consanguinity and
co-operation. In these relationships out of which the wider relations
of a nation were formed, sacrifice was the living force. And it was in
accordance with this principle that the universal family to which
man as man redeemed belonged was bound together in freedom
and in order.

Maurice was confident of the future. "The Eternal Name in

which old priest, lawgiver, and prophet trusted lay beneath the whole universe . . . it had revealed itself . . . it would be at last fully revealed."[60] In due season mankind would acknowledge a universal society. "The principles and wants in man, to which it appealed when it was confined to a little province, . . . must be those which it meets when it has comprehended all kindreds and nations within its circle."[61]

For Maurice, of course, the existential situation of the present could only be represented as a period of conflict. Significantly, the resolution of *Eustace Conway* was set in a struggle never ending in time.

> The strife must continue till your death . . . from first to last it is a strife against principalities and powers. Yet do not be discouraged; the worst of your toil is over, for henceforth you will know who are your enemies, and upon whom you must depend for succour. You have learnt that we are not men unless we are free, and that we are not free unless we are living in subjection to the law which made us so.[62]

It was not, nevertheless, a hopeless struggle. "If there is at the root of all human Society, of Humanity itself, that divine Sacrifice which our Worship sets before us, the Spirit of which it teaches may go with us wherever we go, . . . there must be a light penetrating the gloom."[63] We do not want, Maurice said,

> to dream ourselves into some imaginary past or some imaginary future, but to use that which we have, to believe our own professions, to live as if all we utter when we seem to be most in earnest were not a lie. Then we may find that the principle and habit of Self-sacrifice which is expressed in the most comprehensive human Worship supplies the underground for national Equity, Freedom, Courage; for the courtesies of common intercourse, the homely virtues and graces which can be brought under no rules, but which constitute the chief charm of life, and tend most to abate its miseries. Then every tremendous struggle with ourselves whether we shall degrade our fellow-creatures, men or women, or live to raise them—struggles to which God is not indifferent if we are—may issue in a real belief that we are members one of another, and that every injury to one is an injury to the whole body. Then it will be

F

found that refinement and grace are the property of no class, that they may be in the inheritance of those who are as poor as Christ, and His Apostles were; because they are human. So there will be discovered beneath all the politics of the Earth, sustaining the order of each country, upholding the charity of each household, a City which has foundations, whose builder and maker is God. It must be for all kindreds and races; therefore with the sectarianism which rends Humanity asunder, with the Imperialism which would substitute for Universal fellowship a Universal death, must it wage implacable war. Against these we pray as often as we ask that God's will may be done in Earth as it is in Heaven.[64]

Maurice would have protested against Tennyson's "abstraction" as much as Ludlow's "Platonistic dreams about an Order, and a Kingdom, and a Beauty, self-realized in their own eternity." Yet just beyond the point of ordinary vision, all his life, his gaze had been fixed upon that City and that Kingdom, "still and serene," for all kindreds and races, whose builder and maker is God. Could ye "not see the marvel in his eye"?[65]

GENEALOGICAL TABLE OF THE MAURICE FAMILY

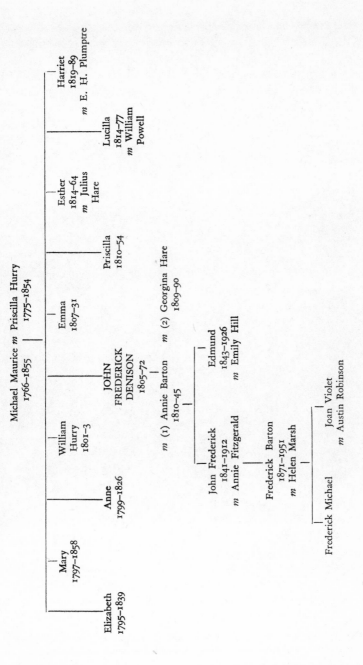

Michael Maurice *m* Priscilla Hurry
1766–1855   1775–1854

Elizabeth
1795–1839

Mary
1797–1858

Anne
1799–1826

William
Hurry
1801–3

JOHN
FREDERICK
DENISON
1805–72

m (1) Annie Barton
1810–45

m (2) Georgina Hare
1809–90

Emma
1807–31

Priscilla
1810–54

Esther
1814–64
m Julius
Hare

Lucilla
1814–77
m William
Powell

Harriet
1819–89
m E. H. Plumptre

John Frederick
1841–1912
m Annie Fitzgerald

Edmund
1843–1926
m Emily Hill

Frederick Barton
1871–1951
m Helen Marsh

Frederick Michael

Joan Violet
m Austin Robinson

Notes

——— ◆ ———

INTRODUCTION

1. F. M. Higham, *Frederick Denison Maurice* (*1947*), p. 121
2. *Life of F. D. Maurice,* II, p. 643
3. loc. cit.
4. loc. cit.
5. loc. cit.
6. Ms. letter, 21 March 1872, Julia Sterling to Emily Hill. (C.U.L., ADD 7793). C.U.L. is used for the Cambridge University Library
7. *Life,* II, p. 642
8. loc. cit.
9. Ms. letter, 28 January 1913, Edward W. Cox to John Frederick Maurice. (C.U.L. ADD 7793). The letter mentions Maurice, quoting from Goethe, "as he looked up . . . his eyes beaming with inspiration, and with a voice trembling with emotion."
10. E.g., see
    C. R. Sanders, *Coleridge and the Broad Church Movement* (1942), pp. 184, 185
    A. R. Vidler, *F. D. Maurice and Company* (1966), pp. 32–7
    C. F. G. Masterman, *Frederick Denison Maurice* (1907), p. 32
    A. M. Ramsey, *F. D. Maurice and the Conflicts of Modern Theology* (1951), pp. 13–20, 22
    H. G. Wood, *Frederick Denison Maurice* (1950), pp. 26–37
    Torben Christensen, *Origin and History of Christian Socialism 1848–54* (1962) pp. 13, 23
11. See *Doctrine of Sacrifice* (1854), p. 322n
12. C. R. Sanders. op. cit., p. 184
13. John Tulloch, *Movements of Religious Thought in Britain during the Nineteenth Century* (1885), p. 264
14. C. R. Sanders, op. cit., p. 185
15. C. R. Sanders, loc. cit.
    Ms. letter, 1 May [1843], F. D. Maurice to Sara Coleridge. Maurice's correspondence with Sara Coleridge is at King's College, London cf. *Kingdom of Christ* 2nd ed. (1842), I, Dedication to the Rev. Derwent Coleridge, pp. v–xxxii

16. C. R. Sanders, op. cit., pp. 185, 196
    Torben Christensen, op cit., p. 23
17. cf. *Life*, II, pp. 243. 244
18. See Rolf Ahlers, *Die Vermittlungstheologie des Frederick Denison Maurice*, (unpublished dissertation in the University of Hamburg, 1967, p. iii
19. *Epistles of St John* (1857), p. 174

I

THE MORALIST IN THE MAKING

1. *Encyclopaedia Metropolitana;* First Division. Pure Sciences. Vol. II (1843), p. 567
2. *Kingdom of Christ* (1838), III, p. 288
3. Ibid., III, p. 11
4. C. R. Sanders, op. cit.. p. 184
5. *Life*, I, pp. 12, 18
6. Ibid., I, pp. 13, 14
7. Lucilla Powell, *Annals of a Family*. Lucilla Powell was the seventh daughter of Michael and Priscilla Maurice, and twin sister of Esther, the wife of Julius Hare. Lucilla married William Powell in 1837. A typed copy of her unpublished memoirs, *Annals of a Family* (composed in 1873), is in the possession of her great grandson, Mr Robert Bayne-Powell
8. *Life,* I, p. 7; cf. Edmund Kell, "Memoir of the late Rev. Michael Maurice," in the *Christian Reformer*, New Series, Vol. XI (July 1855), p. 407
9. Ibid., I, p. 7
10. Edmund Kell, op. cit., p. 413
11. Ibid., p. 414
12. Ibid., p. 416
13. C. F. G. Masterman, op cit., p. 22
14. Ms. letter, 20 July 1837, Annie Barton to F. D. Maurice. (C.U.L. ADD 7793).
15. *Eustace Conway*, I, p. 34
16. Ibid., I, p. 15
17. Ibid., III, p. 169
18. ibid., III, pp. 170, 171
19. ibid., III, p. 224
20. ibid., II, p. 229
21. ibid., II, p. 230
22. ibid., III, p. 18
23. *Life*, I, p. 33
24. ibid., I, pp. 7, 89
25. ibid., I, p. 9
26. *Conscience*, pp. 67, 68
27. S. Nowell-Smith, *Letters to Macmillan* (1967), p. 31

28. *Conscience,* p. 102
29. Ms. letter, 13 August [1867], F. D. Maurice to Edmund Maurice. (C.U.L. ADD 7793)
30. Ms. letter, 26 March [1870], F. D. Maurice to Edmund Maurice. (C.U.L. ADD 7793)
31. Michael Maurice was quoted by Edmund Kell, op. cit., pp. 412-13. cf. Michael Maurice, *An Account of the Life and Religious Opinions of John Bawn* (1824), pp. 35-6, and *The Christian Reformer,* Vol. VIII (August, 1822), p. 256
32. *Life,* II, p. 89
33. ibid., I. p. 20
34. John Malcolm Ludlow, "Some of the Christian Socialists of 1848 and the following years", in the *Economic Review,* Volume III (October 1893), p. 488
35. *Life,* II, p. 531
36. ibid., I, p. 14
37. cf. loc. cit.
38. *Epistles of St John* (1857), p. 11
39. *Life,* I, p. 14
40. Letter, 24 March 1819, Priscilla Hurry Maurice to Esther Parker, in Lucilla Powell, op. cit., p. 166
41. *Social Morality* (1869), p. 31
42. loc. cit.
43. loc. cit.
44. loc. cit.
45. Louisa Twining's Ms. notes in the archives of Queen's College, Harley Street, on Maurice's lectures, "Mental and Moral Philosophy", delivered at Queen's College in 1849
46. *Life,* I, p. 25
47. ibid., I, p. 29
48. ibid., I, p. 18
49. ibid.. I, p. 14
50. Deathbed letters were written in 1816, 1818, and 1819. See Lucilla Powell, op. cit., pp. 155-175
51. *Life,* I, pp. 32-3
52. ibid., I, p. 25
53. Letter, Priscilla Hurry Maurice to Esther Parker, in Lucilla Powell, op. cit., p. 164
54. Letter, 24 March 1819. Priscilla Hurry Maurice to her daughters Elizabeth, Mary, and Anne, in Lucilla Powell, op. cit., p. 172
55. ibid., p. 173
56. Ms. letter, [Autumn, 1843], F. D. Maurice to Sara Coleridge
57. loc. cit.
58. Augustus Hare, *The Story of My Life* (1896), I, p. 71
59. Letter, 24 March 1819, Priscilla Hurry Maurice to Elizabeth, Mary, and Anne Maurice in Lucilla Powell, op. cit., p. 171
60. ibid., p. 169
61. cf. *Life,* I, p. 23

62. Ms. letter, November 1815, F. D. Maurice to [?—?] Jones, (C.U.L. ADD 7793)

63. loc. cit.

64. *Eustace Conway,* I, p. 155

65. ibid., I, p. 154

66. Ms. letter, 17 January 1866, F. D. Maurice to John Frederick Maurice. (C.U.L. ADD 7793)

67. *Life,* I, p. 21

68. ibid., I, pp. 11, 12

69. ibid., I, p. 52. See also "Weak Points" (The Age of Folly, No. 3), *The Metropolitan Quarterly Magazine,* No. 3 (April, 1826), pp. 7, 8. There is unquestionably a self portrait in the description of "Denison", whose "weak point" is "to believe that scorn's slow unmoving finger is always pointed at himself; and so he never can feel comfortable in general society."

70. ibid., I, pp. 33, 34

71. ibid., I, p. 33

72. ibid., II, p. 630

73. ibid., II, pp. 284, 291

74. See Ms. letter, 8 February 1812, Michael Maurice to Dawson Turner. Trinity College, Cambridge, Dawson Turner Correspondence, 0-13-10, No. 14. The tendency toward an exaggerated humility was also apparent in Michael Maurice, who wrote: "Will it not be deemed an intrusion for a person so far distant as myself [to] appear there—also for a Dysent g [*Sic*] teacher—At Lowestoft I have no difficulty in believing that my opinion is not despised . . . But you will remember the difference between my situation in Yarmouth and Lowestoft . . ." There are three letters from Michael Maurice to Dawson Turner in Trinity College Library, Cambridge

75. Augustus Hare, op. cit., I, pp. 71–2

76. cf. C. R. Sanders, op. cit., p. 189

77. *Life,* I, p. 139

78. cf. ibid., I, p. 206

79. cf. ibid., I, pp. 354–63

80. cf. ibid., I, p. 355. Also cf. Ms. letter, 13 November 1850, F. D. Maurice to C. G. Nicolay, (Queen's College, Harley Street)

81. cf. Ms. letter, 21 February [1871], F. D. Maurice to Edmund Maurice. (C.U.L. ADD 7793)

82. Ms. letter, 2 March [1844], F. D. Maurice to Robert Scott. (Pamphlet Room of Pusey House, Oxford)

83. cf. Ms. letter, 15 November 1853, F. D. Maurice to the Board (Queen's College, Harley Street)

84. cf. Ms. letter, 13 November 1850, F. D. Maurice to C. G. Nicolay

85. Ms. letter, 29 June 1858, F. D. Maurice to the students at the Working Men's College (Working Men's College Archives, File Box 1)

86. loc. cit.

87. Ms. letter, 5 July 1869, F. D. Maurice to John Malcolm Ludlow (C.U.L. ADD 7348, art. 8 no. 165)

88. Ms. letter, 3 February 1883, John Frederick Maurice to Leslie Stephen. (C.U.L. ADD 7793)

89. Ms. letter, 19 November [1862], F. D. Maurice to John Frederick Maurice. (C.U.L. ADD 7793)

90. Ms. letter, 13 August [1867], F. D. Maurice to Edmund Maurice, (C.U.L. ADD 7793)

91. *Life,* II, p. 535

92. ibid., II, p. 536

93. ibid., II, p. 535

94. ibid., I, p. 99

95. cf. ibid., I, p. 153. Lucilla Powell, op. cit., p. 80

96. Lucilla Powell, op. cit., p. 95

97. See Bibliography under Priscilla Maurice

98. Priscilla Maurice, *Sickness, its Trials and Blessings* (1850), p. 23

99. Augustus Hare, op. cit., p. 179

100. Lucilla Powell, op. cit., pp. 101, 102
It was an intentional move for Maurice. See Ms. letter, 25 March 1849, Frederick Denison Maurice to John Malcolm Ludlow, (C.U.L. ADD 7348, art. 8, no. 11)

I am perhaps going to be married and to a sick wife. I say *perhaps* for that reason. She was the dearest friend of my wife, owed the formation of her character to her, and was again and again watched by her through sicknesses from which there seemed no chance of her ever rising. When I saw her last January she had a complaint in her throat of which the issue was—even now is—most uncertain. It was with the clear feeling on both sides that our union might never be intended by God and that we might with perfect trust leave Him to decide for us, that we then for the first time bound ourselves to each other. We were both, I believe, surprised at the kind approval with which all our relations received the news.

101. Augustus Hare, op. cit., pp. 82, 83

102. ibid., p. 280

103. S. Nowell-Smith, op. cit., p. 27

104. Augustus Hare, op. cit., p. 82

105. Torben Christensen, op. cit., pp. 211, 212

106. John Malcolm Ludlow, *Autobiography* (C.U.L. ADD 7450, art. 5, vol. 5, chap. 30, p. 16)

107. John Malcolm Ludlow, Ms. *Autobiography* (C.U.L. ADD 7348, art. 1, p. 645n.)

108. Ms. letter, 31 January 1852, F. D. Maurice to John Malcolm Ludlow (C.U.L. ADD 7348, art. 8, no. 56)

109. Ms. letter, 8 May 1852, F. D. Maurice to John Malcolm Ludlow (C.U.L. ADD 7348, art. 8, no. 61)

110. cf. W. Hanna, *Letters of Thomas Erskine* (1877), p. 313

111. cf. Ms. letter, 15 August [1865], F. D. Maurice to Edmund Maurice. (C.U.L. ADD 7793)

F*

112. cf. Ms. letters, 8 March [1871], and 21 March [1871], F. D. Maurice to Edmund Maurice. (C.U.L. ADD 7793)
113. cf. *Life*, I, pp. 97, 235, and II, p. 288. Lucilla Powell, op. cit., p. 81
114. loc. cit.
115. cf. Ms. letter, [Autumn, 1843], F. D. Maurice to Sara Coleridge
116. *Life*, I, p. 77
117. ibid., II, p. 285
118. ibid., II, p. 631
119. loc. cit.
120. cf. *Eustace Conway*, III, pp. 287–8
121. cf. Ms. letter, 26 March [1870], F. D. Maurice to Edmund Maurice. (C.U.L. ADD 7793)

2

THE MORALIST IN ACTION

1. cf. *Eustace Conway*, I, pp. 34–5
2. Ms. letter, 24 August [1867], F. D. Maurice to Edmund Maurice. (C.U.L. ADD 7793)
3. *Ford Madox Brown 1821–93*, Exhibition Catalogue (C.U.L., UC. 6. 265, p. 19)
4. Ford Madox Hueffer, *Ford Madox Brown* (1896), pp. 190–1
5. ibid., p. 100
6. Ms. letter, 2 April [1865], F. D. Maurice to Edmund Maurice. (C.U.L., ADD 7793)
7. Claude Jenkins, *F. D. Maurice and the New Reformation* (1938), p. 23
8. Ms. letter, 1 April 1858, John Malcolm Ludlow to F. D. Maurice (C.U.L., ADD 7348, art. 17, no. 18)
9. Charles Morgan, *The House of Macmillan (1843–1943)* (1943), p. 36
10. ibid., p. 44
11. See below, p. 45
12. *Life*, II, p. 554
13. cf. C. E. Maurice, *Life of Octavia Hill* (1913), p. 120
14. A. M. Ramsey, op. cit., p. 114
15. Ms. letter, 1 March [1844], F. D. Maurice to Sara Coleridge
16. Ms. letter, [Autumn, 1843], F. D. Maurice to Sara Coleridge
17. Ms. letter, 23 November [1843], F. D. Maurice to Sara Coleridge
18. Ms. letter, 1 March [1844], F. D. Maurice to Sara Coleridge
19. loc. cit.
20. *Kingdom of Christ* (1838). *Kingdom of Christ*, 2nd ed. (1842). *Lectures on National Education* (1839). "Moral and Metaphysical Philosophy", in *Encyclopaedia Metropolitana* (1843)
21. *Life*, I, pp. 416, 418
22. ibid., p. 283. John Malcolm Ludlow, *King's College and Mr. Maurice*, p. 4
23. *Life*, I, pp. 354–60. ibid., I, p. 421

24. See *Calendar,* 1967–68, King's College, London, p. 211. Maurice is listed as first Professor of Ecclesiastical History from 1846 until 1853. In a footnote, the *Calendar* says that the title of the chair had been "Professor of Divinity" from 1846 to 1853
25. Janet Elizabeth Courtney, *Freethinkers of the Nineteenth Century* (1920), p. 28
26. Lucilla Powell, op. cit., p. 86
27. Augustus Hare, op. cit., p. 70. See also Ms. letter, 23 September 1888, Augustus Hare to John Frederick Maurice, (C.U.L. ADD 7793). "I have been very glad to include the care of your mother's grave (with ever grateful recollection of her kindness to me as a child) in that bestowed naturally upon the graves of my uncles."
28. Ms. letter, [March 1845], Jane Carlyle to F. D. Maurice. (C.U.L. ADD 7793)
29. *Life,* I, p. 229
30. Ms. letter, 1 May [1843], F. D. Maurice to Sara Coleridge
31. *Life,* II, p. 287
32. ibid., I, p. 403
33. See J. C. Hare, ed., *Essays and Tales,* p. xxxiii.
    There are persons who, by a certain felicity of nature, through a peculiar combination of magnanimity and generosity with gentleness and open-hearted frankness, loving to give the very best of what they have, are gifted with a sort of divining rod for drawing out what is hidden in the hearts of their brethren; and of such persons I have known no finer example than Sterling
34. See *Life,* I, (1884). John Sterling, *Essays and Tales,* edited, with a memoir of his life, by J. C. Hare (1848). Thomas Carlyle, *Life of John Sterling* (1851)
35. *Life,* I, p. 227
36. ibid., I, pp. 56, 59–60. See C. R. Sanders, op. cit., p. 189
37. ibid., I, p. 90
38. Lucilla Powell, op. cit., p. 81
39. *Life,* I, p. 345
40. Introduction to *Remarks on Mandeville's Fable of the Bees by William Law* (1844), pp. iii, iv
41. ibid., p. vi
42. *Life,* I, pp. 380, 381
43. loc. cit.
44. See ibid., p. 545. See also in the Cambridge University Archives, C.U.R. 39.9, art. 53, no. 1, Candidates for Knightbridge Professor, 24 October 1866: Messrs. Ace, Birks, Campion, Maurice, Mayor, Hort, Perowne, Shedden, Venn, Wilson. See also a pencilled notation in *Elections of Professors From 1720,* Vol. II, p. 45. Election of the Knightbridge Professor, 25 October 1866
    The Electors are the Vice-Chancellor [Cartmell (Chr)], the Master of St Peter's College [Cookson], the Regius [Jeremie] and Margaret [Selwyn] Professors of Divinity, the Regius Professor of Greek

[Thompson], the Regius Professor of Modern History [Kingsley], and the Public Orator [W. G. Clark] . . .

Mr Maurice had 4 votes (viz. Prof^r Selwyn, Prof^r Thompson, Mr Clark, Prof^r Kingsley)

Mr Shedden had 1 vote (Dr Cookson)

Mr Hort had 1 vote (Dr Jeremie)

The Vice Chancellor did not vote.

45. *Life,* II, p. 630
46. ibid., II, p. 633
47. Ms. memorandum, F. D. Maurice to Charles Kingsley *re* Lord Ripon's *Duty of the Age,* British Museum Manuscript No. 43621
48. Torben Christensen, op. cit., p. 66
49. cf. A. R. Vidler, op. cit., p. 28
50. *Life,* II, p. 80
51. loc. cit.
52. ibid., II, p. 207
53. ibid., II, pp. 186, 187
54. ibid., II, pp. 198, 199
55. John Malcolm Ludlow, *Autobiography* (C.U.L. ADD 7450, art. 5, vol. 5, chap. 37, p. 7)
56. Ms. letter [1872], Georgina Hare Maurice to John Malcolm Ludlow (C.U.L. ADD 7348, art. 8, no. 184). See also Ms. letter, 26 July 1852 (C.U.L. ADD 7348, art. 8, no. 62). Maurice's dependence on Ludlow is seen in this letter. Mrs Maurice's brother, Reginald Hare, an addict, had arrived at the Maurices' house, uninvited; a bottle of laudanum "enough to destroy several men" had been found in the garden. The children had been sent away. "My wife's life is at stake," Maurice wrote, imploring Ludlow to help him.
57. *Life,* II, p. 551
58. ibid., II, p. 552
59. Ms. letter [1852], F. D. Maurice to John Malcolm Ludlow, (C.U.L. ADD 7348, art. 8, no. 54)
60. Ms. letter, 17 August 1858, John Malcolm Ludlow to F. D. Maurice, (C.U.L. ADD 7348, art. 17, no. 24)
61. loc. cit.
62. *Life,* II, p. 294
63. Ms. letter, 1 July 1859, John Malcolm Ludlow to F. D. Maurice, (C.U.L. ADD 7348, art. 17, no. 29)
64. *Life,* I, p. 350
65. Ms. letter, 3 February 1883, John Frederick Maurice to Leslie Stephen. (C.U.L. ADD 7793)

3

THE DIVINE ORDER: THE FRAMEWORK OF MORALITY

1. Ms. letter, 13 September [1852], John Malcolm Ludlow to F. D. Maurice, (C.U.L. ADD 7348, art. 17, no. 3)

2. A. R. Vidler, op. cit., p. 31
3. A. R. Vidler, loc. cit. See *Life*, I, pp. 132–138. The correspondence to which Vidler refers was actually dated "about February 6, 1832" and "about February 12, 1832", but the Maurices were notoriously lax about dating letters. See also John Tulloch, op. cit., p. 267
4. *Eustace Conway*, III, p. 272
5. Torben Christensen, op. cit., p. 22
6. *Life*, I, p. 90
7. Ms. letter, 21 November 1812, Michael Maurice to Dawson Turner, Trinity College Library, Cambridge; Dawson Turner Correspondence, o–13–10, No. 78. Michael Maurice regularly faced financial crises without losing his enthusiasm for investment. In one letter, making arrangements with his banker, he wrote: "Should I overdraw which I think I shall not, I shall hope to be pardoned; for my debtors instead of discharging—because I was removing—seemed more anxious to have unsettled accounts. . . . If you could part with an unproductive Halesworth concern would a *large actually productive business* of the same kind be desirable? I know one of that description which is obtainable, but not in your neighbourhood . . .".
8. *Life*, I, p. 99
9. loc. cit.
10. loc. cit., p. 99
11. ibid., II, p. 139
12. Lucilla Powell, op. cit., See *Life*, I, p. 18
13. ibid., I, pp. 123, 124
14. Mary Maurice, *Memorials of Two Sisters*, pp. 277–8. The complete entry reads: "Next to my own knowledge of the Saviour, have I desired that my beloved ———— should know him; and none but he to whom all things are naked and opened, can tell the burden which my spirit has known for three years and a half, in the certainty that he was not one who could call God, Father. Now it is removed, my heart's desire is granted, and I could sing aloud all the day long. Oh! . . . And may I ever wonder, and bless my God, for thus gloriously granting this dear one his great salvation." The second edition of *Memorials* repeats the quotation, on page 269, with an "F" at the beginning of the blank and identifies the subject as her brother. Three years and a half takes us back to the summer of 1826, some months after Emma was baptized, some months before Maurice refused to take his Cambridge degree for religious reasons. I am indebted for this information to Mr Peter Allen.
15. Lucilla Powell, op. cit., p. 49. Mrs Powell tells the story of Miss Codrington and Senor Salvador
16. *Eustace Conway*, III, p. 77
17. ibid., III, 274–5. cf. *Life*, I, pp. 134–8
18. *Eustace Conway*, III, pp. 275–6
19. ibid., III, p. 276
20. ibid., III, pp. 278–9
21. *Kingdom of Christ*, I, p. 162
22. ibid., I, p. 165

23. *Encyclopaedia Metropolitana,* First Division, II, p. 589
24. loc. cit.
25. ibid., p. 590
26. loc. cit.
27. *Life,* I, p. 185
28. Ms. letter, 13 September [1852], John Malcolm Ludlow to F. D. Maurice (C.U.L. ADD 7348, art. 17, no. 3), Ludlow specifically mentioned *Moral Metaphysical Philosophy.*
29. *Moral and Metaphysical Philosophy,* I, 2nd ed., revised (1850), p. 150. The quotation is slightly different from *Encyclopaedia Metropolitana,* First Division, II, p. 597
30. Ms. letter, 8 February [1864], F. D. Maurice to Edmund Maurice, (C.U.L. ADD 7793)
31. loc. cit., cf. *Life,* II, p. 463
32. *Life,* I, pp. 135–6
33. ibid., I, p. 167
34. ibid., I, p. 218
35. ibid., II, pp. 349–54
36. ibid., II, p. 354
37. *Apocalypse,* p. vi
38. ibid., pp. vi, vii
39. ibid., p. vii
40. *Life,* pp. 147–52. The similarity of the ideas of Maurice and Stephenson is seen in the fact that Maurice's memoir of Stephenson appears in *F. D. Maurice and Company* as "Memoir by J. A. Stephenson in Life of F.D.M., I, 151". See A. R. Vidler, op. cit., p. 62
41. *Life,* I, pp. 148–50
42. ibid. I, p. 150
43. Joseph Adam Stephenson, *Christology,* 2 vols. (1838).
It is likely that Stephenson himself was influenced by reading Ernst Wilhelm Hengstenberg. A note in *Christology* states: "This title may have been suggested by the work of Professor Hengstenberg of Berlin; a writer for whom Mr Stephenson had a high respect."
See ibid., p. vi.
Hengstenberg's *Christologie* [Stephenson's copy?] is found among Maurice's books in the library at King's College, London
44. ibid., II, p. 141
45. ibid., II, p. 136
46. ibid., II, p. 132
47. loc. cit.
48. *Apocalypse,* p. 181
49. ibid., p. 349
50. ibid., pp. 364–5
51. L. E. Elliott-Binns, *Religion in the Victorian Era.* 2nd ed. (1946), p. 144
52. *Life,* I, p. 167
53. Florence Higham, op. cit., p. 31
54. J. A. Stephenson, op. cit., p. iii
55. ibid., pp. iii–v

56. Lucilla Powell, op. cit., p. 128
57. ibid., p. 43
58. ibid., p. 42
59. ibid., p. 43
60. ibid., p. 56
61. ibid., p. 59
62. ibid., p. 72
63. Florence Higham, op. cit., p. 21
64. Lucilla Powell, op. cit., p. 74. cf. *Life*, I, p. 89
65. ibid., I, pp. 139–40
66. Lucilla Powell, op. cit., pp. 79–80
67. ibid., p. 80
68. *Life*, I, p. 147
69. loc. cit.
70. ibid., I, p. 208
71. ibid., II, p. 243
72. ibid., II, p. 244
73. St Luke 17. 21
74. Ms. letter, 13 September [1852], John Malcolm Ludlow to F. D. Maurice (C.U.L. ADD 7348, art. 17, no. 3)
75. Ms. letter, 24 September [1852], F. D. Maurice to John Malcolm Ludlow (C.U.L. ADD 7348, art. 8, no. 65)
76. John Malcolm Ludlow, *Autobiography* (C.U.L. ADD 7450, art. 5, vol. 5, chap. 37, p. 7)
77. Ms. letter, 24 November [1849], F. D. Maurice to John Malcolm Ludlow (C.U.L. ADD 7348, art. 8, no. 19)
78. *Life*, II, pp. 126–7
79. Memorandum, F. D. Maurice to Charles Kingsley (British Museum Ms. No. 43621)
80. Ms. letter, 13 September [1852], John Malcolm Ludlow to F. D. Maurice (C.U.L. ADD 7348, art. 17, no. 3)
81. Louisa Twining, manuscript notes on Maurice's lectures on "Mental and Moral Philosophy", delivered at Queen's College, Harley Street in 1849–50.
    See Louisa Twining, *Recollections of Life and Work* (1893), p. 152. All the references which follow immediately are to Louisa Twining's notes preserved in Queen's College, Harley Street.
82. Louisa Twining, Ms. notes, Sec. 1
83. Louisa Twining, Ms. notes, Sec. 2
84. Louisa Twining, Ms. notes, Sec. 5
85. Thomas Acland, *Memoir and Letters* (1902), p. 75
86. *The New Statute and Mr Ward*, pp. 19–21
87. Ms. letter, 2 December [1853], F. D. Maurice to [   ] Dangerfield. (C.U.L. ADD 7793).
88. *Life*, I, p. 497

4

THE LAW OF SACRIFICE: THE PRINCIPLE OF MORALITY

1. *Encyclopaedia Metropolitana*, First Division, II, p. 597
2. ibid., p. 590
3. *Epistles of St John*, p. 205
4. cf. *Doctrine of Sacrifice*, p. xxxviii
5. cf. A. M. Ramsey, op. cit., p. 20. Ramsey speaks of "the unique *act* of the Incarnation".
6. Schubert Ogden, *Christ Without Myth* (1962), p. 182
7. Ms. letter [Autumn, 1843], F. D. Maurice to Sara Coleridge
8. loc. cit.
9. loc. cit.
10. Ms. letter, 23 November [1843], F. D. Maurice to Sara Coleridge
11. *Doctrine of Sacrifice*, p. 15
12. ibid., p. 31
13. ibid., p. 16
14. ibid., pp. 43–44
15. ibid., p. xlviii
16. *Epistles of St John*, p. 209
17. ibid., p. 208
18. ibid., p. 209
19. *Sequel to the Inquiry*, p. 247
20. ibid., p. 246
21. *Conflict of Good and Evil*, p. 164
22. ibid., p. 162
23. *Epistle to the Hebrews*, p. 55
24. ibid., pp. 95–6
25. *Doctrine of Sacrifice*, p. 187
26. Romans 7. 19, 24
27. *Epistles of St John*, p. 188
28. ibid., p. 186
29. ibid., p. 190. cf. Ms. letter, 13 August [1869], F. D. Maurice to Edmund Maurice. (C.U.L. ADD 7793). "I have been taught what Evil is, taught to regard it not as an abstraction but as an actual Power working upon me at every moment."
30. *Life*, II, pp. 538–41
31. cf. ibid., II, p. 538
32. ibid., II, p. 16
33. ibid., II, pp. 17, 19
34. *Theological Essays*, p. 442
35. *Sequel to the Inquiry*, p. 257
36. ibid., p. 258
37. loc. cit.
38. St Matthew 6. 15
39. *Sequel to the Inquiry*, p. 261

40. See J. H. Newman, *Diaries*, vol. xx (1970), p. 416.

An illustration is provided by correspondence following a public apology by Maurice to J. H. Newman. Newman, in response wrote: "It has before now surprised and pained me, that you have in print spoken of me in terms which jarred with my recollections of you. I have nothing but kind and pleasant thoughts, of the occasions, in times long past, which you have given me, of intercourse with you. Your letter of the 27th has put all right—it has destroyed the incongruity between the past and the present which was to me so unwelcome; and I thank you for it."

Maurice answered ". . . I have no doubt that I have said many words about you which ought not to have been said. If they have ever given you pain I must ask you to forgive them. I am convinced that the more we care for the Truth and wish to live for it, and the more our own sins are revealed to us, the fewer of such wounds we shall inflict."

41. Ms. letter, 18 [July, 1843], F. D. Maurice to Sara Coleridge
42. Ms. letter, 1 March [1844], F. D. Maurice to Sara Coleridge
43. *The Lord's Prayer, the Creed, and the Ten Commandments*, p. 44
44. ibid., p. 46
45. *Social Morality*, p. 468

5

THE "I": THE SUBJECT OF MORALITY

1. *Epistles of St John*, p. 23
2. *What is Revelation?* (1859), pp. 328–9. See also H. L. Mansel, *The Limits of Religious Knowledge* (1858), pp. 135–6
3. ibid., p. 360
4. *Social Morality*, p. 2
5. ibid., p. 4
6. ibid., p. 28
7. ibid., p. 10.

The use of "individual" is unusual for Maurice. cf. *Conscience*, pp. 6–7. See also R. C. Trench, *Letters and Memorials*, I, p. 190. In a letter to Trench on 30 March 1835, Maurice wrote from his first curacy at Bubbenhall, "I am more and more convinced that we must not use the *personal* and *individual* as synonymous words; but in fact we shall have most sense and lively realization of our distinct personality when we cease to be individual, and most delight to contemplate ourselves as members of one body in one head."

8. *Doctrine of Sacrifice*, p. 182
9. ibid., p. xlv
10. *Encyclopaedia Metropolitana*, First Division, II, p. 620
11. *Social Morality*, pp. 26–7
12. ibid., p. 50
13. Ms. letter 20 July 1837, Annie Barton to F. D. Maurice, (C.U.L. ADD 7793)

14. *Social Morality*, p. 72
15. Ms. letter, 24 March 1819, Priscilla Hurry Maurice to Esther Parker in Lucilla Powell, op. cit., p. 164
16. *Queen's College, London: Its Objects and Methods*, p. 8.
    Queen's College, London, founded 1848, grew out of Maurice's co-operation with his sister Mary and her interest in the Governesses Benevolent Institution.
17. *Social Morality*, p. 11
18. Ms. letter, 24 March 1819, Priscilla Hurry Maurice to Esther Parker, in Lucilla Powell, op. cit., p. 166
19. Ms. letter, [April, 1845], F. D. Maurice to his children. (C.U.L. ADD 7793)
20. *Life*, I, p. 130
21. *Conscience*, p. 63
22. cf. *Lectures on National Education*, p. 2
23. ibid., p. 3
24. ibid., p. 36
25. *Learning and Working*, p. 38
26. ibid., p. viii
27. ibid., p. 109
28. ibid., p. 113
29. ibid., p. 114
30. ibid., p. 121
31. *Eustace Conway*, II, p. 106
32. ibid., II, p. 107
33. loc. cit.
34. S. T. Coleridge, *Table Talk*, 1917 ed., p. 118
35. *Life*, I, p. 207
36. F. J. A. Hort, "Coleridge," in *Cambridge Essays* (1856), p. 305
37. Sara Coleridge, *Memoir and Letters* (1873), I, p. 177
38. Ms. letter, 1 May [1843], F. D. Maurice to Sara Coleridge
39. *Eustace Conway*, III, p. 116. cf. *Kingdom of Christ*, II, p.v. Maurice wrote that he did not wish "to confound the act of perception, or the faculty of perception, with the object perceived; to make the Living Word identical with the Conscience, instead of representing one as necessary to the other."
40. Ms. letter, 18 [July, 1843], F. D. Maurice to Sara Coleridge
41. loc. cit.
42. loc. cit.
43. Ms. letter, 23 November [1843], F. D. Maurice to Sara Coleridge
44. Ms. letter, 1 March [1844], F. D. Maurice to Sara Coleridge
45. Introduction to *Remarks on Mandeville's Fable of the Bees*, p. xxxiv
46. *Encyclopaedia Metropolitana*, First Division, II, p. 657
47. *Kingdom of Christ*, ed. A. R. Vidler (1958), I, p. 57. See also, I, p. 176. "There is an organ in man which speaks of that which is absolute and eternal."
48. R. C. Trench, op. cit., I, p. 127
49. S. T. Coleridge, *Aids to Reflection* (1843), I, p. 90

50. loc. cit.
51. *Conscience*, p. 202
52. *Encyclopaedia Metropolitana*, First Division, II, p. 660
53. loc. cit.

6

THE FAMILY: THE DISCOVERY OF MORALITY

1. *Life*, II, p. 535
2. cf. ibid., II, pp. 313, 314
3. cf. *Eustace Conway*, II, p. 272
4. *A Lecture delivered at the opening of the Lower Norwood Working Men's Institution*, p. 9
5. loc. cit.
6. *Doctrine of Sacrifice*, p. xxxix
7. ibid., p. xl
8. cf. *An address of congratulation to the Rev. F. D. Maurice, on his nomination to St. Peter's, Vere Street; with his reply thereto*, p. 4
9. loc. cit.
10. *Social Morality*, p. 25
11. loc. cit.
12. ibid., p. 26
13. cf. loc. cit.
14. loc. cit.
15. ibid., p. 28
16. ibid., p. 30
17. ibid., pp. 30–1
18. *Epistles of St John*, p. 11
19. *Social Morality*, p. 30
20. Ms. letter, 11 March, [1859], F. D. Maurice to Edmund Maurice. (C.U.L. ADD 7793).
    Several letters "about" Homer are preserved from Edmund's Winchester school years
21. cf. *Life*, I, p. 128
22. Ms. letter, 9 November, [1862], F. D. Maurice to Edmund Maurice. (C.U.L. ADD 7793)
23. Ms. letter, 29 August, [1870], F. D. Maurice to Edmund Maurice. (C.U.L. ADD 7793)
24. Ms. letter, 18 January, [1862], F. D. Maurice to Edmund Maurice. (C.U.L. ADD 7793)
25. Ms. letter, 9 November, [1871], F. D. Maurice to Edmund Maurice. (C.U.L. ADD 7793)
26. Ms. letter, 17 February, [1859], F. D. Maurice to Edmund Maurice. (C.U.L. ADD 7793)
27. Ms. letter, 19 September, [1860], F. D. Maurice to Edmund Maurice. (C.U.L. ADD 7793)
28. Ms. letter, 21 March [1862], F. D. Maurice to Edmund Maurice. (C.U.L. ADD 7793)

170 NOTES TO PAGES 100-109

29. Ms. letter, 14 May, [1862], F. D. Maurice to Edmund Maurice. (C.U.L. ADD 7793)
30. Ms. letter, 28 November, [1864], F. D. Maurice to Edmund Maurice. (C.U.L. ADD 7793)
31. *Winchester College Register, 1836–1906*, p. 151
32. *Life*, I. p. 131
33. Ms. letter, 18 October, [1862], F. D. Maurice to Edmund Maurice. (C.U.L. ADD 7793)
34. Ms. letter, 28 July, [1864], F. D. Maurice to Edmund Maurice. (C.U.L. ADD 7793)
35. Ms. letter, 21 October, [1863], F. D. Maurice to Edmund Maurice. (C.U.L. ADD 7793)
36. loc. cit.
37. loc. cit.
38. Ms. letter, 24 October, [1862], F. D. Maurice to Edmund Maurice. (C.U.L. ADD 7793)
39. cf. *Life*, II, pp. 284–6
40. Ms. letter, 15 March, [1862], F. D. Maurice to Edmund Maurice. (C.U.L. ADD 7793). William Luke, Edmund's tutor at Christ Church, drowned 5 March 1862
41. Ms. letter, 7 December, [1864]?, F. D. Maurice to Edmund Maurice. (C.U.L. ADD 7793)
42. Ms. letter, 2 September, [1870], F. D. Maurice to Edmund Maurice. (C.U.L. ADD 7793)
43. Ms. letter, 28 June, [1866], F. D. Maurice to Edmund Maurice. (C.U.L. ADD 7793)
44. Ms. letter, 24 August, [1867], F. D. Maurice to Edmund Maurice. (C.U.L. ADD 7793)
45. Ms. letter, 30 April, [1870], F. D. Maurice to Edmund Maurice. (C.U.L. ADD 7793)
46. Ms. letter, 23 February, [1862], F. D. Maurice to Edmund Maurice. (C.U.L. ADD 7793)
47. Lucilla Powell, op. cit., p. 53
48 Matthew 19. 4; Genesis 1. 27
49. *Social Morality*, p. 60
50. ibid., p. 59
51. ibid., p. 61
52. F. J. A. Hort. op. cit., p. 318
53. loc. cit.
54. *Life*, I. pp. 498–9
55. *Social Morality*, pp. 63–4.
    cf. "On Sisterhoods", the *Victoria Magazine*, I (August, 1863). pp. 289–301. Maurice discussed religious orders for women which were to be judged by the way their work supported the union rather than the separation of the sexes.
56. ibid., p. 62
57. ibid., p. 64
58. ibid., p. 65

59. *Kingdom of Christ*, III. p. 33
60. *Social Morality*, p. 50
61. loc. cit.
62. ibid., p. 84
63. loc. cit.
64. Ms. letter, 4 January, [1870], F. D. Maurice to Edmund Maurice. (C.U.L. ADD 7793)
65. Ms. letter, 23 January [1870], F. D. Maurice to Edmund Maurice. (C.U.L. ADD 7793)
66. loc. cit.
67. Josephine Butler, *An Autobiographical Memoir* (*1928*), p. 82
68. *Social Morality*, p. 66
69. See "Female Suffrage," *Spectator*, No. 2,175 (March, 1870), p. 298
70. *Social Morality*, p. 65
71. ibid., p. 72
72. loc. cit.
73. cf. ibid., p. 80
74. ibid., p. 81
75. cf. John Malcolm Ludlow, "Some of the Christian Socialists of 1848 and the following years." *The Economic Review*, Vol. III (October 1893), pp. 486–500, and Vol. IV. (January 1894), pp. 24–42
76. Ms. letter, 13 August [1867], F. D. Maurice to Edmund Maurice. (C.U.L. ADD 7793)
77. *Social Morality*, p. 83
78. Ms. letter, 13 August, [1867], F. D. Maurice to Edmund Maurice. (C.U.L. ADD 7793)
79. *Eustace Conway*, I, pp. 282–3
80. Ms. fragment of a speech delivered in Leeds. The fragment is in the possession of the Revd A. R. Vidler.
81. Ms. lecture "On Co-operation", p. 8. See "The President's Lectures on Co-operation at Greenwich–Lecture II", *Journal of Association*, No. 14., Vol. I. (29 March 1852), p. 106.
    The published lectures are summarized and not given *verbatim*. The manuscripts are in the possession of the Revd A. R. Vidler
82. ibid., p. 9
83. Ms. fragment of a speech delivered in Leeds
84. loc. cit.
85. loc. cit.
86. Ms. Lecture "On Co-operation", p. 23. See "The President's Lectures on Co-operation at Greenwich," Vol. I. (22 March 1852), p. 101. See above, n.81
87. ibid., p. 41
88. loc. cit.

7
THE NATION: THE CULTIVATION OF MORALITY

1. Ms. letter I August [1870], F. D. Maurice to Edmund Maurice. (C.U.L. ADD 7793)
2. *Moral and Metaphysical Philosophy,* 2nd ed., revised. (*Encyclopaedia Metropolitana,* 2nd ed., revised, First Division, Pure Sciences, 1850; later published in 1872, separately, in two volumes as *Moral and Metaphysical Philosophy*),see p. 11
3. loc. cit.
4. loc. cit.
5. loc. cit.
6. ibid., p. 12
7. ibid., p. 15
8. *Social Morality,* p. 128
9. ibid., p. 127
10. *Doctrine of Sacrifice,* p. 64
11. *Social Morality,* p. 25
12. See: *Conscience,* p. 150. *Social Morality,* p. 137
13. *Kingdom of Christ,* III, p. 12
14. loc. cit.
15. *Life,* I, p. 249
16. loc. cit.
17. Ms. sermon, preached at St Edward's Church, Cambridge, Quinquagesima Sunday, 11 February 1872, at Evening Prayer. The manuscript of Maurice's last sermon is preserved in the library of Trinity College, Cambridge. The manuscript is incorrectly dated 27 February
18. *A lecture delivered at the opening of the Lower Norwood Working Men's Institute,* pp. 11–12
19. *Doctrine of Sacrifice,* p. 133
20. ibid., p. 4
21. *Epistles of St. John,* p. 87
22. i John 2. 3. *Doctrine of Sacrifice,* pp. 70-1
23. ibid., p. 75
24. *Social Morality,* p. 144
25. ibid., pp. 145-6
26. ibid., pp. 146-7
27. *Kingdom of Christ,* III. p. 13
28. *Social Morality,* p. 150
29. ibid., pp., 151-2
30. *Theological Essays,* p. 23
31. L. E. Elliot-Binns, *Religion in the Victorian Era* (1964), p. 144
32. *Social Morality,* p. 152
33. ibid., p. 154
34. ibid., p. 163
35. ibid., p. 161
36. ibid., p. 178
37. ibid., p. 181

38. Lucien Wolf, *Life of the First Marquess of Ripon* (1921), p. 36
39. loc. cit.
40. Ms. letter, 8 September 1852, F. D. Maurice to John Malcolm Ludlow. (C.U.L. ADD 7348, art. 8, No. 64)
41. loc. cit.
42. loc. cit.
43. Lucien Wolf, op. cit., p. 37
44. Ms. letter, 25 September [1867], F. D. Maurice to Edmund Maurice. (C.U.L. ADD 7793)
45. loc. cit. See *Life of F. D. Maurice,* II, p. 559. The published form of the letter has slight differences, for example the word "sacredness" in this sentence appears as "sanctity".
46. loc. cit.
47. Memorandum, F. D. Maurice to Charles Kingsley (British Museum Ms. No. 43621)
48. Ms. letter, 8 September 1852, F. D. Maurice to John Malcolm Ludlow. (C.U.L. ADD 7348, art, 8, no. 64)
49. Memorandum, F. D. Maurice to Charles Kingsley (British Museum Ms. No. 43621)
50. Ms. letter, 25 September [1867], F. D. Maurice to Edmund Maurice. (C.U.L. ADD 7793)
51. Ms. letter, 8 September 1852, F. D. Maurice to John Malcolm Ludlow. (C.U.L. ADD 7348, art. 8, no. 64)
52. Memorandum, F. D. Maurice to Charles Kingsley (British Museum Ms. No. 43621)
53. Ms. letter, 1 May [1865], F. D. Maurice to John Malcolm Ludlow, (C.U.L. ADD 7348, art. 8, no. 149)
54. J. A. Stephenson, *Sword Unsheathed* (1834)
55. loc. cit.
56. loc. cit.
57. *Social Morality,* pp. 199-200
58. *Life,* II, p. 240
59. *Apocalypse,* p. 370
60. Ms. Letter, 17 January 1866, F. D. Maurice to John Frederick Maurice (C.U.L. ADD 7793)
61. *Life,* I, p. 15
62. Cambridge University Papers, 1869, p. 28. The papers are in the Cambridge University Archives.
63. *Social Morality,* p. 200
64. Ibid., p. 201
65. ibid., p. 199
66. *Kingdom of Christ,* III, p. 74
67. *Social Morality,* pp. 201-2
68. *Kingdom of Christ,* III, p. 59
69. loc. cit.
70. ibid., III, p. 66
71. *Encyclopaedia Metropolitana,* First Division, II (1843), p. 640
72. *Social Morality,* pp. 204-5

73. *Apocalypse,* pp. 374-5
74. *Social Morality,* pp. 206-7
75. *Life,* I, p. 15
76. *Social Morality,* p. 208
77. ibid., p. 204
78. ibid., p. 209
79. loc. cit.
80. ibid., p. 215
81. loc. cit.
82. *Life,* II, p. 418
83. *Social Morality,* p. 217
84. The source of the story is a conversation with Maurice's great grand-daughter, Joan Maurice Robinson, Professor of Economics in the University of Cambridge.
85. *Life,* II, p. 8
86. Ms. lecture "On Co-operation", pp. 16-17. See "The President's Lectures on Co-operation at Greenwich"—Lecture I, *"Journal of Association,"* No. 13 Vol. I, (22 March 1852), p. 101

    Maurice usually objected to the apparently depersonalized use of the word "hands." Lecturing on mechanics' institutes at Northampton, he mentioned that "we were all in danger of *becoming* machines, of getting into a mere habit of performing certain operations without considering how we performed them." See Ms. lecture "On Mechanics' Institutes," delivered at Northampton. The manuscript is in the possession of the Revd A. R. Vidler.
87. Ms. lecture "On Co-operation" p. 20
88. *Commandments Considered,* p. 116
89. Ms. lecture "On Co-operation", p. 21. See "The President's Lectures on Co-operation at Greenwich–Lecture I; *Journal of Association,* No. 13, Vol. I (22 March 1852), p. 101
90. ibid., p. 22
91. *Social Morality,* p. 146
92. ibid., pp. 146-7
93. Henry Sumner Maine, *Ancient Law* (1861), p. 270
94. Ms. lecture "On Co-operation", p. 9. See "The President's Lectures on Co-operation at Greenwich—Lecture II"; *Journal of Association,* No. 14, Vol. I (29 March 1852). p. 12
95. ibid., p. 27. See "The President's Lectures on Co-operation at Greenwich —Lecture II (Continued)"; *Journal of Association,* No. 15, Vol. I (5 April 1852), p. 114
96. See above, Ms. lecture "On Co-operation" . . . (29 March 1852), p. 106
97. *Commandments Considered,* p. 121
98. *Social Morality,* p. 148
99. *Commandments Considered,* p. 124

8

THE UNIVERSAL SOCIETY: FULFILMENT OF MORALITY

1. *Theological Essays*, p. 25. See above p. 165
2. *Eustace Conway*, I, p. 155. See above p. 23
3. *Life*, I. p. 21. See above p. 24
4. *Kingdom of Christ*, I, pp. 14–15
5. loc. cit.
6. *Kingdom of Christ*, II, pp. 266–7
7. Ms. letter, 23 November [1843]. F. D. Maurice to Sara Coleridge
8. Louisa Twining, Ms. notes on Maurice's lectures "On Mental and Moral Philosophy", sec. 5, Queen's College, Harley Street, 1849
9. *Social Morality*, p. 250
10. Louisa Twining, Ms. notes on Maurice's lectures "On Mental and Moral Philosophy", sec. 5
11. *Doctrine of Sacrifice*, p. 133
12. *Kingdom of Christ*, I, 96f
13. ibid., I, p. 114
14. loc. cit.
15. loc. cit.
16. *Gospel of the Kingdom of Heaven*, p. 227
17. *Subscription no Bondage*, Introductory letter, p. i
18. A. R. Vidler, op. cit., pp. 113–14
19. *Kingdom of Christ*, II, p. 289
20. *Social Morality*, p. 224
21. A. R. Vidler, op. cit., p. 66
22. *Theological Essays*, p. 396
23. Ms. letter, 1 March [1843], F. D. Maurice to Sara Coleridge
24. *Kingdom of Christ*, III, p. 252
25. ibid., III, pp. 251–2
26. "Mr Maurice and the Bishop of Grahamstown", a letter printed in the *Spectator*, No. 2,071 (7 March 1868), p. 289
27. loc. cit.
28. Ms. letter, 4 August, [1868], F. D. Maurice to G. W. Rusden. Rusden Mss, Vol. II, Trinity College, Parkville, Victoria, Australia
29. loc. cit.
30. *Kingdom of Christ*, III, p. 350
31. *Epistle to the Hebrews*, p. cxxiv
32. *A. M. Ramsey*, op. cit., p. 34
33. Stephen Neill, *The Church and Christian Union* (1968), p. 26
    Bishop Neill refers to Rahner's essay in *Zeitschrift* für Katholische Theologie (1947), reprinted in Rahner's *Schriften zur Theologie*, vol. II (1960), pp. 7–94
34. *Stephen Neill*, op. cit., pp. 26–7
35. Dietrich Bonhoeffer, *Ethics* (1955), ed. by Eberhard Bethge, p. 71
36. ibid., p. 72
37. ibid., p. 78

38. Ms. letter, 12 September [1859], F. D. Maurice to Edmund Maurice. (C.U.L. ADD 7793)
39. *Life*, II, p. 256. cf. ibid., II, p. 549
40. *Kingdom of Christ*, I, p. 156
41. ibid., I, p. 328
42. Ms. letter, 2 May 1907, John Frederick Maurice to [   ] Jacob
43. "On Church and State", a letter published in *The Daily News*, 25 September 1868
44. loc. cit.
45. H. R. Niebuhr, *Christ and Culture* (1952), p. 226
46. Ms. sermon, St Edward's Church, Cambridge, Quinquagesima Sunday, 11 February 1872, preached at Evening Prayer
47. Ms. sermon, St Edward's Church, Cambridge, preached at Morning Prayer, Sixth Sunday in Lent, 2 April 1871. The manuscript of this sermon, as well as that preached in St Edward's Church, 26 March 1871, is in the Church Archives.
48. *Gospel of St John*, p. 94
49. *Life*, I, pp. 134–8
50. ibid., I, p. 137
51. *Conflict of Good and Evil*, p. 51
52. *Social Morality*, p. 452
53. *Conflict of Good and Evil*, pp. 202–3
54. *Apocalypse*, p. 423
55. *Conflict of Good and Evil*, pp. 202, 212
56. Louisa Twining, Ms. notes on Maurice's lectures "On Mental and Moral Philosophy", sec. 1, Queen's College, Harley Street, 1849
57. *Conflict of Good and Evil*, p. 127
58. loc. cit.
59. *Apocalypse*, p. 456
60. Ms. sermon, St Edward's Church, Cambridge, Quinquagesima Sunday, 11 February 1872
61. Preface to *Handbook of the Geography and Statistics of the Church*, by *J. E. T. Wiltsch* (1859), pp. vii, viii
62. *Eustace Conway*, III, p. 287
63. *Social Morality*, p. 481
64. ibid., pp. 482–3
65. See Alfred, Lord Tennyson, *The Mystic*, lines written in vindication of Maurice.

> Angels have talked with him and showed him thrones;
> Ye knew him not; he was not one of ye;
> Ye scorned him with an undiscerning scorn;
> Ye could not see the marvel in his eye,
> The still serene abstraction.

Bibliography

\

———•◆•———

A
MANUSCRIPT SOURCES

1. *Bayne-Powell, Robert*: The typescript of *Annals of a Family*, the memoirs of Lucilla Maurice Powell, in the possession of Mr. R. Bayne-Powell includes letters of Priscilla Hurry (Mrs. Michael) Maurice.

2. THE BODLEIAN LIBRARY, OXFORD
   Five letters by Maurice are in the collection of the Bodleian Library.

3. THE BRITISH MUSEUM
   Maurice's memorandum to C. Kingsley about Lord Goderich's *Duty of the Age* is in the British Museum Collection, No. 43621. The collection also contains letters from F. D. Maurice to the Kingsleys, to Gladstone, and to others. Recently the Macmillan Archives which contain Maurice letters have been placed in the British Museum, Department of Manuscripts. British Museum ADD Ms. 44809–Minute book, containing titles of Maurice's papers read to Gladstone's essay society.

4. CAMBRIDGE UNIVERSITY ARCHIVES

   a. *Cambridge University Registry*, 39.9 [C.U.R.]
      The Cambridge University Archives has a letter from Maurice explaining that he did not normally use his full name, John Frederick Denison.

   b. *Elections of Professors from 1720*
      Two volumes. These records of elections to professorships are in the Cambridge University Archives. A pencilled notation about Maurice's election as Knightbridge Professor appears in Vol. ii.

5. CAMBRIDGE UNIVERSITY LIBRARY
   a. *Ludlow MSS (ADD 7348)*
      The collection contains letters to J. M. Ludlow from F. D. Maurice, his widow, and his son, J. F. Maurice, 1847–72. There are letters from Ludlow to Maurice, 1852–71, and Ludlow's manuscript *Autobiography.*
   b. *Maurice MSS (ADD 7793)*
      Mr F. M. P. Maurice has deposited an extensive collection of letters in the Anderson Room. There are six letters from Maurice to his son, J. F. Maurice, 1856–66, and approximately 116 letters and fragments from Maurice to his younger son, Edmund. There are a number of other letters from Maurice and concerning Maurice.

6. HAMPSHIRE RECORD OFFICE
   Blachford MSS. The collection contains a letter from F. D. Maurice, 1855, about the death of Charles Mansfield.

7. KING'S COLLEGE, LONDON
   a. *Pamphlet Box,* 106.H.
      Personal Documents of F. D. Maurice
      Ordination as Deacon (1834)
      Ordination as Priest (1835)
      License and Declaration as Minister of Oxford Chapel, Marylebone, (1860)
      Declaration on admission to Donative of St Edward's, Cambridge, (1871)
      Appointment as Preacher in the Chapel Royal, Whitehall, (1871)
   b. *Relton Library,* Bx 5037–M4–R
      Five letters from F. D. Maurice to Sara Coleridge, 1843–44.
   c. *Official Publications,* 3
      The collection contains "Correspondence between the Principal of King's College, London and the Rev. Prof. Maurice". (Privately printed). King's College also has a manuscript sermon preached at St Peter's, Vere Street.

8. PUSEY HOUSE, OXFORD
   A letter from Maurice to the Rev. Dr Robert Scott (later Master of Balliol and Dean of Rochester) gives Maurice's estimate of courses he gave to medical students at Guy's Hospital.

9. QUEEN'S COLLEGE, HARLEY STREET, LONDON
   Thirteen letters from Maurice to C. G. Nicolay, and others, are in the archives of Queen's College. Queen's College also has a manuscript of a sermon preached by Maurice on 16 October 1870, and a bound volume of notes made by Louisa Twining on Maurice's lectures "On Mental and Moral Philosophy", 1849–50.

10. RAMSEY, ARTHUR MICHAEL

Archbishop Ramsey has several interesting letters by Maurice in his possession.

11. ST EDWARD'S CHURCH, CAMBRIDGE

Ms. Sermons, preached 26 March 1871 and 2 April 1871, are in the archives of St Edward's church.

12. TRINITY COLLEGE, CAMBRIDGE

a. *Dawson Turner Mss*

The collection contains three letters from Michael Maurice to Dawson Turner, 0-13-3, No. 22; 0-13-10, Nos. 14, 78.

b. *Houghton Mss*

Letters to Lord and Lady Houghton; Houghton, 16, 133–44.

c. Several letters from F. D. Maurice are in the collection of Trinity College. The library also has the manuscript of Maurice's last sermon, 11 February 1872. A covering letter from Bishop John Macmillan (married to Maurice's granddaughter) may indicate that other Maurice manuscripts were sent to institutions connected with Maurice at the death of his son, Major General Sir John Frederick Maurice.

13. TRINITY COLLEGE, PARKVILLE, VICTORIA, AUSTRALIA

Rusden Mss

Volume II contains a letter from Maurice to G. W. Rusden, 4 August [1868].

14. VIDLER, ALEC ROPER

The manuscripts of two addresses "On Co-operation", two addresses on "Working Men's Colleges", addresses "On Mechanics' Institutes", "On the Word *Civilization*", and fragments of a speech delivered in Leeds, and of an address "On the Historical Plays of Shakespeare", are in the possession of the Rev. A. R. Vidler, Rye, Sussex.

15. WORKING MEN'S COLLEGE

A collection of letters and documents concerning Maurice is in the archives of the Working Men's College, Crowndale Road, London.

B

PUBLISHED WORKS BY F. D. MAURICE

The works listed here are in the order of their first publication. Where possible the earliest available edition of any work has been consulted. When reference is made to another edition, it is mentioned in the notes. In those cases where a book is mentioned in the notes by an abbreviated title, this is added in brackets.

Attention should be called to G. J. Gray's *Bibliography of the Writings of F. D. Maurice*, to the bibliography in the third edition of *The Life of F. D. Maurice*, and to the bibliography given in J. W. Cox's Cambridge Ph.D. dissertation, "God Manifesting Himself: a study of some central elements in the theology of F. D. Maurice".

The Metropolitan Quarterly Magazine [Edited by F. D. Maurice and Charles Shapland Whitmore of Trinity College, Cambridge.] 3 numbers published. The following articles are by Maurice:

"The Age of Folly" (No. 1), *The Metropolitan Quarterly Magazine*, I, No. 1 (November 1825), pp. 1–8

Review of *A Treatise on Christian Doctrine*, by John Milton. *M.Q.M.*, I, No. 1 (November 1825), pp. 9–24

"The New School of Cockneyism" (No. 1). *M.Q.M.*, I, No. 1 (November 1825), pp. 34–62

"The Age of Folly" (No. 2). *M.Q.M.*, I, No. 2 (January 1826), pp. 257–279

"A Supplementary Sheet to Bentham's Book of Fallacies". *M.Q.M.*, I, No. 2 (January 1826), pp. 353–377

"Weak Points" (The Age of Folly, No. 3). *M.Q.M.*, II, No. 3 (April 1826), pp. 1–10

"On Pastoral Poetry" (No. 1). *M.Q.M.*, II, No. 3 (April 1826), pp. 30–45

Review of *The Diary of Mr Papster from the year 1790 to 1827. Found in the National Museum, and published by order of his Majesty, by Mr Henry Burntcoal* . . . (Extracted from *M.Q.M.*, No. 861). *M.Q.M.*, I, No. 3 (April 1826), pp. 85–100

"The New School of Cockneyism" (No. 2). *M.Q.M.*, II, No. 3 (April 1826), pp. 219–30

"Memorabilia of the General Election" (The Age of Folly, No. 4). *M.Q.M.*, II, No. 4, pp. 248–59

"Female Education". *M.Q.M.*, II, No. 4, pp. 265–282

"On Pastoral Poetry" (No. 2). *M.Q.M.*, II, No. 4, pp. 360–70

"A Circular Letter to the Editors of the Edinburgh, Westminster, and Quarterly Reviews". *M.Q.M.*, II, No. 4, pp. 488–96

"Montgomery's *Pelican Island*". *Westminster Review*, October 1827

"Theobald Wolfe Tone's Memoirs". *Westminster Review*, January 1828

"Sketches of Contemporary Authors" (No. 1). *The Athenaeum*, 16 January 1828 (The following are titles in the series "Sketches of Contemporary Authors", which appeared in subsequent issues of *The Athenaeum*):

"Mr Jeffrey and the Edinburg Review" (No. 2), 23 January 1828
"Mr Southey" (No. 3), 29 January 1828
"Mr Cobbett" (No. 4), 12 February 1828
"Mr Wordsworth" (No. 5), 19 February 1828
"Mr Moore" (No. 6), 22 February 1828
"Mr Brougham" (No. 7), 29 February 1828
"Percy Bysshe Shelley" (No. 8), 7 March 1828
"Sir Walter Scott" (No. 9), 11 March 1828
"Sir James Mackintosh" (No. 10), 18 March 1828
"Maria Edgeworth" (No. 11), 28 March 1828
"Lord Byron" (No. 12), 8 April 1828
"James Mill" (No. 13), 18 June 1828
"Mr Crabbe" (No. 14), 30 July 1828

Review of S. L. Blanchard's *Lyric Offerings*. *The Athenaeum*, 30 July 1828
Review of T. Davies' *Estimation of the Human Mind*. *The Athenaeum*, 6 August 1828
Review of Hare's *Guesses at Truth*. *The Athenaeum*, 13 August 1828
"The Hamiltonian System". *The Athenaeum*, 27 August 1828
"Intellectual Arithmetic" (Reviews of Hutton's *Theory and Practice of Arithmetic* and Reynolds' *Practical Arithmetic*). *The Athenaeum*, 27 August 1828
Review of M. Ancey on Infant Education. *The Athenaeum*, 3 September 1828
"Lord Byron's Monument". *The Athenaeum*, 24 September and 1 October 1828
"The London University and King's College". *The Athenaeum*, 15 October 1828
"Spanish and Italian Refugees". *The Athenaeum*, 5 November 1828
"The Spanish Exiles". *The Athenaeum*, 26 November 1828
"The Universities of Europe and America". *The Athenaeum*, 3 and 17 December 1828
"Mr De Quincey and the London University". *The Athenaeum*, 24 December 1828
Review of Hare's *Children of Light*. *The Athenaeum*, 31 December 1828

A Contributor to *Lardner's Biographies,* London, 1829

Eustace Conway: or The Brother and Sister, a Novel. 3 volumes. Richard Bentley 1834 [*Eustace Conway*]

Subscription No Bondage, or the Practical Advantages afforded by the Thirty-nine Articles as Guides in all the Branches of Academical Education. by Rusticus. J. H. Parker 1835 [*Subscription No Bondage*]

Letters to a Member of the Society of Friends. [The Rev. Samuel Clark.] By a Clergyman of the Church of England. W. Darton & Son. Published in 12 parts, commencing January 1837. [See 1838]

The Kingdom of Christ: or Hints on the Principles, Ordinances, and Constitution of the Catholic Church in Letters to a Member of the Society of Friends. 3 volumes. Darton and Clark 1838 [*Kingdom of Christ*]

"The Responsibilities of Medical Students". A Sermon preached in the Chapel of Guy's Hospital on 4 March 1838. Darton and Clark 1838

Has the Church, or the State, the Power to Educate the Nation? A Course of [6] *Lectures* (delivered during June and July, 1839). J. G. & F. Rivington 1839. [*Lectures on Education*]

"Moral and Metaphysical Philosophy". An Article in *Encyclopaedia Metropolitana: or, Universal Dictionary of Knowledge, on an original plan: comprising the twofold advantage of a Philosophical and an Alphabetical Arrangement, with appropriate engravings.* Edited by the Rev. Henry John Rose, B.D. First Division. Pure Sciences, Vol. II. B. Fellowes 1843, pp. 545–674. [*Encyclopaedia Metropolitana*]

The Educational Magazine. New Series. Edited by F. D. Maurice. London, 1840–1

"Introductory Lecture". By the Professor of English Literature and Modern History at King's College, London, delivered, Tuesday, 13 October 1840. *The Educational Magazine* (New Series), November 1840, pp. 273–88

Reasons for not joining a party in the Church: a letter to the Ven. Samuel Wilberforce, Archdeacon of Surrey; suggested by the Rev. Dr Hook's letter to the Bishop of Ripon on the State of Parties in the Church of England. J. G. F. & J. Rivington, Dated from Guy's Hospital, 22 April 1841

Three Letters to the Rev. W. Palmer on the Name "Protestant": on the Seemingly Ambiguous Character of the English Church: and on the Bishopric at Jerusalem, with an Appendix. G. Rivington 1842. [*Three Letters to the Rev. W. Palmer*]. [2nd ed.: John W. Parker 1842]

The Kingdom of Christ; or, Hints to a Quaker respecting the Principles, Constitution, and Ordinances of the Catholic Church. The 2nd Ed., revised and altered. 2 volumes. J. G. F. and J. Rivington 1842

Christmas Day and Other Sermons. J. W. Parker 1843

On the Right and Wrong Methods of Supporting Protestantism: A Letter to Lord Ashley respecting a certain proposed measure for stifling the expression of opinion in the University of Oxford. J. W. Parker 1843 [*Methods of Supporting Protestantism*]

Introduction to *Remarks on Mandeville's Fable of the Bees,* by Wm. Law. Macmillan 1844

The New Statute and Mr Ward: A letter to a non-resident Member of Convocation. J. H. Parker, Oxford, 1845 [addressed to Archdeacon S. Wilberforce]

Thoughts on the rule of conscientious subscription, on the purpose of the Thirty-nine Articles, and on our present perils from the Romish system. John Henry Parker, Oxford 1845 [also addressed to Archdeacon S. Wilberforce]

"A Lecture Delivered at the Church Schoolmasters' Association". On the Progress and Prospects of Education. *The English Journal of Education,* II (January 1845), pp. 1–12. (Delivered on 21 December 1844)

"Who are with Christ, and who against Him?" A Sermon preached in the Temple Church on the third Sunday in Lent, 1844. In *Practical Sermons,* Part IV. Ed. A. Watson. J. W. Parker 1845.

"A Few Words on the New Irish Colleges". By Nemo. Houlston Stoneman 1845

The Epistle to the Hebrews: being the Substance of Three Lectures Delivered in the Chapel of the Honourable Society of Lincoln's Inn, on the Foundation of Bishop Warburton. With a Preface containing a Review of Mr Newman's Theory of Development. J. W. Parker, London, 1846 [Epistle to the Hebrews]

"The Education Question in 1847". A letter addressed to the *Editor of the English Journal of Education* (December 1846). Appeared again in *English Journal of Education,* I. New Series (January 1847, pp. 3–9.)

"The Prophet Elijah". A Sermon. In *Practical Sermons,* Volume III, Part xviii. Ed. A. Watson. J. W. Parker, London, 1846

The Religions of the World and their relations to Christianity, considered in eight lectures founded by the Right Hon. Robert Boyle. J. W. Parker, London, 1847

"Thoughts on the duty of a Protestant in the present Oxford election". A letter to a London clergyman. J. W. Parker, London 1847

G

"A Letter [to the Rev. Arthur P. Stanley] on the Attempt to Defeat the Nomination of Dr Hampden". W. Pickering, London, 1847. F. Macpherson, Oxford, 1847

"The Government Scheme of Education". *English Journal of Education*, New Series, I, 1847, pp. 203–8

"Moral and Metaphysical Philosophy", pp. 545–674 of the *Encyclopaedia of Mental Philosophy*. J. J. Griffin & Co. Originally published in the *Encyclopaedia Metropolitana*. It was revised and reprinted in 4 parts; Part I, 1850; II, 1854; III, 1857; IV, 1862. Collected in 2 vols., with new Preface, 1873

"A Sermon by the Rev. F. D. Maurice, M.A., Chaplain of Lincoln's Inn, and Professor of Divinity, King's College, London, preached in the Parish Church of All Saints, Southampton, on Easter Monday, 1848: together with an address delivered at the opening of the New Schools in Your Buildings, and the Form of Service used on the occasion." J. W. Parker, London, 1848

The Lord's Prayer. Nine Sermons preached in the Chapel of Lincoln's Inn in the months of February, March, and April, 1848. J. W. Parker, London, 1848

Politics for the People: a weekly paper in 17 numbers and 2 supplements, from 6 May 1848, to 29 July 1848. Edited by F. D. Maurice and J. M. Ludlow. J. W. Parker, London, 1848. (The following are the articles by Maurice:)

"Prospectus", pp. 1–2

"Fraternity", pp. 2–5

"Dialogues in the Penny Boats", No. 1, "Between a Templar, Silk Mercer, A Coalwhipper, and Myself", pp. 18–21

"Dialogues in the Penny Boats", No. 2, "The Universities and Working Men; between a Student from Oxford, a Carpenter, and Myself", pp. 81–3

"Dialogues in the Penny Boats", No. 3, "Education", pp. 154–7

"Liberty". A Dialogue between a French Propagandist, an English Labourer, and the Editor, pp. 49–53

"Equality". A Dialogue between a Young Frenchman, a Statesman from America, and an English Mechanic, pp. 97–100

"Mr Lovett's Address to the Middle Classes, p. 110

"Rough Notes of some Lectures on Modern History", pp. 113–15

"A Word on Emigration—Lord Ashley's Motion", pp. 137–8

"Recollections and Confessions of William Millward". In two parts, pp. 161–76, 257–72

"To the Reader", pp. 177–8

"Is there any Hope for Education in England?" By a Clergyman. I, pp. 193–6; II, pp. 209–11; III, pp. 234–9; IV, pp. 241–6
"More Last Words", pp. 283–4

Queen's College, London, its Objects and Methods.
Francis and John Rivington, London, 1848. [Republished in *Introductory Lectures at Queen's College*, London, by F. D. Maurice, C. Kingsley, and others. J. W. Parker, London, 1849]
Preface to *The Saints' Tragedy*, by Charles Kingsley. J. W. Parker 1848
Letter to Archdeacon J. C. Hare, inserted in Hare's letter to the Editor of the *English Review. (Thou shalt not bear false witness against thy neighbour.)* J. W. Parker 1849

Introductory Lectures delivered at Queen's College, London, by F. D. Maurice, C. Kingsley, and others. J. W. Parker 1849

Lecture I. "Queen's College; its Objects and Method", pp. 1–27. [Originally published separately in 1848]
Lecture XII. "On Theology", pp. 245–63
"Address at the End of the First Term", pp. 346–52

The Religions of the World, 2nd Ed. J. W. Parker 1849 [1st ed. 1847]
The Prayer-Book considered especially in reference to the Romish System; Nineteen Sermons preached in the Chapel of Lincoln's Inn. J. W. Parker 1849 [2nd ed. 1851; 3rd, with the *Lord's Prayer*, 1880]
"Is a Decision of the Privy Council a reason for secession, or for retiring into Lay Communion?" A letter to a Clergyman of the Evangelical School. By another Clergyman. Signed A. B. George Bell 1849
Introductory Lecture delivered at the Opening of the Metropolitan Evening Classes for Young Men [16 January 1849]. J. W. Parker 1849
Queen's College, London: A Letter to the . . . Bishop of London, in reply to the article in No. CLXXII of the Quarterly Review, entitled "Queen's College, London". J. W. Parker, 1850. [*Queen's College, London*]

Tracts on Christian Socialism. George Bell, 1850.
(The following are the Tracts by F. D. Maurice:)

No. 1. *Dialogue between Somebody (a person of respectability) and nobody (the writer)*
No. 2. *History of the Working Tailors' Association, 34, Castle Street, Oxford Street*
No. 3. *What Christian Socialism has to do with the Question at present agitating the Church*

No. 7. *A Dialogue between A & B., two Clergymen, on the Doctrine of Circumstances as it affects Priests and People*

No. 8. *A Clergyman's answer to the question "On what grounds can you associate with men generally?"*

Tracts by Christian Socialists, No. 1. *On English History*, by a Clergyman (1850). (The other tracts are by Charles Kingsley and J. M. Ludlow.)

Moral and Metaphysical Philosophy, Part I. Ancient Philosophy, anterior to the time of Christ, 2nd ed., revised. J. J. Griffin. 1850. [1st ed., 1847]

The Church a Family: Twelve Sermons on the Occasional Services of the Prayer-Book. Preached in the Chapel of Lincoln's Inn. J. W. Parker 1850. [*The Church a Family*]

The Christian Socialist: a Journal of Association. Conducted by several of the Promoters of the London Working Men's Associations. Edited by John Malcolm Ludlow. Working Printers' Association, London, 1850–1. Afterwards

The Journal of Association, edited by Thomas Hughes.
(The following articles are by Maurice:)

"Correspondence on Education Between a Member of Parliament and a Clergyman", volume I, pp. 21f, 33f, 50, 75f, 86, 106f, 138f, 146f

"To Our Friends of *La République*". In volume I, pp. 41f

"The *Guardian* and Christian Socialism", Vol. I, pp. 161f, 178f

"The Experiences of Thomas Bradford, Schoolmaster". (Serialized fiction, incompleted.) In Vol. I, pp. 215f, 223f, 232, 239f, 247f, 263f, 279f

"The *Times* and Socialism", p. 217

"The Author of *Yeast* [C. Kingsley] and the *Guardian*". In volume I, pp. 257f

"Mr Maurice's Reply to the Congratulation of the Central Board". In volume II, p. 65

"Reasons for Co-operation": a Lecture delivered at the office for promoting Working Men's Associations, 11 Dec., 1850. *To which is added "God and Mammon", a sermon to young men, preached in St. John's District Church, S? Pancras.* 19 January, 1851. J. W. Parker 1851. [*Reasons for Co-operation*]

On the Reformation of Society and How all Classes May Contribute to It: a lecture delivered in the Town Hall of Southampton, on the Opening of the Working Tailors' Association, 18 Bernard Street, on Monday, 31 March 1851. Forbes and Knibb Southampton 1851. J. Tupling, London, 1851. [*Reformation of Society*]

The Old Testament: nineteen sermons on the first Lessons for the Sundays from Septuagesima Sunday to the third Sunday after Trinity. Preached in the Chapel of Lincoln's Inn. J. W. Parker 1851

"The President's Lectures on Co-operation at the Greenwich Literary and Scientific Institution". In *"The Journal of Association"*, edited by Thomas Hughes, 22, 29 March and 5 April 1852. (The lectures are summarized and not given *verbatim.*)

The prophets and kings of the Old Testament: A series of sermons preached in the Chapel of Lincoln's Inn. Macmillan, 1853

Sermons on the Sabbath-Day, on the Character of the Warrior; and on the Interpretation of History. Macmillan. 1853. [*Sermons on the Sabbath Day*]

Lying and Truth: the Old Man and the New. A sermon preached in the Church of St. Bartholomew, Moor Lane, in Adventtide, 1852. Macmillan. 1853. [*Lying and Truth*]

National Education: a Sermon, preached at St Mark's College, Chelsea, on Sunday, 6 March 1853, in aid of the Funds of the National Society. J. W. Parker 1853. [*National Education*]

Theological Essays. Macmillan 1853

The Word "Eternal" and the Punishment of the Wicked: a letter to the Rev. Dr Jelf. Macmillan 1853 [*The Word "Eternal"*]

The word "Eternal", and the Punishment of the Wicked: a letter to the Rev. Dr Jelf . . . 5th thousand, with a new preface. Macmillan 1854

Letter to the Council of King's College, dated 7 November 1853. Inserted in the "Postscript" to the *Spectator*, XXVI, No. 1324 (12 November 1853), p. 1084

Moral and Metaphysical Philosophy, Part II. Philosophy of the first Six Centuries. 2nd ed., revised. R. Griffin & Co. 1854

Scheme of a College for Working Men. [February 1854].

Lectures on the Ecclesiastical History of the First and Second Centuries. Macmillan 1854 [*Ecclesiastical History*]

The Unity of the New Testament: a synopsis of the first three Gospels and of the Epistles of St James, St Jude, St Peter, and St Paul. J. W. Parker 1854 [*Unity of the N.T.*]

The Doctrine of Sacrifice deduced from the Scriptures: a series of Sermons. Macmillan 1854 [*Doctrine of Sacrifice*]

The concluding essay and preface to the second edition of Mr Maurice's Theological essays. Macmillan 1854

The Communion Service from the Book of Common Prayer, with select readings from the Rev. F. D. Maurice, M. A. Edited by the Right Rev. John William Colenso, D.D., Lord Bishop of Natal. Macmillan 1855

Death and life: a sermon preached in Lincoln's Inn Chapel on the 25th of March, 1855. Macmillan 1855

G*

Lectures to Ladies on Practical Subjects. Macmillan 1855 (The following are by Maurice:)
The preface
"Plan of a Female College for the Help of the Rich and the Poor", pp. 1–25
"The College and the Hospital", pp. 26–52

Plan of a Female College for the help of the rich and the poor: the substance of a lecture delivered at the Working Men's College . . . to a class of ladies, on Monday, 21 May Macmillan 1855
Administrative Reform, and its connexion with Working Men's Colleges. Macmillan 1855 (Delivered at the Working Men's College, London, 31 May 1855.)
The Patriarchs and Lawgivers of the Old Testament: a series of Sermons preached in the Chapel of Lincoln's Inn. 2nd ed. Macmillan 1855 (Ist ed. *The Old Testament*, 1851) [*The Patriarchs and Lawgivers*]
Learning and Working. Six Lectures Delivered in Willis's Rooms, London, in June and July, 1854. The Religion of Rome, and its influence on Modern Civilization. Four Lectures Delivered in the Philosophical Institution of Edinburgh, in December, 1854. Macmillan 1855. [*Learning and Working*]
The Working Men's College, 31 Red Lion Square, London. Christmas, 1855. (Report at the end of the first year.) (Among the papers at Pusey House, Oxford.)
The Gospel of St John. A series of discourses. Macmillan 1857. [*Gospel of St. John*]
"Essay on Archdeacon Hare's Position in the Church, with Reference to the Parties that Divide it." An introduction to *Charges to the Clergy of the Archdeaconry of Lewes . . .* by J. C. Hare, Archdeacon of Lewes. 3 volumes. Macmillan and Co., 1856. (Afterwards republished in *The Victory of Faith*, by J. C. Hare 1874.)
"The Denison Case". A letter to the Editor from the Rev. F. D. Maurice. *Fraser's Magazine for Town and Country.* LIV, No. 324 (December 1856), pp. 732–5.
"The Teacher of the Gentiles." Sermon by Maurice, preached at Lincoln's Inn, the First Sunday after Epiphany, 16 January 1853 (Text: Ephesians 3. 8–11). *In British Eloquence: The Literary, Political and Sacred Oratory of the Nineteenth Century, Sacred Oratory. Sermons by Eminent Living Divines of the Church of England.* Series I. R. Griffin & Co. 1856, pp. 101–17.
"The Sabbath Day." An Address to the Members of the Working Men's College, 31 Red Lion Square, on Sunday Excursions. R. Clay 1856

Speech at the distribution of prizes in St Mary's Medical School, Thursday, 1 May 1856. (In the *Report of the Proceedings at the distribution of prizes in St. Mary's Medical Hospital, 1 May 1856.* Published by direction of the School Committee, 13 May 1856.)

Moral and Metaphysical Philosophy—[Pt. 3, *with title:*] *Mediaeval philosophy; or, a Treatise of moral and metaphysical philosophy from the 5th to the 14th century.* (Enc. Metrop. Cabinet ed., vol. 36) Richard Griffin and Company, London and Glasgow, 1857.

"Milton considered as a Schoolmaster". A Lecture delivered at the Royal Institution, 30 January, 1857, p. 6.

The Worship of the Church. A Witness for the Redemption of the World. A Sermon, to which is prefixed a letter to F. S. Williams, Esq., in answer to a pamphlet entitled *Thoughts on the Doctrine of Eternal Punishment with reference to the views of the Rev. F. D. Maurice and the Neo-Platonists,* Macmillan 1857. (The letter dated May 1857). [*Worship of the Church*]

The Epistles of St John: a series of lectures on Christian Ethics. Macmillan 1857. [Epistles of St John]

Sermons preached in Lincoln's Inn Chapel. Six volumes. Issued to subscribers only. J. E. Taylor, London, 1857-9

The Indian Crisis. Five Sermons by Frederick Denison Maurice, M. A., Chaplain of Lincoln's Inn. Macmillan 1857

The Worship of God and Fellowship among Men: a series of Sermons on Public Worship at Christ Church, Marylebone (1858). The following sermons are by Maurice: "Preaching, a call to Worship" and "The Bible, a revelation of the beginning and end of Worship"

"Christian Civilization". A speech delivered at the Young Men's Christian Association in Cambridge on Thursday, 25 March 1858. Reported in *The Cambridge Chronicle and University Journal,* No. 4975 (27 March 1858), p. 8

Speech at the Working Men's College, Cambridge, 26 March, 1858. In *Proceedings at a Meeting of the Working Men's College, Cambridge,* 26 March, 1858. Reprinted from *The Cambridge Chronicle and University Journal,* by request of the "Committee of Students"

Three Sermons Preached at Special Evening Services, at St Margaret's, Westminster, by the Rev. William Cureton, D. D., Rector of St Margaret's: the Rev. William Scott, M.A., Incumbent of Christ Church, Hoxton: and the Rev. Frederick Maurice, M. A., Chaplain of the Hon. Society of Lincoln's Inn (on Trinity Sunday, 30 May 1858, on the text Galatian 4. 6). Rivingtons 1858

The Working Men's College Magazine, Vol. I (January to December, 1859, 12 numbers). (The following articles are by Maurice:)

"Introductory Lecture on the Studies of the [London] Working Men's College." (Delivered on 27 December 1858.) No. 1 (1 January 1859), pp. 1–8

"Address at a Meeting of Working Men's Colleges at Manchester, 5 January 1859." Supplement (February 1859), pp. 28–35

"Lectures on 'The Studies of a College'." (Summary.) No. 4 (1 April 1859), pp. 69f

"Recruiting for a College." No. 7 (1 July 1859), pp. 109f

What is Revelation? A series of Sermons on the Epiphany; to which are added letters to a student of theology on the Bampton lectures of Mr Mansel. Macmillan and Co., Cambridge, 1859. [*What is Revelation?*]

Preface to *Handbook of the Geography and Statistics of the Church,* by J. E. T. Wiltsch. Two Volumes. Bosworth & Harrison, London, 1859

War: How to prepare ourselves for it. A Sermon preached in the Chapel of Lincoln's Inn. (On 20 November 1859.) Macmillan 1859

"Mr Kingsley and the *Saturday Review*", *Macmillan's Magazine,* I, No. 2 (December 1859), pp. 116–19

Sequel to the Inquiry, What is Revelation? In a series of Letters to a Friend; containing a reply to Mr Mansel's "Examination of the Rev. F. D. Maurice's Strictures on the Bampton lectures of 1858". Macmillan 1860. [*Sequel to the Inquiry*]

A Lecture delivered at the opening of the Lower Norwood Working Men's Institute (2 January 1860). W. Kent & Co., London, 1860

A Sermon preached to the 19th Middlesex Volunteer Rifle Corps, at Christ Church, Marylebone, on the Second Sunday in Advent. Macmillan 1860

"Lord Macaulay", *Macmillan's Magazine,* I, No. 4 (February 1860), pp. 241–47

"On the Revision of the Prayer-Book and the Act of Uniformity," *Macmillan's Magazine,* I, No. 6 (April 1860), pp. 417–28.

Working Men's College Magazine, Volume II, (Nos. 13–24, January through December, 1860). (The following items are by Maurice:)

"A Letter to the Teacher of a Boxing Class on Prize Fighting", *Working Men's College Magazine,* Vol. II, No. 17 (1 May 1860), pp. 75–8

"College for Working Men". (Extracts from a printed statement bearing the date of 7 February 1854) Nos. 21 (1 September) and 22 (1 November), *Working Men's College Magazine*, Vol. II, pp. 146ff, 165ff.

"The Suffrage considered in reference to the Working Class and to the Professional Class", *Macmillan's Magazine*, II, No. 8 (June 1860), pp. 89–97

"Female School of Art; Mrs Jameson", *Macmillan's Magazine*, II, No. 9 (July 1860), pp. 227–35

Review of *History of England*, by J. A. Froude, volumes V and VI. *Macmillan's Magazine*, II, No. 10 (August 1860), pp. 276–84

The Faith of the Liturgy and the Doctrine of the Thirty-nine Articles. Two sermons, the substance of which was preached at St Peter's, Vere Street, on 9 September 1860. Macmillan and Co., Cambridge, 1860. [*Faith of the Liturgy*]

Address of congratulation to the Rev. F. D. Maurice, on his nomination to St Peter's, Vere Street; with his reply thereto (dated 27 November 1860). London, 1860.

"History and Casuistry", *Macmillan's Magazine*, Vol. II, No. 12 (October 1860), pp. 505–12

"More Political Ethics: The Neapolitan Revolution and the Fugitive Slave Law", *Macmillan's Magazine*, Vol. II, No. 13 (November 1860), pp. 65–8

Sermons. 1st Series. 2 Volumes. Smith, Elder and Co., London, 1860. [A Re-issue of the 6 vols. of Sermons, 1857–9.]

Sermons. 2nd Series. 2 Volumes. Smith, Elder and Co., London, 1860

Sermons. 3rd Series. 2 Volumes. Smith, Elder and Co. 1860

Working Men's College Magazine, Volume III (Nos. 25–37, January to December 1861). (The following items are by Maurice:)

"Personal Explanation", *Working Men's College Magazine*, Vol. III, No. 26 (1 February 1861), pp. 13ff

"A Letter to The Editor in reference to College Dances", No. 26 (1 February 1861), p. 28

"The Bible and the College: a letter to R. B. Litchfield", No. 27 (1 March 1861), pp. 29–32.

Extract from "A Sermon preached to the 19th Middlesex (Working Men's College) Volunteer Rifle Corps," No. 28 (1 April 1861), p. 55 (the entire sermon has been published separately as given above).

"Letter to the Promoters of a Working Men's College" [addressed to
J. S. Henderson, Esq., Secretary of the Ayr Working Men's College,
dated from 5 Russell Square, W.C., 3 June], No. 31 (1 July 1861),
pp. 98–100.
"Baron Bunsen", *Macmillan's Magazine*, III, No. 17 (March 1861), pp.
372–82.
"Dr. Lushington, Mr Heath and the Thirty-nine Articles", *Macmillan's
Magazine*, V, No. 26 (December 1861), pp. 153–6.

Tracts for Priests and People by various writers. Macmillan 1861–2.
(Maurice contributed to the following:)

No. II. *The Mote and the Beam: a Clergyman's Lessons from the
Present Panic*
No. VI. *The Sermon of the Bishop of Oxford* [S. Wilberforce] *on
Revelation, and the Layman's Answer.* I. *A dialogue on Doubt.* By
J. M. Ludlow. II. *Morality and Divinity.* By the Rev. F. D. Maurice
No. X. *Politics, Ancient and Modern.* Part II, *Do Kings Reign by the
Grace of God?* By . . . F. D. Maurice. (Part I, *The Prophets of the
Old Testament* is by Sir Edward Strachey.)

A Letter to the Writer, by F. D. Maurice, affixed to Tract No. XIV,
The Incarnation, and Principles of Evidence, by Richard H. Hutton
*Lectures on the Apocalypse; or Book of Revelation of St John the
Divine.* Macmillan 1861. [Apocalypse]
Moral and Metaphysical Philosophy—[Pt. 4, *with title:*] *Modern
philosophy; or A treatise of moral and metaphysical philosophy from
the 14th century to the French Revolution* . . . Griffin, Bohn, and Co.
1862
"The New Morality: Worship of Majorities, a letter to the Editor",
Macmillan's Magazine, No. 30 (April 1862), pp. 504–6
Dialogues between a Clergyman and a Layman on Family Worship.
Macmillan 1862. [*Family Worship*]
The Sacrifices which we owe to God and His Church. A sermon
preached at St Peter's, Vere Street, on Sunday, 2 November [1862.]
Macmillan 1862
Acquisition and Illumination. Part of a New Year's address to the
pupils of some evening classes (1863). (Lecture XII in *The Friendship
of Books.*)
"Dr Pusey and Professor Jowett". Two letters published in *The Times*,
Nos. 24,487 and 24,490 on 20 and 24 February 1863
"Dr Newman and Dr Pusey." A letter published in *The Times*, No.
24,493 on 27 February 1863

The Claims of the Bible and of Science. Correspondence between a Layman and the Rev. F. D. Maurice on some questions arising out of the controversy respecting the Pentateuch (1863). Macmillan 1863. [*Claims of the Bible and of Science*]

"On Sisterhoods", *The Victoria Magazine*, I (August 1863), pp. 289–301. (This article does not appear in other bibliographies of Maurice's works.)

"Christmas Thoughts on Renan's *Vie de Jésus*", *Macmillan's Magazine*, IX (January 1864), pp. 190–7.

"The Oxford Protest." A letter published in *The Times*, No. 24,812 on 5 March 1864. (Later republished; Liddon, Henry Parry.) *Life of Edward Bouverie Pusey*, Vol. IV (1860–82). Longmans, Green 1897, p. 57.

"Dr Pusey and the Declaration of Faith." Two letters published in *The Times*, Nos. 24,815 and 24,818, 8 and 14 March 1864. (Later republished by Liddon, *Life of Edward Bouverie Pusey*, pp. 59f.)

"Corruption at Elections: Mr Christie's Suggestions", *Macmillan's Magazine*, X (July 1864), pp. 192–8

The Clergyman's Self-Examination concerning the Apostles' Creed. [Anonymous.] Macmillan 1864

The Gospel of the Kingdom of Heaven, A Course of Lectures on the Gospel of St Luke. Macmillan 1864 [*Gospel of the Kingdom of Heaven*]

Introduction to *Post Tenebras Lux*, by the Rev. G. D. Snow. Smith, Elder & Co. 1864

"The Bishop of Capetown and Spiritual Jurisdiction." A letter published in *The Times*, No. 24,994 on 4 October 1864

"A Letter to a Colonial Clergyman on some Recent Ecclesiastical Movements in the Diocese of Cape Town and in England", *Macmillan's Magazine*, XI (December 1864), pp. 97–112

What Message have the Clergy for the People of England? A Letter to the Right Hon. and Right Rev. the Bishop of London in reference to the controversy on the future state of sinners. Macmillan 1864

The Conflict of Good and Evil in our Day. Twelve letters to a Missionary. Smith, Elder and Co. 1865 [*Conflict of Good and Evil*]

"A Few Words on the Pope's Encyclical Letter," *Macmillan's Magazine*, XI (February 1865), pp. 276–8.

"A Word more on the History of Caesar and on Certain other Histories, written and acted", *Macmillan's Magazine*, XII (May 1865), pp. 23–31

The Commandments considered as Instruments of National Reformation. Macmillan 1866. [*The Commandments*]

Casuistry, Moral Philosophy, and Moral Theology. An Inaugural Lecture delivered in the Senate House, Cambridge, on Tuesday, 4 December, 1866. Macmillan 1866. [*Casuistry, Moral Philosophy, and Moral Theology*]

The Workman and the Franchise: Chapters from English history on the representation and education of the people. Alexander Strahan, 1866. [*The Workman and the Franchise*]

To J.R. formerly a pupil in the Working Men's College, now a Tradesman in New York. 1866

"Meditations and Prayers concerning the Church of Mankind." *From Present-Day Papers, on Prominent Questions in Theology,* edited by the Right Rev. Alexander Ewing, D.C.L., Bishop of Argyll and the Isles. First Series. Daldy, Isbister & Co., 1867

Letters to the Bishop of Argyll and the Isles (A. Ewing), from Hamilton Villa, Weston-super-Mare (6 October 1867), affixed to "Reconciliation", by A. Ewing. From *Present-Day Papers . . .* , First Series, pp. 45ff. Daldy, Isbister & Co. 1867

"Use of the Word Revelation in Scripture." From *Present-Day Papers . . .* , edited by A. Ewing. Second Series (1867). Daldy, Isbister & Co. 1867

The Light of Men. A Sermon preached in Great St Andrew's Church, Cambridge, on Advent Sunday, 1868, *on behalf of the Cambridge Industrial School.* Macmillan 1868 [*The Light of Men*]

"The Irish Church Establishment." *Contemporary Review,* VII, (February 1868), pp. 54–65

"Mr Maurice and the Bishop of Grahamstown", a letter printed in the *Spectator,* No. 2,071 (7 March 1868), p. 289 (This article does not appear in other bibliographies of Maurice's works).

"The Dean of Cork [W. C. Magee] and the Irish Establishment", letter published in the *Contemporary Review,* Vol. VII, (April 1868), pp. 586–90.

"Baron Bunsen. Reviews of *Memoirs of Baron Bunsen,* by his widow, 2 vols.; and *God in History,* by Baron Bunsen," *Macmillan's Magazine,* XVIII (June 1868), pp. 144–50.

The Ground and Object of Hope for Mankind: four Sermons preached before the University of Cambridge in November 1867. Macmillan 1868. [*Hope for Mankind*]

The Conscience: Lectures on Casuistry delivered in the University of Cambridge. Macmillan 1868. [*Conscience*] Second edition, Macmillan 1872

"On Church and State." A series of letters published in *The Daily News* on 14, 17, 22, 27 August, 2, 9, 16 and 25 September 1868

Review of "Few Words on the Irish Church Question", by W. G. Clark, *Cambridge University Gazette,* 11 November 1868, pp. 23–4

"Walter Savage Landor and Henry Crabb Robinson." Reviews of *W. S. Landor,* a Biography by J. Forster, two volumes; and H. C. Robinson's *Diary,* edited by Sadler, three volumes. *Macmillan's Magazine,* XX (August 1869), pp. 355–65.

Social Morality: twenty one lectures delivered in the University of Cambridge. Macmillan 1869. Preface signed at Cambridge, 22 Nov. 1869. Second edition, 1872. New edition, Macmillan 1893. [*Social Morality*]

"The Moral Sciences. A Reply to the Rev. F. J. A. Hort." *Cambridge University Gazette,* 28 April 1869, p. 141.

The Warrior's Prayer. A Farewell Sermon preached to the Congregation of St Peter's, Vere Street, on Sunday, November 7, 1869 (from the text: Psalms XXXV.1). Macmillan 1869. [*The Warrior's Prayer*]

"Speech on the Abolition of the University Tests", *Cambridge University Gazette,* 1 December 1869, p. 254

"Dr Newman's Grammar of Assent." *Contemporary Review,* XIV (May 1870), pp. 151–72

"Female Suffrage." A letter printed in the *Spectator,* No. 2,175 (March 1870), p. 298

"The Infallibility of the Scriptures", *Spectator,* No. 2,176 (12 March 1870), pp. 331f

"The Thirty-nine Articles and the Broad-Church", *Spectator,* No. 2,179 (2 April 1870), pp. 434f. A reply to Leslie Stephen

"A Few More Words on the Athanasian Creed", *Contemporary Review,* XV (October 1870), pp. 479–94

Christian education. Two sermons preached on behalf of the Old Schools of Cambridge, on the morning and evening of Sunday, 20 November 1870. Macmillan 1870. [*Christian Education, Two Sermons*]

A Few Words on Secular and Denominational Education, in a letter to the members of the Working Men's College, etc. Macmillan 1870 [*A Few Words on Secular and Denominational Education*]

The Lord's Prayer, the Creed, and the Commandments. A Manual for Parents and Schoolmasters. To which is added, *The Order of the Scriptures.* Macmillan 1870.

Mediaeval Philosophy: or, a treatise on moral and metaphysical philosophy from the fifth to the fourteenth century. Second Edition, revised (1853). (Contains a preface of interest which is not reproduced in the later editions of Maurice's *Moral and Metaphysical Philosophy*.) Macmillan 1870

"On the Mode of Dealing with Words which Occur Most Frequently in Treatises on Mental Philosophy." *Contemporary Review*, XIX (January 1871), pp. 260–80

"The Purchas Judgement and the Bishops", *Spectator*, No. 2,231 (1 April, 1871), pp. 382–3

"The Recent Judgements and Mr Maurice", *Spectator*, No. 2,233 (15 April, 1871), pp. 446–7

On the Words "Nature", "Natural", and "Supernatural". Metaphysical Society's Papers, 21 November 1871 (Privately Printed.)

"Report of the Address delivered at the Commencement of the College Session, 1871–2. Appended to *Service and Rest, A Sermon, in memory of F. D. Maurice*, by L. D. Bevan. S. Standring, London 1872

Sermons Preached in Country Churches. Macmillan 1873

The Friendship of Books and (11) *other Lectures*. Edited with a preface by T. Hughes. Macmillan 1874 [*The Friendship of Books*]

The Life of Frederick Denison Maurice chiefly told in his own Letters. Edited by his son Frederick Maurice. Two volumes. Macmillan 1884. [*Life*]

Lessons of Hope. Readings from the Works of F. D. Maurice. Selected by J. Llewelyn Davies. Macmillan 1889

The Acts of the Apostles. A Course of Sermons. Macmillan 1894

"Three Letters Concerning Ruskin's *Notes on the Construction of Sheepfolds*." From Literary *Anecdotes of the Nineteenth Century*, Vol. II, edited by W. Robertson Nicoll and Thomas Wise (1895)

C

SELECTED BIBLIOGRAPHY OF OTHER SOURCES CONSULTED

THIS LIST CONTAINS ONLY THOSE BOOKS TO WHICH REFERENCES ARE MADE

Acland, Sir Thomas, *Memoir and letters*. Ed. by his son, A. H. D. Acland. Chiswick Press: Charles Whittingham and Co. London. Printed for Private Circulation, 1902

Ahlers, Rolf, *Die Vermittlungstheologie des F. D. Maurice*, (unpublished dissertation in the University of Hamburg) [Hamburg 1967.]

Bonhoeffer, Dietrich, *Ethics*, edited by Eberhard Bethge. S.C.M. Press 1955. Translated by Neville Horton Smith from the German *Ethik*. Chr. Kaiser Verlag, Munich, 1949

Brown, Ford Madox, Exhibition Catalogue (Cambridge University Library, Uc.6.265). The catalogue is of an exhibition organized by the Walker Art Gallery, Liverpool, 1964. The Curwen Press

Butler, Josephine Elizabeth (Mrs. G.), *An Autobiographical Memoir.* Third Edition. Arrowsmith 1928

Calendar, 1967–8, King's College, London

Cambridge Essays, contributed by Members of the University, 1856. J. W. Parker 1856

Carlyle, Thomas, *The Life of John Sterling.* Chapman and Hall 1851

Chadwick, Owen, *From Bossuet to Newman. The Idea of Doctrinal Development.* Cambridge University Press 1957

Christensen, Torben, "F. D. Maurice and the Contemporary Religious World." From *Studies in Church History, Volume III,* G. J. Cuming, p. 69. E. J. Brill, Leiden, 1966

Christensen, Torben, *Origin and History of Christian Socialism* 1848–54. Universitetforlaget, Aarhus 1962

Clark, Samuel, M.A., *Memorials from Journals and Letters of Samuel Clark, M.A.* Ed. by his Wife. Macmillan 1878

Coleridge, Samuel Taylor, *Aids to Reflection.* Ed. Henry Nelson Coleridge. Two volumes. With an appendix to Volume II, *On Rationalism,* by Sara Coleridge. William Pickering 1843

Coleridge, Samuel Taylor, *The Table Talk* and Omniana, ed. Coventry Patmore. Oxford University Press 1917

Coleridge, Sara, *Memoir and Letters of Sara Coleridge.* Ed. by her daughter. Two Volumes. Henry S. King and Co. 1873

Courtney, Janet Elizabeth (Mrs W. L.), *Freethinkers of the Nineteenth Century.* Chapman and Hall 1920

Davies, John Llewelyn, Introduction to *Lessons of Hope: Readings from the works of F. D. Maurice.* Selected by J. L. Davies. Macmillan 1889

Elliott-Binns, Leonard Elliott, *Religion in the Victorian Era,* Lutterworth Press 1964

Erskine, Thomas, of Linlathen, *Letters of Thomas Erskine of Linlathen from 1800 till 1840,* ed. William Hanna. David Douglas 1877

Erskine, Thomas, of Linlathen, *Letters of Thomas Erskine of Linlathen from 1840 till 1870.* Ed. William Hanna. David Douglas, 1877

Ford, Ford Madox [Hueffer], *Ford Madox Brown. A Record of His Life and Work.* Longmans, Green 1896

Gray, George John, *Bibliography of the writings of F. D. Maurice.* [With Ms. letters etc., addressed to the compiler.] Macmillan 1885

Hanna, William, *Letters of Thomas Erskine of Linlathen.* Ed. by William Hanna, D.D. Two Volumes. David Douglas 1877

Hare, Augustus John Cuthbert, *The Story of My Life,* Volume I. George Allen 1896

Hare, Julius Charles, *Essays and Tales, by John Sterling, collected and edited, with a Memoir of His Life.* J. W. Parker 1848

Hengstenberg, Ernst Wilhelm, *Christologie des Alten Testaments und Commentar über die Messianischen Weissagungen der Propheten*. Ludwig Oehmigke, Berlin, 1829

Higham, Florence May (Mrs C. S. S.), *Frederick Denison Maurice*. S.C.M. 1947

Hort, Fenton John Anthony, "Coleridge", *Cambridge Essays, contributed by Members of the University*, 1856. J. W. Parker 1856

Hueffer, Ford Madox, (Ford Madox Ford). *Ford Madox Brown, A Record of his Life and Work*. Longmans, Green 1896

Jenkins, Claude, *F. D. Maurice and the New Reformation*. S.P.C.K. 1938

Kell, Edmund, "Memoir of the late Rev. Michael Maurice", *Christian Reformer*, New Series, Vol. XI (July 1855), pp. 407–17

Law, William, Remarks on the Fable of the Bees. With an introduction by the Rev. F. D. Maurice. With an appendix containing the poem of the Fable of the Bees, Mandeville's Introduction, etc. on the Origin of Morality. Cambridge: Printed at the University Press, for D. & A. Macmillan, 1844

Leinonen, Hannes, *Frederick Denison Mauricen Sosiaalietiikka Hänen Teologisten Peruskatsomustensa Valossa*. Helsinki 1951

Ludlow, John Malcolm, *King's College and Mr Maurice*, (No. 1). The Facts, by a Barrister of Lincoln's Inn. D. Nutt 1854

Ludlow, J. Malcolm, "Some of the Christian Socialists of 1848 and the following years", *The Economic Review*, Volumes III (October, 1893), pp. 486–500, and IV (January, 1894), pp. 24–42

Maine, Henry James Sumner, *Ancient Law*. John Murray 1861

Mansel, Henry Longueville, *An examination of the Rev. F. D. Maurice's Strictures on the Bampton Lectures of* 1858. By the Lecturer [i.e. H. L. Mansel]. John Murray 1859

Mansel, Henry Longueville, *The Limits of Religious Thought Examined in eight lectures, preached before the University of Oxford in the year MDCCCLVIII*. Oxford: for John Murray 1858

Masterman, Charles Frederick Gurney, *Frederick Denison Maurice*. (Leaders of the Church, 1800–1900. Ed. George W. E. Russell) Mowbray 1907

Maurice, Charles Edmund, *Life of Octavia Hill as told in her letters*. Macmillan 1913 [*Life of Octavia Hill*]

Maurice, John Frederick, *The Life of Frederick Denison Maurice chiefly told in his own letters*. Ed. by his son Frederick Maurice. Two Volumes, 2nd edition. Macmillan 1884 [Life]

Maurice, Mary Atkinson, *Aids to Development*. 2 Vol. London, 1829

Maurice, Mary Atkinson, *Memorials of Two Sisters* [Anne C. M. and Emma L. M.] Edited [or rather written] by the author of "Aids to Development", etc. [i.e. M. A. Maurice.] R. B. Seeley and W. Burnside 1833

Maurice, Michael, "An account of the life and religious opinions of J. Bawn", *The Christian Reformer*, Vol. VIII (August 1822), pp. 256f

Maurice, Michael, *An Account of the Life and Religious Opinions of John Bawn* . . . Also answers to some objections frequently advanced against Unitarians. W. Browne 1824

Maurice, Michael, "Memoir of the Late Michael Maurice", *Christian Reformer*, Vol. XI (July 1855) pp. 407–17

Maurice, Priscilla, *Hints On The Service For The Visitation Of The Sick*. Francis and John Rivington 1845

Maurice, Priscilla, *Sickness, Its Trials and Blessings* [By P. Maurice] With an introduction by R. C. Trench. Francis and John Rivington 1846

Maurice, Priscilla, *Sickness, Its Trials and Blessings* [By P. Maurice] Francis and John Rivington 1850. Other editions, 1868, 1869, 1877 [1876], 1880 [1879], 1884, 1885

Maurice, Priscilla, *Help and Comfort* for the sick poor, etc. Rivingtons 1853

Maurice, Priscilla, *Prayers for the Sick and Dying*. By the author of "Sickness, Its Trials and Blessings". Francis and John Rivington 1853

Maurice, Priscilla, *A Few Words to A Nurse On Entering An Hospital*. Francis and John Rivington 1853

Morgan, Charles, *The House of Macmillan* (1843–1943). Macmillan 1943

Neill, Stephen, *The Church and Christian Union*. The Bampton Lectures for 1964. Oxford University Press 1968

Newman, John Henry, *The Letters and Diaries of John Henry Newman. Volume XX*. Nelson 1970

Niebuhr, Helmut Richard, *Christ and Culture*. Faber and Faber 1952

Nowell-Smith, Simon, *Letters to Macmillan*. Macmillan 1967

Ogden, Schubert Miles, *Christ Without Myth;* a study based on the theology of Rudolf Bultmann. Collins 1962

Ramsey, Arthur Michael, *F. D. Maurice and the Conflicts of Modern Theology*. Cambridge University Press 1951

Ripon, George Frederick Samuel Robinson, 1st Marquis of Ripon, *The Duty of the Age*. J. J. Bezer 1852

Ripon, George Frederick Samuel Robinson, 1st Marquis of, *Life of the First Marquess of Ripon,* by Lucien Wolf. In Two Volumes. John Murray 1921

Sanders, Charles Richard, *Coleridge and the Broad Church Movement: Studies in S. T. Coleridge, Dr Arnold of Rugby, J. C. Hare, Thomas Carlyle and F. D. Maurice.* Durham, N.C.: Duke University Press 1942. [*Coleridge and the Broad Church Movement*]

Stephenson, Joseph Adam, *The Christology of the Old and New Testaments.* Two volumes. J. G. and F. Rivington 1838

Stephenson, Joseph Adam, *The Sword Unsheathed: The Polity of the Church of England, the Polity Enforced by St Paul.* L. B. Seeley and Sons, 1834. Pamphlet 70180, Pusey House Collection.

Sterling, John, *Essays and Tales, Collected and edited with a memoir of his life, by J. C. Hare.* 2 Vols. J. W. Parker 1848

Trench, Richard Chenevix, *Richard Chenevix Trench, Archbishop: Letters and Memorials.* Edited by the author of "Charles Lowder". Two Volumes. Kegan Paul, Trench & Co. 1888

Tulloch, John, *Movements of Religious Thought in Britain during the Nineteenth Century.* Longmans, Green & Co. 1885

Twining, Louisa, *Recollections of Life and Work.* London, 1893

Venn, John Archibald, *Alumni Cantabrigienses.* Part II, From 1752 to 1900. Volume IV. Cambridge University Press 1951

Vidler, Alec Roper, *F. D. Maurice and Company.* Nineteenth-Century Studies. S.C.M. 1966

Vidler, Alec Roper, Maurice (Frederick Denison). *The kingdom of Christ, or Hints to a Quaker respecting the principles, constitution and ordinances of the Catholic Church.* New ed., based on the 2nd ed. of 1842; ed. A. R. Vidler, 2 Vols. S.C.M. Press 1958

Vidler, Alec Roper, *The Theology of F. D. Maurice* (Hale Lectures for 1947). S.C.M. 1948

Vidler, Alec Roper, *Witness to the Light.* The Hale Lectures for 1947. Charles Scribner & Sons, New York, 1948

Wainewright, John Bannerman, *Winchester College 1836–1906, A Register edited by John Bannerman Wainewright.* Winchester: P. & G. Wells, 1907. [*Winchester College Register*]

Wiltsch, J. E. T., *Handbook of the geography and statistics of the Church.* Transl. by J. Leitch. With a preface by F. D. Maurice. 2 Vols. Bosworth & Harrison 1859

Wolf, Lucien, *Life of the First Marquess of Ripon.* In Two Volumes. John Murray 1921

Wood, Herbert George, *Frederick Denison Maurice.* Cambridge University Press 1950

Index